People of the Noatak

CLAIRE FEJES

ILLUSTRATED BY THE AUTHOR

People of the
NOATAK

VOLCANO
· PRESS ·

Volcano, California

Copyright © 1966, 1994 by Claire Fejes. First published as a Borzoi Book by Alfred A. Knopf, Inc.
First Volcano Press, Inc. edition, 1994, with a new foreword by Iggiagruk William Hensley.
Printed in the United States of America.

Library of Congress Cataloging-in-Publication Data
Fejes, Claire.
   People of the Noatak / Claire Fejes: illustrated by the author.
      p. cm.
   Reprint. Originally published: New York: Knopf, 1966.
   ISBN 1-884244-00-9: $15.95
   1. Eskimos–Alaska–Noatak–Social life and customs. 2. Eskimos–Alaska–Point Hope–Social life and customs. 3. Noatak (Alaska)–Social life and customs. 4. Point Hope (Alaska)–Social life and customs. I. Title.
E99.E7F4 1994
979.8'7–dc20   93-47388
                                                                     CIP

Volcano Press participates in the Cataloging-in-Publication program of the Library of Congress. However, in our opinion, the data provided above by CIP for this book does not adequately nor accurately reflect the book's scope and content. Therefore, we are offering our librarian and bookstore users the choice between CIP's treatment and an Alternative CIP prepared by Sanford Berman, Head Cataloger at Hennepin County Library, Edina, Minnesota.

Alternative Cataloging-in-Publication Data
Fejes, Claire, 1920-
   People of the Noatak. Illustrations by the author.
Volcano, CA: Volcano Press, copyright 1994.
   Reprint of the 1966 Knopf edition, with new Foreword by Iggiagruk William Hensley.
   Illustrated with maps and drawings.
   PARTIAL CONTENTS: Sheshalik–white whale. Women at work. Beluga: Beluga:-Point Hope. Baleen, ivory, and whalebone. –Nalukatuk. –Black whale. –The river. Kotzebue. Noatak River.
   1. Northwestern Alaska–Description and travel. 2. Noatak River region, Alaska–Description and travel. 3. Inuit in art. 4. Inupiat–Social life and customs. 5. Women artists–Northwestern Alaska–Personal narratives. 6. Point Hope, Alaska–Description and travel. 7. Women's autobiographies. I. Title. II. Title: Noatak people. III. Volcano Press.
917.987 or 979.87 or 970.3 I

Photograph of cover painting by James H. Barker, Fairbanks, Alaska

The author will share her proceeds from PEOPLE OF THE NOATAK with the University of Alaska Scholarship Fund for Eskimo Students.

Please enclose $15.95 for each copy of PEOPLE OF THE NOATAK ordered. For postage and handling, add $5.00 for the first book and $1.00 for each additional book. California residents please add appropriate sales tax. Contact Volcano Press for quantity discount prices and for a current catalog.

Volcano Press, P.O. Box 270, Volcano, CA 95689 • 209-296-3445 • FAX: 209-296-4515

 PRINTED ON RECYCLED PAPER

To Joe,

WHO ENCOURAGED ME

TO GO INTO THE ARCTIC TO PAINT

and to Mark and Yola

FOR THEIR UNDERSTANDING.

Acknowledgments

I am deeply grateful for the help and encouragement of the many friends who have contributed to this book especially to the people of Noatak, Point Hope, and Kotzebue. My deepest thanks go to my ahpah, Jimmy A. Killigivuk, for permission to use his stories, legends, and songs and other material about Point Hope and to all the Eskimos who extended such warm hospitality and friendship to me in the Arctic.

My thanks to Edwin Hall, Jr., anthropologist of Yale University, who lived at Noatak and who read part of my manuscript and who allowed me to use his Noatak legends and notes on Erahooruk; to Ethel Mills for her information about Noatak and to Enoch Sherman and Juanita Norton for information about Kahhoaruk; to Hildur Keturi, for her wisdom and valuable criticism throughout the book; to Linda Badten, Reverend John E. Gurr, S.J., and Cliff Campbell who read the complete manuscript and offered suggestions; to Howard Rock, editor of *Tundra Times*, Thomas and Dorothy Richards, Reverend and Mrs. John Thomas, Reverend and Mrs. Keith Lawton, and many others who answered innumerable questions and made helpful suggestions; to Angus Cameron and the staff at Knopf; to Rockwell Kent, Ben-Zion, and to the University of Alaska, especially Charles J. Keim, Dean of Arts and Letters, who encouraged me to paint as well as write; my thanks to Elizabeth Wills, Margaret Everly, Janet Brumberg, Jo Ann Wold, and Virginia Poore, who helped me during the early stages of the book. Just as the title of the book cannot encompass all I covered in the book neither can I adequately thank all those who have aided me.

The political and economic life of the Eskimo is changing as more and more young Eskimos receive higher education and skilled training. Eskimos are encouraged to enter all phases of life and employment away from the villages to achieve better living standards, It is inevitable that many will not return. I began my trip north as an artist, but I began to write in the hope that my experiences may be of some value to the future generations of Eskimo children so that they will not forget their rich, proud heritage.

CLAIRE FEJES

Fairbanks, Alaska

Foreword

In her book, *People of the Noatak,* Claire Fejes eloquently captures the life of the Inupiat in Northwest Alaska before outside influences changed our lives. Her drawings, in a few simple strokes, evoke fond images dear to the heart of all Inupiat.

As a boy, I grew up along the delta of the Noatak River. Our family enjoyed the bounty of Nature—the shee fish, muskrats, seals, rabbits, ducks, ptarmigan, berries, and other traditional food. Life in the "city" of Kotzebue was much too difficult because of the lack of firewood and the distance from game. One of my earliest memories was of a terrible summer storm up the coast from Sisaulik at Anigaq when we had to move into the shelter cabin because our tent was about to blow away.

Several years later, as a college freshman in Fairbanks, I met Claire. Rosie Mitchell, whom I knew from Kotzebue, introduced me to her. I had met only one other artist as a boy and could not quite understand how they made a living painting pictures. Claire's family was friendly, talkative, and musical.

At the time I met her, I did not know how deeply Claire's visit to the Kotzebue area had affected her life. Having grown up in the traditional culture she was observing, it was not a novelty to me. As I grew to know Claire, and as I began to be more conscious of the world, it became clearer to me why she was so inspired to paint the scenes that portrayed our everyday life.

The people in her sketches and those she describes in her book are our friends and relatives. Many are no longer with us but they live in our hearts and memories and, thanks to Claire, others can know them.

People of the Noatak is an excellent portrayal of the Inupiat people before great changes came about—before television, newspapers and radios, before the effects of statehood, before the advent of big oil. Claire had the good fortune of catching a glimpse of the Inupiat world when traditional values and roots were still strong. We were fortunate to have her share our life along the gravel beaches of Sisaulik.

IGGIAGRUK WILLIAM HENSLEY
Co-chairman of the Alaska Federation of Natives
November, 1993

Preface

In 1946 we moved from New York City where I had been exhibiting in the A.C.A. Gallery, to Fairbanks, Alaska. I became an artist in a pioneering community, a frontier town at the end of the railroad.

My life changed completely in 1958 after I left my family and home for a Noatak hunting camp on the edge of Kotzebue Sound. Sheshalik was the beginning of the great adventure of my life.

I did the best drawings of my life sitting on the floor of Otoonah's house, or standing in deep snow drawing the Tigara landscape. I still remember the north wind blowing, the dogs howling and the everlasting scent of seal oil which I grew to love. It was my good fortune to be in the Arctic at that time to experience their culture.

Eskimos lived with a tested philosophy of life of which I knew nothing. Inspired by their lives, I began to paint at home. Sometimes a canvas became a sacred place and I was just the instrument. I continually strived towards their wisdom, to balance the harmony between my work and life. Arctic life released within me new images, and paintings poured out in a flood of colors.

I did not know then that painting Arctic life would remain the strongest creative force of my life; that I would continue to travel to northern villages with my paint box and sleeping bag; that I would travel the Yukon River into Indian villages and into the Arctic Refuge. My paintings now hang in Alaska, in collections and in museums throughout the United States, Europe and Japan.

Due to my habit of journal keeping I was able to write this book, first published in 1966. I felt it was important to record what I had witnessed, for there was no Inupiat written language then in Alaska. In 1972 the Inupiat established a new writing system with the Alaska Native Language Center. Therefore Sheshalik became Sisualik and Tigara is now Tikigaq.

The friends I met in the Arctic became my friends for life. Puyuk (Della Keats) and her sister Leela, Killigivuk and Otoonah, David Frankson, Nick Hank and many others are now buried in Arctic soil but their voices live on in this book.

My deepest thanks to The Puffin Foundation for their grant enabling this new edition to be published after twenty-eight years.

CLAIRE FEJES
Fairbanks, Alaska 1994

SIBERIA

ARCTIC OCEAN

ALASKA

BERING STRAIT

POINT BARROW
Barrow

Kotzebue

ST. LAWRENCE I.

KONGAKUT R.

BROOKS RANGE

COLVILLE

Demarcation Point

BERING

Nome

NUNIVAK I.

St. Michael

Anvik

Holy Cross

Nulato

KOYUKUK R.

YUKON R.

Arctic Village

Wiseman

Bettles

CHANDLAR R.

SHEENJEK R.

COLEN R.

OLD CROW

PORCUPINE R.

Fort Yukon

Fairbanks

YUKON R.

KUSKOKWIM R.

Kantishna

MT. McKINLEY

TANANA R.

Dawson

SEA

NUSHAGAK R.

ALASKA RANGE

Anchorage

Valdez

YUKON R.

CANADA

ALASKA PENINSULA

KODIAK I.

GULF OF ALASKA

Skagway

Juneau

Sitka

Ketchikan

Cape Lisburne

Point Hope (Tigara)

KIVALINA R.

BROOKS RANGE

Kivalina

Noatak

ARCTIC CIRCLE

Sheshalik

Kotzebue

NOATAK R.

KOTZEBUE SOUND

KOBUK R.

TREE LINE NORTHERN LIMIT

TREE LINE WESTERN LIMIT

Nome

map by palacios

Miles
0   100   200

Contents

Main Characters

POINT HOPE (*cont.*)

Otoonah, wife of Killigivuk, mother of Anahkaloktuk

Chester Seevek, Ah-gaik's father

Sunshine Tuckfield, mother of Ikkaheena

Tigluk, husband of Anahkaloktuk, brother of Dinah Frankson

Tingook, famous dancer

Billy Weber, husband of Alice, son of Keepororuk and Hilda

Alice Weber, wife of Billy, village of Point Hope nurse

NOATAK

Judith Allen, Quavuk's daughter

Charlie, Quavuk's husband

Erahooruk, oldest woman at Noatak

Gordon, Leela's husband

Horace, Ikkaheena's husband

Jack, Okukchuk's husband

Kahhoaruk, mother of Noyuk

Kanayak, Mary's husband

Leela, wife of Gordon, mother of Rosie, sister of Okukchuk

Mary, Kanayak's wife, mother of Daisy (adopted)

Noyuk, married to Cyrus Norton's brother in Noatak

Okukchuk, wife of Jack, mother of Mary, sister of Leela

Puyuk, Gordon's sister

Quavuk, Charlie's wife, mother of Judith Allen

PART I

Sheshalik –

White Whale

CHAPTER 1

Flight

Far, far will I go . . .
. . . far away beyond the high hills,
Ajajai, ajajai,
Where the birds live,
Far away over yonder, far away over yonder.

"IT IS MIDNIGHT in June and the Arctic sun is behind clouds. I am alone in my tent at Sheshalik. The wind lashes the tent and I can hear the sea nearby and the cry of an occasional loon. There are no trees here, only tundra which stretches for miles back to the foothills leading to distant low mountains.

"Even though the evening sky is light as day, the night air is cold. Shivering, I crawl deeper into my sleeping bag, listening to the melancholy cry of the huskies."

So began the journal of my stay at Sheshalik, Alaska, among a nomadic tribe of Eskimos. Only the night before, in Kotzebue, every white person I spoke to had warned me about the mosquitoes, lack of drinking water, and absence of toilet facilities at Sheshalik; but every Eskimo I met said longingly, "I wish I were going with you." Sheshalik was a seasonal Eskimo whaling camp and white people seldom visited there.

Two days before I had been home with my husband and two children in Fairbanks where we had lived for fifteen years. After the war and three years in the U. S. Air Force in Alaska, Joe brought me from New York City to live in a gold mining camp in the Alaskan wilderness. Later we moved to Fairbanks and settled down to raise a family. I had studied art in New York and painted every chance I could. From the beginning I was interested in painting Eskimos, for people's faces and movements had always fascinated me.

Our Eskimo neighbors in Fairbanks have adopted our ways and are slowly being assimilated into our culture, but I had heard different tales of Eskimos in the North following the hunt as generations had before them. I wanted to paint them in their own environment instead of against my studio background. With the growth of statehood the economic pattern was changing and the way of the primitive Eskimo was becoming a thing of the past.

Looking at a map of Alaska's vast areas I picked out one place and then another, discarding them if a school or mission was located there for I preferred a place remote from white civilization.

One day I stopped at the home of Charles Lucier, an anthropologist who had spent a summer in the Arctic collecting Eskimo myths. When I told Charlie of my desire to paint Eskimos from a remote place, he said: "I know just the place for you, but you may not like it. There is no bathroom, drinking water is hard to find, no soft beds or houses, only tents. There is no corner store if you forget to bring something."

I said instinctively: "That's the place I want to go."

"It's a place called Sheshalik, meaning 'place with belugas' in Eskimo."

"Shesh-AL-ik"—I pronounced it several times, finding it difficult to repeat, rolling it around on my tongue. "Where is it?"

"It's above the Arctic Circle on Kotzebue Sound near the mouth of the Noatak River," Charlie said. "They're a nomadic people who hunt caribou and fish at Noatak in the winter but in the spring travel down the Noatak to Sheshalik for sea-mammal hunting. After that they move to Kotzebue and camp there for fishing and berry picking, then in the fall return to Noatak again."

I asked Charlie what I would need. "Bring your own food; there is no store except at Kotzebue, and be sure you boil the water before you drink it. You'll need a sleeping bag, gas stove, and yes, be careful with the wood there—it's all driftwood and very scarce."

Charlie's wife, an Eskimo girl, showed me a photograph of her cousin who lived at Sheshalik. Black braids framed her smiling face, and as I looked at her I felt a strange kinship. The decision grew in me to go.

"How would you take care of yourself? You can't even put up your own tent" was the first thing Joe said.

"I'll learn; I'll practice."

Joe understood my need. He worried about my safety, but once he saw how badly I wanted to go he helped me to prepare. The first thing he did, with the help of our eleven-year-old son Mark, was to show me how to put up the small mountain tent. Mark had camped out with other boys in below-zero weather and knew how to take care of himself. Every summer our family went camping and fishing in wilderness places but Joe had always put up the tent.

After Joe and Mark had explained everything to me, they pulled the tent down and left it to me to put it up by myself. The family watched, teasing and giving advice: "Turn it inside out." "Straighten the sag." "Pull the ropes tighter."

I decided to spend a few nights in the tent for practice. Although it was June the temperature at night was forty-five degrees. Our Yola wanted to sleep with me in the tent, so we bedded down in the back yard. In a few hours Yola left to crawl into her own warm bed, leaving me with aching bones and a longing to join her. What the neighbors thought when they saw me crawling out each morning, disheveled and wearing heavy woolen socks, jeans, and a sweater, I will never know.

As with most women, mechanical things were mysterious. What if the stove should blow up? Even such a simple thing as making oatmeal presented problems. I finally learned, with Joe's help, how to operate my "cookstove," a secondhand pressure gas stove. Then Joe helped me pack groceries, simple things like oatmeal, rice, dry soups, hardtack, canned meat, coffee, and cheese. In a separate duffel bag were packed, along with underwear, jeans, socks, and sweaters, a pair of knee-high rubber boots. My painting supplies went into a metal box, and into another bag went sleeping bag, tent, stakes, ax, camera, matches, a few pots, and a fry pan, can opener and knife, together with calico material and skin sewing needles for gifts. Arrangements were made for the family's meals and Yola was sent to stay with her best friend. I was grateful for an understanding family.

The Fairbanks area had an urban population of 35,000, modern facilities, and comfortable homes. It was the end of the Alaska Railroad and the Alaska Highway. The only transportation to the Arctic from Fairbanks was by plane, unless I wanted to take a dog team in winter.

When I went to the airlines and asked for a ticket to Sheshalik, no one knew where it was. I decided to take a round-trip ticket to Kotzebue and charter a flight to She-shalik from there.

I walked out of the airline office slightly dizzy and very happy. In spite of my elation, though, a few unexpressed doubts remained. Turning the corner I ran into a dear friend, a lively gray-haired woman of about seventy, whom we know fondly as "Mom."

"Mom, at last I'm doing what I have always dreamed of." I spilled out the details breathlessly.

"Good," was all she said.

"But Mom, what if the Eskimos won't accept me," I said doubtfully. I wanted the reassurance of a world traveler, and Mom was certainly that, for every winter she took off on a tramp steamer for a different port.

"Claire," she said, "people are the same the world over. I remember the year I was let down in Mau Mau country at midnight and it was dark and raining. I didn't know a soul, couldn't speak their language, and didn't know where to stay, but someone took me in. I managed."

With that we laughed and I answered: "I don't know the Eskimo language but at least it won't be dark. It's the time of the midnight sun; the sun will be out twenty-four hours a day!" My last reservation had disappeared.

The next day, with the family to see me off, I flew from Fairbanks to Kotzebue, a distance of about 450 miles. The plane was an old DC-3 and most of the seats had been taken out to make room for cargo. A dog team and ten dogs were tied up next to a load of canned stuff, and the Eskimo owner of the team was the only other passenger.

We flew over jagged mountains, winding rivers, and great lakes which made grayish abstract patterns in the wilderness. As we crossed the Arctic Circle it seemed to become rougher and colder in the plane.

There were no signs of habitation except a few villages scattered sparsely, about one every hundred miles, settled near a river, a small dark confusion of cabins huddled in a vast hilly landscape, with thin smoke rising. A herd of caribou roamed the hillside foraging for lichen. Finally we were above the flat treeless tundra and circling low over a large lagoon, landed on Kotzebue's small runway.

Kotzebue, the Eskimo metropolis, had about ninety white people in 1958 in comparison to its 1,200 Eskimos. In summer the Eskimos from the neighboring villages come to Kotzebue, swelling the population to about 2,500. Its main street was crowded with ramshackle houses made of old logs, shiplap, tin, plywood, or anything the sea drifted in, with several houses a combination of all of these things. Colors ranged from orange and yellow to patches of dark green or raspberry, but mostly they were just the beaten gray of old timber. Few of the timbers were straight, the doors sagged and the roofs tipped. Wooden racks facing the beach were filled with drying meat, fish, seal, or beluga (white whale), turning black and attracting flies. The beach was littered with rusty oil drums, tents, bits of driftwood. An ugruk head (large bearded seal) and one very old beluga smelling of decay lay rotting at the edge of the water. Boats in all states of repair and condition lined the beach, some with new outboard motors.

At one end of town was the Standard Oil building and the Native Hospital and School; at the other end stood the Federal Aviation Agency; and in the middle of town was the graveyard. On the main street facing the sea was Rotman's Store and Hotel, Wien's Airline Hotel, Hanson's Trading Store, and Eckhardt's, a fascinating old building which housed a hodgepodge of Eskimo artifacts, arctic supplies, clothing, and everyday drug items. All of these buildings except Eckhardt's had plumbing and running water. The rest of the village managed with "honey buckets," the name given to containers which served for toilets.

Five churches were scattered about the community, all of them pulling and praying for the soul of the Eskimos. The village sprawled close to the sea, bustling with hunting activity all year round. The appearance of Kotzebue Eskimos contrasted with the decrepit housing. Vigorous, active people of all ages greeted strangers with hearty smiles, while the many dog teams tied near houses were not as hospitable but growled and threatened newcomers.

I spent a sleepless night on a soft bed in Rotman's Hotel. Restless and excited, I anticipated the adventure ahead of me. In the morning I was up early and went downstairs for coffee, which was served over a counter at the back of Rotman's mercantile store. There I met an old-time Kotzebue polar-bear guide and jade prospector, who tried to discourage me from making the trip. "Too many mosquitoes, too rough," he said, looking me over. But when he saw I could not be discouraged, he suggested a way for me to become acquainted with the Eskimos. He said that on arriving at Sheshalik I should set up my tent away from the main camp and begin to paint, not saying a word to anyone. Just like people anywhere, the Eskimos in their curiosity might then seek me out. He suggested my having bubble gum for the children. I did not know what to expect at Sheshalik or how I was going to get there from Kotzebue, except by chartering a bush flight, but I was determined to be as self-sufficient as possible.

My luck began when an Eskimo hunter from Sheshalik came to Kotzebue for supplies and loaded his boat outside of Rotman's. He was leaving at once, and when he offered to take me as a passenger I accepted without hesitation and helped to load my bags into his boat. Unobtrusively I placed a paper bag in my pocket in case of seasickness, remembering the miserable seasickness I had experienecd on the boat trip from Seattle to Alaska.

The Eskimo's homemade wooden boat, about twenty feet long, had a small Johnson motor. In the boat were two Eskimo men, a woman, and a boy sitting among many assorted boxes, barrels, and cans. The men were in a hurry to be off, as the sea looked rough, so I climbed in and sat down next to the Eskimo woman. The boat moved out into Kotzebue Sound, the Bering Sea in front of us and the unknown ahead.

The woman wore a faded blue parka with an immense wolverine fur around her head, and out of the ruff poked a round friendly face. Lifting her brows, she smiled, revealing white wrinkles over the bridge of her short sunburnt nose.

"I am Okukchuk," she said in English with pride. "We are Real Eskimos."

"I am Clara and I live in Fairbanks." Unconsciously I had used the name I was given at birth. "I'm not a tourist, I'm an artist, and we have lived in Alaska for fifteen years."

Okukchuk looked searchingly into my eyes as we talked. I understood. It was the look Alaskans use to size up the mettle of a newcomer. We chatted about our families, and I learned that she was fifty-five years old and had seven grandchildren. She informed me that there were about 275 people at Sheshalik.

Several miles out all traces of Kotzebue disappeared and our little boat was on its own. Dark stormy clouds formed overhead and a windy gale whipped up the waves as the choppy sea roughly tossed our boat about. I pulled my fur ruff closer around my face as the velocity of the wind increased, making us feel as if we were going to be flung out of the boat. In order to balance the boat Okukchuk seated herself in the bottom between my legs and I put my arms tight around her comforting hulk.

The storm increased until the spray drenched us, filling the boat with water. The hunter steering the boat covered us with a tarpaulin and put a reassuring hand on my shoulder, which was a comfort, as I had little experience with boats and was strictly a landlubber. When the water threatened to engulf us again, Okukchuk, who was more experienced but less confident, began to scream as if it were the end, "Eeregee, eeregee, eeregee!" We threw our weight on the opposite side to keep the boat from overturning and got a good soaking in the process. The young boy frantically began to bail out the water with a tin can.

I shoved my dripping wet hair off my face and caught Okukchuk's eye, and suddenly it all seemed very funny. Ordinarily I would have been seasick in a rowboat on a calm pond, but here I was, wet as a muskrat, in the middle of the sea, my life in the hands of strange Eskimos and not a life jacket in sight. It was a relief to laugh, and we laughed as we rolled to balance the boat, we laughed as we began to bail out the water in earnest, we laughed hysterically at the sea, but not a sound came from the man struggling to guide the boat. It was just the beginning of my trip; I knew I was not destined to drown! The waves did not subside but seemed to get rougher and rougher. Suddenly Okukchuk lifted her head and pointed straight ahead. "Look," she shouted. I looked but could see nothing at all.

A few minutes later, staring constantly in the direction she pointed, I saw through the gray fog a faint distant glimmer of white spots.

The swells were too big to allow us to land near the camp, so the men beached the boat far below Sheshalik in a sheltered cove.

Stepping from the boat, I realized that I was on my own, with no husband to help and no one to speak for me but myself. Perhaps here among the real Eskimos I would find out what I was really like as an individual and as an artist.

I felt I had shed the other world and had been initiated into Eskimo life. Every defense, every preconception was stripped away, as though I had undergone a sort of baptism of the sea.

CHAPTER 2

Sheshalik

There is joy in
Feeling the warmth
Come to the great world
And seeing the sun
Follow its old footprints
In the summer night.

MY FIRST VIEW of Sheshalik was of two small dark figures walking toward us on the flat tundra. They seemed infinitesimal against the blue sky. The flat shore jutting out against the sea looked like the edge of the world. Far, far off were the green foothills and a fringe of white mountains.

A few stunted willows about one foot high were the tallest vegetation; there were no trees at all, no shade or shelter between the earth and the sky. A person here was exposed directly to all elements. We marched single file along a beaten path with the bags on our backs, across the tundra. A few children ran to meet us and a boy offered to help carry a duffel bag, so I walked along with my paint box, the tool of my trade.

The row of small white dots on the landscape turned out to be tents puffing in the wind. There were about forty tents lined up beyond the shore of this sandy gravel spit that jutted out into the sea. In front of the tents were the drying racks already full of black meat; behind each tent, tied to a stake, were the husky dogs of each family. As the dogs continually howled, snarled, and fought, I stayed well away from them. Bits of scattered seal fur and intestines were spread on the gravel beach and seal guts lay at the shore line washed by sea water.

Just as we passed an Eskimo family, I offered to change packs with the small boy who had been stoically carrying my duffel bag. When I tried to fling the bag casually over my shoulder, I received a rude shock: I could not lift it after several tries. Finally I bent down and awkwardly hoisted the bag onto my back, something a boy half my size had done easily! It was embarrassing to show my lack of strength with the Eskimos looking on.

One by one the Eskimos dropped out of the path as each came to his particular tent. I doggedly followed Okukchuk, staggering under my load. She asked me then if I would like to sleep in her tent, but determined to be self-sufficient I thanked her for her generous offer and declined. Pointing out an area right next to hers she said that I could put my tent there.

Okukchuk turned out to be the village matriarch and one of the hardest-working, respected members of that small band. If I had dropped in by plane and set the tent away from the others, as the jade prospector had suggested, it would have taken all summer just to become acquainted. As it was, I camped in their very midst and was made welcome.

As news of my arrival had already traveled throughout the camp, a crowd of women, children, and dogs assembled to watch me as I began to set up the small mountain tent.

It was fortunate that I had practiced putting up the tent at home and that Joe had cautioned me to turn the green side inside so that the white side would draw the heat rays. The tent, although small, fitted in with the white tents of the Eskimos. Joe had also cut some extra long wooden stakes which I hit with the side of the ax to drive them squarely into the ground. Then I blew up the air mattress, talking to Okukchuk all the while—a difficult feat. My tent and air mattress drew many comments in Eskimo, and I learned later that they thought it was a little play tent because it was so small. Within the tent I arranged sleeping bags on one side, groceries and clothing on the other, the small Army-type gas stove and paint box went outside and the precious can opener in the air vent to enable me to find it quickly.

My quarters made up, I crawled out of my tent. Coming toward me was a woman bent under a load of driftwood. It was difficult to tell her age because she was toothless. Her face had a determined, capable look, with one eye squinting like an old sailor's. She wore wrinkled work pants, a jacket of fake leopard material probably found in a missionary's box, and high sealskin mukluks of a beautiful design. As she threw down her bundle of driftwood her perceptive eyes examined me from under her rumpled hair. This was Puyuk.

Following in her footsteps was a little girl with a runny nose, also carrying driftwood. According to Puyuk, Alunik was not her real daughter but her sister's child, who had been given to her because the sister had previously given birth to two dead children and to break the ill luck gave away the third child.

Okukchuk's head suddenly appeared through her tent

flap and she invited us in. "I have a hot fire going," she said, picking up my wet fur parka and spreading it out to dry on her tent pole. She had taken me under her wing.

In the center of the tent a fire was burning in a square iron stove, over which hung a few cooking utensils, neatly arranged. It was good to be near a fire; the chill of the boat trip was still in my bones.

There was a gravel and pebble floor spread over the original moss turf, and along the right wall of the tent, facing the sea, was a cotton-filled mattress laid over springy cut willow tops. Over the bed hung some printed cotton material which could be used as a curtain for privacy. The tent poles and the mattress had been brought down from Noatak on the boat with all the dogs and equipment. Another bed consisted of a caribou-skin hide for a bed mat with a log placed at the end.

Okukchuk's sister, Leela, came in followed by five children, none of whom were her own. The children sat around watching me intently, but I paid little attention to them so that they could become accustomed to me. The kind bronzed face of Leela held my rapt attention. Her head was framed by dark braids and her expression had an eloquent gentleness. Leela's nose was almost lost in high round cheeks, and her body, massive with good strong legs, had the solidity of sculpture. Leela is one of the women I'd like to paint, I thought. She looked fruitful, like the mother of the earth.

Since the weather was comparatively warm, the women were all wearing summer parkas and the children miniature variations. The summer parka, or "calico," made of sailcloth or calico in solid bright colors, is a most practical dress. Rows of colored rickrack trim the long ruffle above the knee and the hem falls about ten inches above the ground. Because it is cut straight and has long sleeves set in below the shoulder for freedom of action it fits comfortably. The material is heavy enough so that mosquitoes cannot bite through it.

Everyone became still in the tent, even the children, as Okukchuk spoke, "I heard in Kotzebue that one of the Sage boys from Kivalina drowned on hunting trip. He fell in icy water when he sat on end of boat looking through telescope for beluga." Her movements were unhurried and purposeful as she made the coffee and gave each of us a cupful.

There was a very long silence after which Leela with a long sigh said: "Ehhhhhhhhhhhh." It was a sound I was to hear again and again and seemed to express a deep resignation. At last Puyuk said: "The boat must have hit ice."

"No," Leela said. "Maybe he hit himself on the head."

Okukchuk reported softly: "He wore rubber boots."

At that there was a longer silence. I gathered that wearing rubber boots was the wrong thing to do since the water then sucked him under.

At last Leela said: "The men have not come home yet from ugruk hunting. It is two days now that Gordon is gone."

Okukchuk told us: "I had a letter from Jack." And to me she said: "Jack is my husband. He works for wages this summer instead of hunting so we have money this winter."

Leela stood up to go and the children clustered around her. Pouring some boiling water from the kettle into her cup, she swished it around and then tossed it out onto the gravel floor. "Tomorrow is Sunday and no one works; we go to church."

I asked if painting was work and Pukyk interceptedly firmly, "You just go ahead and paint."

As I left Okukchuk's tent, Puyuk called to me: *Suirsauktut ilurasi qaikapsi.* Leela translated: "We are happy to have you. Just come to our tent when you want."

Back in my tiny tent, I opened a can of cold beef stew, as I had not eaten since early morning. Okukchuk stopped by and insisted that I heat my dinner on her stove since it was already hot. When I offered to share the stew with her, she said she never ate until she was hungry, but I put some on a plate for her anyway to taste. With each spoonful she said something which sounded like "Up-pie, up-pie." It is Eskimo for "That's enough."

Okukchuk and I took a long walk past the white tents and staked-out huskies. Dotting the flat green landscape were innumerable blue lakes upon which small ducks swam unconcernedly. Arctic tern and sea gulls circled the camp. We passed poles stacked tent fashion marking the old graves of two men who had died at Sheshalik. Far off in the distance the low hills looked snow covered, but Okukchuk said the "snow" was white limestone.

Our feet stepped on an extraordinary carpet of nature's weaving. Hundreds of small tundra flowers, tiny blue forget-me-nots, fragrant violets, sweetpeas, yellow poppies, buttercups, and bluebells made random patterns. Wild blue iris grew in swampy places and creeping black crowberry hugged the earth. We walked a good distance then sat down near some willows. This was the signal for hordes of squirming mosquitoes to attack. I had always heard that mosquitoes do not bother Eskimos, but Okukchuk was bitten as well as I.

"I hate mosquitoes," she said as she slapped herself. We walked back to the tents and saw in the distance two white huskies, who had escaped their chains, racing and cavorting on the tundra like wild wolves.

Near the sea Leela was cutting up an ugruk with her ulu, her hands stained with blood. The triangular ulu had been cut from an old saw blade and fitted into a hand-carved ivory handle, a tool superbly suited to the job.

In front of the tent three little girls were playing hopscotch by making an indentation in the gravel and jumping skillfully over the squares. Two other children were swinging on a board suspended from the meat racks, and on the beach boys were seesawing with a wooden log over an old rusty drum. A butterfly flew by just over their heads. "BUT-terfly, BUT-terfly!" one child called in wonder. Most of the children wore outsize wolverine fur ruffs around their faces, their parkas reached the knees or farther, and their hands were hidden in the sleeves so that from the back they resembled large lollipops.

I was weary. My senses were filled with the scent of the sea mingled with that of seal meat. Colored pebbles, tundra flowers, and the vivid clothing of the people merged in abstract images. The Eskimos' bronzed faces seemed ageless, as naturally worn as the stones washed by the sea.

The midnight sun hung over the mountains and the mosquitoes sounded thick as they bumped the tent. A man in one of the tents shouted harshly to the dogs to quiet them. Creeping lower into the sleeping bag, I threw the fur parka over my feet and listened.

Soon the wind lashed the tent and over the sound of the sea I heard the dogs singing and the fearful cry of a loon. Closing my eyes I felt the intensity and purity of the sky permeating my thoughts as a benediction upon us all.

Boom! Boom! Boom! Loud drum beats broke the stillness of the Sunday morning announcing the start of church services. Waking early, I washed with cold water and dressed in a sitting position. Housework consisted of pushing back the sleeping bag and leaving the tent. Ah, the simplicity and luxury of it! Okukchuk's head appeared through the tent flap and she called, "I have hot water in my tent if you want coffee."

I took a box of oatmeal and instant coffee and joined Okukchuk who was frying sourdough pancakes. After coffee, I put a little hot water from the teakettle into my cup and sloshed it around to clean it out, pouring the water onto the gravel floor as I had seen Leela do.

"You don't have to do that," said Okukchuk. "Leela does that because she takes medicine—she is on home rest for TB and is spitting blood." I remembered Leela working late the night before when she should have been resting.

Okukchuk and I walked to Leela's tent and found her

in her slip, lathered with soap, scrubbing herself over a small basin of water. When she was finished, she put on her best blue calico parka and neatly braided her hair. All of the women were in their best Sunday calicos, hair neatly combed; scrubbed clean of the scent of seal. Jeans and sweater made up my costume, for I had not brought a skirt with me; over the sweater was a red windbreaker and on my head a kerchief to keep my hair from blowing. It had not seemed necessary to bring any lipstick or adornments, nor had I missed them; on the contrary, they would have seemed in poor taste.

White mountain ranges formed a natural setting for the large church tent. An American flag waved from the top and at the entranceway an old man in a fur parka greeted everyone. We marched between two rows of staked huskies straining at their ropes, but I felt protected with Leela and Okukchuk on either side. An empty gasoline can was offered me as a chair, but since everyone was sitting directly on the gravel floor I refused and squeezed in among the women. Old women sat in the back, leaning against the tent walls. The men were on one side of the tent and teen-agers and children sat in every available space.

In 1898 the Friends of California established a church at Kotzebue, then a mission at Noatak and converted the whole village.

Strong, sonorous notes filled the tent and Puyuk's face beamed at mine as she presided at a small organ. She was transformed by having exchanged her everyday work clothes for a colorful parka, white mukluks, and neatly braided hair.

The woman next to me whispered: "The Friends church in Kotzebue gave us the organ, and we bring it to Sheshalik by boat. Puyuk taught herself to play it."

One of the old men led us in the Lord's Prayer in Eskimo:

> *Ahpapta keelangmeetoatin,*
> (Our Father which art in heaven,)

Ahtkin nahgooruk.
(Hallowed be thy name.)

Oomeeyagootin kaikpun.
(Thy kingdom come.)

Peetkootin talvahnyaktuk
(Thy will be done in earth,)

Noonameeloo keelangmeeloo.
(as it is in heaven.)

Following the prayer, we all sang hymns, the two sides of the room taking harmony. I shared a hymnbook with one of the woman who sang in a high thin chant which sounded Oriental. The Eskimos' voices, lifted in song, expressed the joy and the sorrow of the old hymns. In this seventh day they rested from their toil.

During testimonial time Leela rose and spoke in Eskimo, in a soft, serious melodious voice that never faltered, pleading like a mother to her children. When she finished, Okukchuk translated in one sentence: "Leela told us all to love one another."

Sitting Eskimo style with my feet outstretched put a hard strain on my muscles and I began to squirm. Eskimo legs are shorter and have been trained for centuries to sit in this manner.

After the service the young people and teen-agers went to Sunday school held on the tundra under the sky, while the older people stayed on for a special service. Everyone laughed when they overheard me telling Puyuk that I was old too.

The elders studied printed tracts about Samson and Delilah which were translated for them into Eskimo. In their earnestness the old people drew little signs that looked like hieroglyphics on their papers, since no written Eskimo language exists.

Apparently there was no leader in the church; there seemed to be no real leader outside of the church. I remembered what Okukchuk had said to me that morning: "We Eskimos help one another always. We are not like white people."

There were not many men in church; most of them were still out hunting. A few of the women's faces were fierce and stern looking, but these same faces would return a smile immediately in an open greeting. They seemed to say: "We are women, you and I."

Black lines were tattooed on some of the older women's chins, first one stripe having been put down the middle of the chin when a girl was young and the other two stripes added when she married. The tattooing was done with a bone needle which pulled sooty thread through the skin. Under the missionaries' influence this practice was stopped.

Leela and most of the older women had worn their teeth short from chewing sealskin for mukluks, and when they smiled they revealed an arc with the shortest teeth being the two center ones. Their skin, warm bronze, had orange-ocher undertones, but their necks were pale. Most women wore their hair parted in the center and braided on either side and a few wore colored kerchiefs on their heads.

Although the wind had died down and the day was getting warm, the old women wore fur ruffs around their heads. As for the men, they wore hip-length parkas made of heavy drill or store-bought jackets, shirts, and pants, and most wore handmade mukluks.

The service ended with these Eskimo words: *Ouluk-neeningahneenuklam, pugnumeeuneen, taymoongahsoolee, noonahmun, eesooeechoamun. Amen.* (As it was in the beginning, is now, and ever shall be, world without end. Amen.)

Walking out of church ahead of me was an old blind woman with an expressionless pale face and a drooping mouth. I noticed a young, pink-faced albino girl who squinted badly, as if the light were painful.

Around the corner of the tent, sitting on the earth, was an ancient wrinkled woman curled up asleep in the sunshine, who woke when I passed and looked up with the eyes of a mischievous child. She spoke to me in Eskimo, then seeing that I could speak only English she went back to sleep. Answering an impulse as she looked at me, I took some paper out of my pocket and began to sketch her quickly, but she was so very old and couldn't understand what was asked of her. I felt inadequate, as if I were an intruder on an ancient privacy, and so could not finish the sketch. Nevertheless, it was the first inevitable step to recording my impressions of the people of Sheshalik.

CHAPTER 3 # Women at Work

Mark you there yonder?
There come the men
Dragging beautiful seals
To our homes,
Now is abundance
With us once more....

LEELA'S HUSBAND, GORDON, pulled his boat up to the beach after returning from a five-day hunting trip. He tugged at the ugruks and seals, dragging them up for Leela and Puyuk to butcher. Gordon was Puyuk's brother, and part of his hunt went to her.

A small spotted seal with tawny silver fur lay pathetically on its side. "It was alive," Gordon said. "Can't live without mother."

Puyuk and I picked it up and stroked its soft fur while Gordon, his share of the work done, sat down and rested. He was a square stocky man with a strong face which gave the impression of utter simplicity and integrity.

"Years ago," Gordon said, "the Selawik and Shungnak Eskimos also came to Sheshalik to hunt beluga." He pointed to the beach in front of us. "One thousand beluga were there one time—the sea just covered with white whales— right where we stand. Now, not many belugas!"

He talked to me about the past at Sheshalik when the Eskimos used kayaks and paddled, not outboard motors. "When the dog teams pulled the *umayaks* [large skin boats] along the edge of the river from Sheshalik to Noatak, at the end of the trip the dogs' feet were raw and bloody from the rough gravel." He explained, "They used the dogs in those olden days to pull the load against the swift river current."

Leela and Puyuk began to cut meat from the seals, first stripping the skin with ulus, then expertly weaving through the bone joints in big chunks, cutting through the seal ribs and taking out the liver. With red gory hands they hung the red-purple meat on the rack, where it would blacken and dry in the continuous sunlight. The colors of the vivid bloody carcasses contrasted sharply with the blues and bright oranges of the women's dresses. The soles of their mukluks became stained with the blood of the seals.

All up and down the beach women and men were busy working. Okukchuk, who pitched in to help, stripped ugruk with her ulu, cutting it in smaller pieces on the rack so that the wind and sun would dry the meat faster. She picked up another ugruk hide, cut slits around the edge, and then drove wooden stakes through the slits to stretch the ten-foot hide out on the grass. Bending over the hide with her knees straight, she scraped the fat from the fleshy side.

Gordon pulling a seal

Each hide would provide the bottoms for ten or twelve pairs of mukluks, which Okukchuk would give as gifts to her family and friends for Christmas. After scraping off the fat, Okukchuk would soak the hide in seal oil to remove the hair, to make the skin supple. Then she would carefully cut each sole and chew, and pleat it with her teeth.

Quavuk, the Sunday school teacher, was cutting layers of blubber into small pieces and storing them in a seal poke, working fast. She flayed it rapidly with her ulu, revealing such skill and such a keen knowledge of anatomy that not a single drop of blood spilled on her clothing.

Quavuk's face was strong, with a well-defined jaw and eyes that looked straight at one. She pointed to a bent old man sitting in front of the next tent.

"When I was younger, he took care of me; now I take care of him." He was a blind, sick, and helpless old man, spending his last days in the sunshine, spitting his life's

blood into a can. "I have to feed him and move him everywhere."

A young boy with freckled white skin and light hair ran
by.

"You see my boy Billy, he's my grandson; I adopted
him when my daughter died. Two of my own children I
gave away when there was little food."

Many of the families cared for children not their own.
It was difficult to distinguish who belonged to whom; everybody was related to everyone else in the village.

Working up and down the beach were many women,
all bending from the waist. I tried to bend like that to cut
some of the seal, using Puyuk's ulu, but after a few minutes
the blood rushed to my head and I felt dizzy. Yet these
woman stood for hours in this position, with mosquitoes
buzzing around them and the sweat running down their
faces, working over the stench of the meat, never complaining or seeming to tire.

The days that followed were sunny and clear as I
roamed the beach and became better acquainted with my
neighbors. I was silent, observing the scenes and adjusting
my life and thought to the Eskimo ways.

I did not take a stick of driftwood from the beach,
knowing that it was scarce. The lakes around the camp were
all mosquito infested and the water was undrinkable, so the
men brought ice from an iceberg situated two miles away.
When a hunter brought a boatload of ice chunks, I helped
him unload it into a barrel, for only then did I feel a right to
use it. The ice then melted in the sun and was used for
drinking water by the people in the camp.

One afternoon I walked a few miles out to examine one
of the numerous lakes dotting the tundra, until the only
living things within sight were three ducks swimming lazily
on one of the lakes. Loneliness swept over me and I became
aware of the vast uninhabited spaces. I wondered how a
man alone with his dog team felt coming across the mountains on the winter snow. Walking back to the beach, I

passed some children fishing; others were gathering shells and one of them brought me a lovely starfish. Most of the children were still very reticent and shy. I listened to them as they talked in Eskimo; it sounded short and choppy and very pleasant to my ears.

When I asked one of the little girls how to mail a letter, she took me by the hand and led me over to where the women were cutting up ugruk. Ethel, the Eskimo post-mistress of Noatak, wearing a pink parka spotted with blood, was skinning a seal.

"I'm real dirty," she said, laughing, as she piled the fat into a blown-up sealskin poke. The poke was the Eskimo "refrigerator," an excellent year-round storage container for meat, berries, oil, and other foods. She explained that since the chunks of seal blubber were greasy, they melted away in the poke and turned to oil.

"I also store meat and oil in barrels," Ethel explained, "but barrels are hard to get. Eskimos like to dip their dried meat into the seal oil in the winter," she said, "because it keeps us warm."

Wiping her hands, she got up to show me her "post office." Since most of the village of Noatak had moved to Sheshalik, she had just moved the "post office" with it. Located in the back of her tent, it occupied a small space crammed full of papers. I bought some stamped airmail envelopes for the same price that I paid in the United States. As I started to go, Ethel told me proudly of her daughter who was studying to be a nurse at the Mt. Edgecumbe Native School in Sitka.

"I'm a kind of nurse too," she added. "I'm a Noatak midwife."

Her son liked to draw pictures so I invited him to come to my tent for some art materials, the idea having occurred to me that I might give the children art lessons. Up to now I had not touched a paintbrush, but as more children gathered around me I decided to hold an Arctic art class.

I reached into my tent to get a box of crayons and some

white wrapping paper and found that children of all ages were coming to join the group. Distributing a torn piece of paper and a crayon to each child, I soon had seventeen children kneeling and sitting in all positions on the gravel outside my tent. They rested the paper on pieces of wood, gallon cans, barrels, or any other smooth surface while they shared each precious crayon.

Laboriously they drew scenes from their experiences— the sea, the seals, the beluga, the people in parkas. One girl drew the row of white tents; another sketched the people entering the church tent with the American flag on top. A boy drew an iceberg with a seal on it and hunters in a boat nearby; still another drew hunters in a boat with a plane overhead.

The women working along the beach looked up every once in a while, pleased that their children were happy. I too was glad that I had found work to do and could contribute a little to the group. And this proved to be no one-day art class—unknown to me the children had enrolled for the semester, or for the duration of my stay at Sheshalik. Before I awoke each morning, they would be chattering outside the tent. Dressing first, then swabbing cold water on my face, I would stumble, half-awake, out of the tent, stall for time (at least until I had a cup of coffee) and then art class would begin.

As the teen-agers became interested, the class swelled in numbers and sprawled over a larger and larger area. The crayons began to get shorter and shorter and we were finally reduced to our last scrap of wrapping paper, which had been doled out in small torn squares. There was no place to get more paper, so I asked the children if they could bring some scraps of plain material from home. None was available, but one girl brought a diaper. The boys refused to color on diapers, but I said firmly that I always used diapers to paint on and that they were fine. So, six children to the diaper, lying on their bellies on the gravel, they pressed heavily with crayon stubs. In deep concentration they drew wild flowers all over every available inch of material until it was beautiful. They carefully picked up each little bit of wax crayon from the gravel and placed it back in the box when they were through.

The next day we gathered small white clam shells and then snail shells along the beach. The boys punched holes in the shells with the three-cornered fur needles I had bought. The girls threaded the shells for necklaces and were intrigued with this new activity.

We invited the blind woman to come out of her dark tent and sit with us and the children held her hand to guide her till she sat down in our midst. We gave her the shells to feel and she threaded a few of the larger ones which the children had gathered. She sat in the sun, in her butter-yellow parka, her pale face beaming, happy for the children's brightness and laughter. I did a sketch of her and gave it to her to keep, even though she could not see the drawing. After a treat of bubble gum and crackers, the class ended. I let the children take the needles home to their mothers.

We roamed the tundra for all kinds of wild flowers and placed them in water in curved pink shells. The children's names were as varied as the wild flowers: Daphne, Ahlook, Ruby, Ahayuk, Beverly, Ditkak, Diglook, To-suk, and Tick-asook. They called me "Cara," with a hard K sound.

A little seven-year-old girl named Frances caught my attention; among all the lovely shy faces, hers was the shyest. Like a little untamed animal, she had a wildness and timidity; evidently she had not seen many strangers and her shyness amounted to fear. Finally I coaxed her to make a flower necklace, and tempted by it she drew nearer.

The wind blew her raven-black hair against her wolverine ruff and she looked up at me with her first bashful smile. As her trust grew she followed me wherever I walked, holding my hand. I began an oil painting of her and she sat for several hours, neither one of us saying a word. She sat unmoving and so rapt that I did not realize an audience had collected, nor did I realize what a sunburn I was getting. The painting showed a stony-faced girl with a wing of jet black hair, squinting in the sun. I do not believe they had ever seen oil paints in use before and while the painting remained outside my tent to dry, a great many of the people walked by to examine it. Now the villagers could see what my work was; whether they thought it was useful or useless, I never knew.

After that day, Frances and I were inseparable. I would stuff my sketch pad and pencil in the pocket of the orange calico which Okukchuk had given me to wear (so that I would be dressed like the other women) and would walk with Frances along the beach, chatting with the women as they worked. I found myself walking like an Eskimo, with a sort of rolling gait necessary over bumpy and uneven ground. Now my pencil was sketching everything I could see and I tried to be unobtrusive so that my work would not disturb theirs. It seemed that my drawing was selfish and did not in any way help the people, considering that all their efforts were directed toward hunting and processing as much food for the winter as possible.

There were now several professed child artists at Sheshalik, and every time I turned around I bumped into a child drawing in the earth with a stick. One day the temperature reached seventy; it was brilliant, clear, and hot, one of those rare days savored in the Arctic. The children knew best how to spend it. They abandoned art class and ran to the water, the girls in their slips or whatever they had on and the boys naked, to swim in the sea. Running in and out, shaking themselves and splashing the husky pups who ran in after them, they were completely free. I rolled up my jeans and waded in but the water was too icy for me.

Some of the women were washing clothes; they built fires outdoors with driftwood under large tubs and then hung the clothes on makeshift lines to dry. Others cooked meat for the dogs in large tubs and then rendered blubber over outdoor fires. Every now and then the peace was shattered by dogs who had decided to fight. The women built small grass smudge fires near their work to smoke the mosquitoes away and as they crouched near the fire and worked close to the earth, the scene was reminiscent of some ancient age.

The heat of the day intensified the stench of the meat drying on the racks. The scent wafted back to the tents all day, penetrating everything; it was in our hair and skin, the thick sickening odor of wild meat drying.

Okukchuk's daughter, Mary, and her husband, Kanayak, were cutting the fat blubber from the beluga muktuk. She handed me a chunk of muktuk that had been packed in oil, and I ate it while she watched me carefully to see my reaction, for too many white people had spurned the hard-won food. It was oily and something like pigs' knuckles, requiring strong teeth. (Later I was to acquire a taste for raw muktuk, preferring it to the cooked.) Then Mary offered me dried black seal meat and it tasted similar to jerky, the dried deer meat of our early settlers in the West.

Mary explained that the seal meat is packed in a seal-skin poke with half of it sun-dried and half of it boiled, then blubber is added to the mixture. A delicacy is *ooshak*, or ugruk flippers. The flippers are placed in fresh blubber and left in a warm place for two weeks until the fur comes off. As little Ditkak told me, "You eat the seal's bare feet, with or without cooking." (Vilhjalmur Stefansson, the great Arctic explorer, wrote that he preferred the flippers to any other part of the seal.)

Most of the meat was simply boiled; they used salt now, although a long time ago they did not. Mary chewed on the muktuk as we chatted, and I observed how thin she was and how tired she seemed from the late hours and hard work.

"I'll never forget my beloved Aunt Leela," said Mary softly. "When I was sick and couldn't chew my mukluks, Leela came and did it, even though she had lots of work to do. Some of the women use pliers to pleat mukluks, but not Leela—she says they're not as good."

Kanayak had one eye shut from a hunting accident. One night he had fixed my stove without saying a word. He had been out hunting with another man who owned a boat and ammunition; Kanayak furnished the gun, thus receiving a share of the meat.

At Noatak he was expert at making dog sleds, and he explained to me how he steamed the wood, just so, to bend it. When he and Mary ran their dogs in the Kotzebue dog races the previous winter, Mary had taken third place in the women's races. I urged them to run in the Fairbanks races but knew as I spoke that it would be too expensive to fly into Fairbanks with ten dogs. "Our dogs are heavy work dogs, but they race too," said Mary.

Kanayak has also worked in the canneries in southeastern Alaska. We talked of the possibility of setting up a salmon or shee-fish cannery at Noatak, one of the few places the large shee fish was found. One shee fish made eight 1-pound cans and was considered a delicacy in Fairbanks restaurants. We also spoke of canning muktuk, but he thought a hunting limit might then be set on beluga. In Kotzebue, however, some of the people pickle muktuk and it is sometimes offered on the airline hotel menu.

Kanayak and Mary's daughter, Daisy, who had been given them because they had no children, ran past the tent. The previous night I had seen her playing well after midnight with a group of other children. Cutting some raw muktuk, Daisy bit into it with her sharp white teeth, then gave me some to chew on. The children ate it like bubble gum; it had a nutty chewy flavor.

All the time I was in the camp, I never heard Mary or any of the other women rebuke or say a harsh word to their children, nor did the children seem to fight with one another. There was a refreshing absence of nagging, yelling, and bullying between parent and child. Love seemed to surround these children from birth and to envelop them, love given not only by mother and father, aunt and uncle, but by everyone in camp.

Some of the mothers told me their daughters had babies but were not married; the baby was either kept or given to someone who loved it and would rear it as her own.

Mary and Kanayak conversed softly in Eskimo. They had no radio at camp but often sang together in the evening.

The men were still out hunting but there were no boats in view. I brought out crackers and made coffee for the women who were working nearby. Okukchuk was making a seal poke and I was too enthralled watching the operation to think of sketching. First she cut off the seal's head; then after skinning and scraping it, she turned the hide inside out and sewed all the openings closed except for a small hole at top. Inserting a small hollow bone into the hole, she blew up the seal poke to dry; then she rubbed ashes on the blown-up form. The hair acted as an insulator and the dried poke became an excellent airtight container.

An experienced Eskimo housewife, Okukchuk said: "Whale meat tastes much better in a seal poke than if I pack it in a barrel." I admired the ease with which she worked; she did everything smoothly, evidently enjoying her labor. It made me feel ashamed of the way I tackled unpleasant jobs; Okukchuk knew the art of doing necessary menial jobs with grace.

Okukchuk sipped coffee and talked about her husband, who was known as a good provider and hunter. "When he was here last year, we go down the river and fish for salmon together. Sometime in winter we go by dog team and visit my cousins at Point Hope for the whale feast. My husband and me hunt caribou by dog team, we do everything together."

"What is the whale feast?" I asked.

Her eyes lit up. "Whale feast, or *nalukatuk*, lots of good

things to eat, dancing, blanket-tossing, happy time for Point Hopers. I have many cousins there to visit."

"Do you have nalukatuk at Noatak?"

"No, no whale at Noatak. Besides we Friends don't dance."

Okukchuk plucked a Brandt (goose) for her dinner and Puyuk picked up her sewing. "Would you like to hear a very old-time story about Point Hope and our people, the Noatagmiut?" Puyuk asked.

"Misigaq told me this story. His grandfather was Noatagmiut but his grandmother came from the coast."

Puyuk looked at me, then sucked the end of the caribou sinew thread and rubbed it back and forth on her cheek to get it even.

"A man and woman lived beside people, like we at Sisualik. This couple had two children, a boy and a girl.

"Before the man and woman went to visit people they tied the children by a rope long enough to let them go in and out of the house. They were afraid to let them go far. Then these parents went to get something to eat from the people close by.

"When the father and mother were gone the boy and girl, the ones who were tied, began to cry. Those two cried when they went outside but didn't see their parents.

"Ulului was the boy's name. The grandmother was inside while the children were crying. They cried and cried. They were crying and saying: *Ululuinya geruq.*

"And that Ulului sang, 'Ulului cried.'

"And that girl sang, 'Ulului cries. Ulului cries.'

"The old woman thought someone was with the children, because she heard singing: 'That boy has bow and arrow, that girl has fancy parka.'

"The old woman asked, 'Ulului, what are you saying?' She knew a person was out there, for she heard someone talk to that girl.

"Ulului was crying, 'I should go to my mama.'

"Then the grandmother heard no more voices. She

knew Ulului was gone. She thought someone took him to his mama.

"The parents stayed a little while at the other camp. Then Ulului's mother came home and they began to look for Ulului, even around Sisualik.

"Those people couldn't find Ulului. They looked for him for many days, but they didn't find him. It was summer; there were no tracks to follow. Then they didn't care to search more. They went back to living.

"Then that girl, Ulului's sister, began to be a young woman. It was maybe ten years since Ulului disappeared.

"Then finally that boy came to them. He wasn't wearing any clothes, not even boots. He didn't know from where he came. Those parents asked him from where he came, who he belonged to, and what his name was. Then he told them his name was Ulului. When they asked he told them his mother wasn't very far from him. Then the father ran with a spear to seek that woman.

"Ulului followed his father. Even he didn't put on clothes. He wouldn't have let his foster mother be killed; for when she raised him he was very pleased that she let him suck.

"A bear raised Ulului. That's all about the bear that I know, but maybe the story is longer at the beginning and end. That's the way I heard it," Puyuk concluded.

CHAPTER 4   *Beluga!*
Beluga!

Here I stand,
Humble, with outstretched arms,
For the spirit of the air
Lets glorious food sink down to me.

A FEW MILES OUT on Kotzebue Sound, two white beluga leaped playfully in the water. How beautiful they were, these white queens, as they arched up and down, dove in and out, and spouted water high in the air. When they leaped out of the water, their sleek white bodies reflected the dazzling sunlight. Beyond the beluga, white icebergs broke the surface of the sea.

Gordon and another hunter, wearing white drill parkas, were getting ready to go after the whales. Into the boat they put two guns and about four harpoons and approximately thirty-five fathoms of rope; five gallon cans with the hunters' initials on them and three blown-up seal pokes would serve as floats to mark the area where a killed whale had sunk.

Gordon told me: "We shoot them first, then harpoon them. Then we follow beluga for miles; even if he goes underwater we follow trail."

Nearby Puyuk had been cutting whale scraps for her dogs, and now she saw me watching the hunters get ready to go. She looked at my face and read the unspoken message upon it; she asked Gordon in Eskimo if I could go with them on the hunt. He answered without looking up, "We might have to stay all night and besides she might get scared and cry out. Better if she don't go."

Puyuk translated for me and I understood that if they did not shoot anything, it might be considered my fault. The men started the motor and left, Gordon standing stoically, feet apart, steering the boat. We watched until the boat became a dot on the quiet sea and disappeared.

Sensing my disappointment Puyuk tried to cheer me up by describing a beluga hunt she had been on. She made the motions for me with her hands to make it vivid: the beluga swimming up and down, the boats going down and up, the mother whale coming up for air with baby under her flipper, the mother rolling over on her side so that the baby could nurse with his nose in the air (otherwise his lungs would fill with water). Then her hands threw an imaginary harpoon. "They shot her," she exclaimed. "I felt so sorry for her."

She went on to picture the excitement out on the sea, with maybe twenty boats surrounding a school of whales and the men shooting in all directions and flinging harpoons. "It's a wonder no one gets shot," she said.

Puyuk took me over to one of the boats, next to which an old couple sat watching the sea. The old man puffed on a pipe contentedly. He had built the boat in 1931. "This inside piece is carved from tree roots." It was a beautiful strong boat, still useful.

With his hand he caressed the old wood. "My grandfather always use kayak. He make kayak out of split walrus hide, then sew with caribou sinew twisted with beluga sinew. When sinew gets wet, gets bigger. Small stitches, no water comes in. Like that one!" He pointed down the beach to a kayak which had a hole in the top for one person. The hunter usually wore a waterproof coat made from the guts of the ugruk, with a hood and drawstring around the face. The hem of the coat was tied with rope over the hole in the kayak so that when the kayak turned over, no water could get in. The men at Sheshalik now preferred the speedier wooden boats with motors.

The old man shook his head sadly. "Those noisy motors scare the beluga away. . . ."

"Beluga! Beluga!" shouted an old woman, puffing as she climbed the slope to the beach.

We could see the boats slowly coming home. "If the boats come in fast, there is no beluga," a woman explained.

It had been two days since Gordon had left, and on the horizon we could see the small shiny spots of the hunters' boats. Out in the bay they had surrounded the cavorting beluga and driven them into shallow water where killing was easier.

The women rushed to the beach, standing there against the blue sea, ulus ready, one hand up to shade their eyes as they tried to see how many beluga their husbands had caught. The sky cast a violet shadow over the sea as the sound of the motors came closer.

Gordon and his partner brought in five beluga. As they climbed out of their boat Gordon matter-of-factly said: "We caught them four miles out. Fourteen bulls around one female!" The man did not strut; this was not sport but food—seventy-five hundred pounds of food!

To pull a whale ashore they simply tied a rope through its nose and then all hands, including mine, yanked hard. In front of me were seven men and one woman pulling another beluga, their arms outstretched in the shape of a cross, the people silhouetted in their dark parkas against the white whale and the blue sea. A stark scene which begged to be painted!

After the whale was beached a hunter in a faded blue parka with a hood covering his head took a pan, dipped it into the sea, and reverently poured water over the whale's blowhole as we all watched. In the old days they used to pacify the whale spirit by pouring fresh sea water into the blowhole; this was a solemn repetition of the ancient ritual. (Eskimos believed that the whales were very wise; they knew men's thoughts and allowed themselves to be killed because they were thirsty for fresh water. A good hunter always gave the whale a drink; this way other whales would hear of it and allow themselves to be caught too.)

This done, the children rushed excitedly from one whale to another, cutting off pieces of the flipper, the choice muktuk, with their knives. They held the knives dangerously between hand and mouth, narrowly missing their noses. The little ones curiously poked their fingers into the whale's blowhole and into the bloody bullet wounds, while some of the children leaped over the body and others mounted it in "cowboy" play.

One little girl offered me some flipper with the blood still fresh on it, telling me, "Me like muktuk, plenty good." As I chewed the muktuk, I admired the beautiful whale from the sea with its white skin soft to the touch.

The hunters measured the length of each whale and noted it down, as there was a contest to see who caught the largest one. Gordon's largest beluga measured sixteen feet. Leela and Puyuk began to cut the beluga while they were still warm, and along the beach other women bustled with the same activity. About twenty whales must have been caught that night; it was the height of the season.

Two thirteen-year-old boys had gone out with their uncles on their first whale hunt and the men had given them one baby gray beluga for their share. Laughing, one of the hunters said: "Here, you might get married some day and need this meat." Then he proceeded to show the boys how to butcher it.

The women plunged elbow deep into their work, cutting the whale in the prescribed pattern. First they made a deep incision right down the spine horizontally, then they cut off big slabs vertically. Knowing they could use another hand, I asked Gordon for his knife, which was a *sah-vick,* a large murderous-looking tool he had made himself. I began to work on the other side of the whale that Puyuk was butchering. We made deep cuts into the outer muktuk, which is about two and a half inches thick, fleshing off huge chunks measuring about fourteen inches long. Then we made an incision, or handle, at the top of each piece for easier lifting, as the meat was slippery. Puyuk and I carried the muktuk to the sea, cleansing it of blood and loose gravel in a kind of baptism, then carried it to a pile on the beach. The next day the meat would be cut into smaller squares for sun drying.

The cool night air caused the warm whale flesh to steam. We all worked feverishly, our hands bloody and our knives covered with slime. The sea was red with the blood of the whales, and above the horizon the sky was a pale red-violet. It was long past midnight at Sheshalik and bright as day.

After we had removed the blubber we cut off the heads and the flippers. Puyuk showed me exactly where to cut between the bones on the broad rudder-like tail flippers, and I severed the tail. Then she took out the pink bladder of

the whale, blew it up, tied it, and gave it to Alunik, who tossed it into the air like a balloon.

When we reached the last and largest beluga, Puyuk pointed to it with her knife and stated, "This one is pregnant!"

We began to cut away the muktuk, Puyuk on one side and I on the other; and when we reached the red flesh underneath, she took charge and cut away the lungs and the heart with her ulu. I, who could not bear the sight of my child's bloody knee, realized that this mother's dark-red flesh was meat and sustenance. It was fitting that Puyuk, a midwife, should tend this pregnant beluga. Her knife cut deeper and deeper and the pale violet intestines slid out along with the embryo in the sac. Carefully Puyuk cut the membranes to reveal a beluga baby almost ready for birth, gray, smooth, very clean and perfect.

Puyuk bent her head; the sun's rays illuminated her hands and face as she lifted her knife and with one dramatic stroke severed the umbilical cord. It was an unforgettable scene.

Gordon, watching me, explained that a long time ago when food was scarce, the old women ate the embryo along with any roots, meat, or berries they could find. The missionaries stopped the practice of eating the embryo.

Soon there was nothing left of the whales on the beach but twenty bloody, skinned beluga heads lying in a row. The bones were thrown to the dogs, but the gray embryo lay untouched on the gravel.

As we ended our task the sky turned bright crimson as if it were on fire. The June midnight sun shone over Sheshalik. The beluga blood in the sea matched the red of the horizon as a new day dawned.

It was two thirty in the morning and the sun was bright in the sky when I went back to my tent, leaving some of the women still cutting meat. When I passed Mary's tent she invited me in. "I listened for your footsteps," she said. "Do you want some soup?" I was cold and hungry and thankful for the steaming bowl of soup that she set down in front of me. It was dark brown and had rice in it; the meat was the fresh heart and muktuk of a whale killed that evening. The muktuk was tender, something like cooked mushrooms; and the heart reminded me of beef heart, only tougher.

Kanayak came in with four hunters, who sat tiredly on the gravel floor of the tent with their mukluk'd legs crossed. The white hoods of their parkas were pulled back to reveal very black hair. Mary gave each a bowl of steaming hot soup, setting it down with great courtesy, and then large mugs of hot tea and pilot bread. The men relaxed, leaning back on their elbows in a repose known only to men who use all of their muscles.

Kanayak told how one of them had got a beluga with just a harpoon, no gun. "The harpoon rope to the beluga got tangled around his leg and he nearly was pulled in after it. But lucky for him," he said, "he got his leg out just in time." I looked at the lucky hunter, but he was busy eating his soup. He hadn't eaten much or slept for days and was glad to be alive.

"It happened here at Sheshalik," Kanayak began, sipping his hot tea from a mug without a handle. "Leela's grandfather drowned in such an accident. The rope became twisted around his leg and pulled him right in the water. He was dragged with the whale and we never saw him again. A year later at Point Barrow they found a body tied to the belly of a dead beluga. The rope was tangled around and around the whale and the man."

The hunter near Kanayak lifted his head and nodded. "We think it was him."

We all sat silent for a moment. Then I realized that the "Ehhhhhh" was coming from my own throat as well as from Mary's. The fire had gone out; it was time to get some sleep. It was about four in the morning when I crawled into my tent and fell flat on my sleeping bag with my feet hanging out of the entrance. I dreamed of whales swimming without heads, and of Ahab in *Moby Dick* wrapped up in a rope tied to the white whale.

I awakened only once to hear the peculiar singing of the huskies. It was a melancholy strain, a weird wolf-like howl.

CHAPTER 5

Timeless Days

Ready and willing, eager for work
—Away up inland—
I am always gladly at hand
Whatever needs to be done. . . .

THE WEATHER had grown cooler, but the sky remained clear; only a few hazy clouds marred its brilliance. I never ceased to marvel at its intensity; if I could paint it that color no one would believe me—it looked so theatrically blue. It never darkened in the evening, but the sky beyond the sea turned a violet haze. Then came the

night of June 21, the longest day of the year, when the sun
set only to rise again over the mountains, making day hardly
distinguishable from night. Yet as an artist I noticed one
marvelous difference; the midnight-sun glow illumined each
figure with a light that Rembrandt would have loved and
understood. It bathed the people in a translucence that
transformed everything into molten gold; it touched a
child's full round cheek and burned yellow and crimson
lights in it, and lit the arm of a woman wearing orange as a
golden torch.

Every night I found myself hating to go to bed. I got up
early, but night was the exciting time; everyone was out
then. Every position the people took delighted me; it was a
joy to watch them move. They had an earthy, permanent
quality, as if rooted to the soil. Perhaps the fact that they
always worked on the earth and used no elevation further
enhanced this impression. I wanted to capture their time-
lessness. As they hovered near a fire, or bent over a whale,
or cut a seal, they had natural grace of movement, without
self-consciousness. I loved their faces, which were without
guile or vanity; nature had kept them eternally young, eternally true.

Even the very old, like Erahooruk, the old woman I had
seen sitting by the church tent, sat on the wet, cold, gravelly
beach after midnight, fishing. They threw out their nets,
pulled them in, and took out the fish with gnarled fingers.
Every time I passed Erahooruk on the beach she grinned up
at me. I wanted to say, "Grandma, it's after midnight, don't
you know its too cold and damp for an old woman? You
could get rheumatism!" She wouldn't have understood English, and besides I never would have said it; instead I
helped her disentangle some whitefish from her net, smiling
admiringly at her as she threw back two young flounder.
When I walked on, she was still throwing her net into the
water.

Quavuk was pulling in her net too; she pulled with a
clean, sure, classic gesture. When she spoke her eyes opened

wide and her brows lifted toward the center of her forehead. She was an ageless fifty with the simplicity of a young
girl. Her smooth high-boned cheeks had a ruddy healthy
color and her nose was strong and straight. Her dark hair
was parted in the middle and knotted low at the back of her
neck. From early morning till late at night she worked, with
only about five hours of sleep a day. The women said of
Quavuk: "She has had much sorrow in her life and works
hard all the time." When she was very young her mother
died; her uncle took care of her, the one she was now caring
for in his helplessness because she had not forgotten his
kindness to her. She was both midwife and Sunday school
teacher, and she told me with simplicity, "Jesus died for us,"
as she offered me one of her fishes.

She agreed to pose for me after church, and I painted
her as she sat majestically on the beach with the sea behind
her. She had washed and changed from her greasy, ugruk-
cutting, calico parka and her everyday waterproof sealskin
work mukluks. Her face radiated beauty of spirit; my brush
seemed helpless—paint was not enough.

After about three quarters of an hour we went into her
tent because the mosquitoes were biting us. Quavuk led the
way in, picking up clothes her grandson had dropped and
carrying out a potful of urine. Nearby was a hand-operated
sewing machine, a stove, and a bed covered with a polar
bear hide. Quavuk offered me coffee and a doughnut fried in
seal oil, and it was so good I had another, for I had not
eaten any sweets for a long time.

I asked if she could fry hotcakes in seal oil. She answered: "It burns too quick, but sometimes the men use it to
grease the motors of the boats." Then she said shyly: "The
women wonder why you left your family. Did your husband
let you come? Did he give you the fare?"

"He let me come," I answered. "You see, I am an artist.
I wanted to paint Eskimos as they really are, and I earned
the money for the trip by giving art lessons."

She accepted my explanation. As I painted, her eyes

kept closing, for she had been up the night before cutting whale. I left her as she finally fell asleep; it was the healthy sleep of one with an easy conscience who had labored long in the open air.

The next morning I was awakened by a peculiar howling of the dogs; they sounded as if they were singing in unison. Although it was only five thirty A.M., I heard the sound of a motor overhead and guessed it might be a plane landing. I wanted to talk to the pilot about the flight back to Kotzebue so I dressed quickly, but the plane had flown over and away. It was probably on an emergency call to the men who work on the DEW line farther north. I wanted to ask the pilot when he returned if I could ride with him on the mail run to Kivalina, Noatak, and then on to Kotzebue.

I smelled the aroma of the coffee Quavuk was making on her primus stove out of doors. A large pot of cornmeal boiled on the stove, and I offered to flip the pancakes she was frying while she ran off with a bowl of cornmeal for the old man. The sourdough hotcakes were the size of the huge fry pan; every tent had a bowlful of the sourdough yeast mixture constantly in some stage of preparation. There was flour in the tents even though the Eskimos may have had few other store groceries. About two cupfuls of sourdough yeast was kept over for the next day. The sourdough yeast mixture consisted of flour and water and yeast and was the basis for biscuits, bread, and doughnuts, although the women did not bake bread often at camp because it took a hotter fire and more driftwood than the smaller biscuits.

I traded Quavuk some canned stuff for a fresh-caught whitefish which I fried for dinner that evening over my little stove together with some canned potatoes. I left the frying pan outside my tent to soak, and the next day it was gone; the loose dogs must have run off with it.

There was a lassitude in the camp; the women were exhausted, passive. I felt the attitude affecting me and let myself drift through the day, forcing nothing, quietly part of everything, unthinking. It was a change not having to think but to do; such a rest. I knew now why physical work was so healing for people—it demanded activity, yet left the mind idle; the body went through the motions.

Two days later when the mail plane came, landing on the water on floats, everyone gathered around it. One of the women tried to give the pilot a few jars of muktuk. "There are two families left at Noatak who are starved for fresh muktuk; we want to send them some."

The pilot said he had too big a load this time and couldn't take the muktuk. He told the hunters he had seen lots of beluga coming that way. One man replied: "Leave it to Wien [Airline] to drive them here!"

Kanayak asked the pilot if he would take me on the mail run with him. "I have too big a load this time for either muktuk or passenger," the pilot said. "Maybe next time." Familiar with the way of bush pilots, I knew I would just have to take my chances when he came again. The schedule depended on the weather, but the pilot said: "I'll try to be back Monday."

No beluga today. The hunters were sleeping while their wives worked to cut up the meat. Each white chunk of beluga was cut into six-inch-square pieces and hung on racks to dry, each square linked by flesh to another and making a colorful pattern of white-pink next to the black ugruk already drying. The inner flesh of the beluga, which was a dark wine color, was cut in strips to dry, while the yellow fatty blubber was placed in barrels or pokes.

Okukchuk and Mary rigged up a worktable by laying a board across two rusty barrels, but most of the women still preferred to work bending over the ground, head down and knees straight.

The women kept at their various jobs, processing the beluga, despite the rain that plagued us day and night. We had been lucky not to have had rain up till now, for there was no shelter out of doors and my tent was too small for me to stay in for any length of time except to sleep. It was cold and damp and the prospect of breakfast in the rain was unappetizing, so I went into Okukchuk's tent to cook my mush on her stove.

As I drank coffee I set out my watercolor paints. I was planning to sketch and paint the interior of the tent, when the flap opened and Puyuk's head appeared. She had been working in the rain all morning and now came in for a cup of coffee. She sat drinking it near the opening of the tent, not near the fire, as if she didn't want to get too comfortable since she knew she had to go out again.

"If I had a hat on, I would take it off to you," I said, standing with my back to the stove and shivering with the cold. I asked: "Aren't you cold working out there?" Then I realized how idiotic it sounded. Puyuk didn't even bother to answer me. She went on drinking her coffee, holding the mug with strong, capable hands. It meant something; she had more than earned it. She sipped her coffee and looked at me and I shall never forget that look; the image burned.

"Please, dear Puyuk," I said, "just drink your coffee; I know you have work to do. Just until you finish your coffee, may I please paint you?"

In a few quick strokes I captured Puyuk's look forever. It was the quickest watercolor I had ever done. Puyuk's expression in answer to my question is in that painting. It is the final answer every Eskimo gives to a white person of another civilization—who has enough to eat. She had spent her life working in the cold. But what could I know of this —of hard continous work such as she did or of the struggle for food just to survive?

My body was exhausted as were the other women's. I admired their adeptness and patience, for they doled out their strength a little at a time, instead of wasting it all at once. They had a right to be proud of being Eskimo.

One afternoon I noticed heavy smoke pouring out of Leela's stovepipe. Her tent had the only screened window in the whole camp and through it I saw her round brown face.

"You come in, have tea," Leela greeted me. When I admired her screened window she explained: "I spent all day making it and now I can see the hills. It cools off the tent when the stove gets too hot."

She dusted her stove with a large goose wing, then thrust two chunks of driftwood into the firing section. Her body moved easily as she stirred up a batch of sourdough biscuits and shoved the pan of dough into the oven to bake. I asked her if she ever put sugar or an egg into her biscuits.

"No, no money for sugar or eggs," she replied, kneeling by the stove and feeding the driftwood into the flames. I felt ashamed for having asked.

Leela's motherly face was damp from the exertion as she poured the tea into mugs and lovingly set the biscuits on a flat wooden board in front of me.

"I work hard," she said, laughing. "All my children married but three. All the time I work, so my kids have enough to eat and won't be hungry." Then, holding her stomach, she laughed. "That's why I'm so fat." Her humor, like Okukchuk's, seemed always on the surface, ready to bubble up.

Her eleven-year-old son was the boy who had helped me carry by bag into Sheshalik the day I arrived. Leela asked him to close the flap of the tent and he jumped up immediately to do it. "What an obedient boy," I commented, remembering how often I might have to tell my son to do something. "When my son was a baby, I never scolded him," she said. "I was so glad to have him, my son."

Her pretty daughter, Rosie, a teen-ager in jeans and saddle shoes, home from Mt. Edgecumbe School, came into the tent. She had Leela's natural dignity although her hair was up in pincurls. A typical teen-ager home on summer vacation, she would have fitted in with teen-agers across the United States. She helped with the dishes but did not often do the really bloody job of cutting up the seals.

Rosie told me: "When Mama was real sick with TB she taught me how to cut seal and I did it." It was Leela who discouraged her from this kind of work, who wanted her to have an easier life and encouraged her to study hard in school.

After Sheshalik, Leela and Gordon were planning to change their life by moving from the village of Noatak to Shungnak as missionaries. Rosie would be hundreds of miles away in a high school, her education arranged by the U. S. Bureau of Indian Affairs.

Leela busied herself with some white sinew she was drying. "It is from the back of the beluga—the strongest thread to sew mukluks." Leading the way outdoors, Leela said over her shoulder: "The spinal cord makes good rope. I'm going to make rope from sealskin if you want to watch. We call it *aklunaepaek*."

Gordon had rigged up a makeshift tent with poles and canvas over their assortment of seal pokes, barrels, and washtubs. It had taken Leela many days of soaking the sealskin in oil to remove the hair, and many hours of scraping the skin while plagued by mosquitoes just to prepare a length of rope. The finished sealskin would be cut into a continuous circle and hung to dry in coils.

Since the smoke fire did not keep the mosquitoes away, I added more dried grasses to it as I had seen the women do. I offered to get Leela some mosquito repellent and, since her hands were full of seal oil, I rubbed it on her lovely old face. She said: "You'll get your hands dirty." All the women chided me when I cut whale or seal meat, "You'll get your hands dirty!" "Good," I wanted to shout!

She worked steadily, her big body stooped over the tub of stinking hides. Gordon, who had been watching us, came over and sat down near me. "I take a look at your face when you come and I see you are honest—we know what you are like from your face."

Before I could answer him, he went away. I wanted to tell him that I too had come here to see the faces of an honest people and that I had found them.

A few days later two new people came into the camp and pitched their tent near mine. Quavuk asked if I would like to go with her to meet the newcomers, who were Eskimo missionaries from Noatak. They had come from Sealing Point, where they had tended the reindeer herd.

Many children and two other adults were already in the tent. The missionary's wife smiled warmly and shook hands with me; then looking at us she said to Quavuk: "She looks like your sister."

The remark was close to the truth. I had brought no mirror and did not know if anyone in camp had one, but in Okukchuk's orange parka, with my face burned brown from the constant sun, I must have resembled the other woman. I wore no makeup and had acquired a rolling gait from walking on the uneven tundra.

A plate with dried seal was passed around by the good-humored missionary's wife who was holding her wrist which was bandaged with a rag. When I asked her about it, she showed me an ugly infected red swelling, fortunately nothing resembling blood poisoning. The only thing I had brought for such an emergency was an antisceptic lotion and Band-aids, so I cleaned up the sore as best I could and left the lotion with her.

The women donned fur parkas as the evenings grew cooler and I sketched their forms as they strolled and visited, carrying their babies on their backs by means of a belt tied around the waist. Ten-year-old girls also paraded with their brothers and sisters on their backs, the babies' legs clinging tightly to the girls' sides. They wore their mothers' parkas, which were usually too large for them, with their "babies" buried deep in the protection of the fur hood or peeping out shyly.

Small children were still running wild on the tundra, chasing one another in a delirium with the pups yipping after them. They called out, "Hi, Cara!" and by now I knew their names and greeted them also.

When Sunday night arrived I began to pack my things in preparation to leave, dividing the unused groceries among the women. I went to Puyuk's tent to say good-bye, leaving little Alunik the Kleenex and some dried apricots that she loved. I promised her a doll, as I had not seen any of the children in camp playing with dolls. Puyuk picked up Alunik's small ulu and handed it to me as a present. She told me she would hook some trout and send them to me, frozen, by plane in the winter, and we promised to write each other.

That night I crawled into my tent cold and exhausted; it was raining again and I struggled to sleep. My feet were icy and it was impossible to get warm, even with heavy wool socks, flannel pajamas, and two sleeping bags. I got up to put on a sweater and a kerchief as even my head was cold. But I knew that not all the discomfort was physical; most of it was caused by the exciting pace of events and lack of sleep. Not wanting to miss any experience and absorbing everything, I had worn myself out and had lost weight from the unaccustomed activity and change of diet.

Finally falling into a heavy slumber at about four in the morning, I was awakened by the choking and coughing of a baby in a nearby tent. It sounded as if she could not catch her breath and was having a convulsion. I struggled with the impulse to go and help, wanting to yet thinking that the mother knew what to do, that I knew nothing, and that my presence would be superfluous. I could not remember how to treat a convulsion. It was frightening to hear the gasps of the baby. I lay as if paralyzed. I could hear women's voices and while I was still deciding what to do, the baby quieted down and I heard no more.

I slept again and awoke at nine o'clock, worn and tired in every bone; my air mattress had developed holes and I was practically sleeping on the gravel. I had worried all night about the sick child. Some of the children did not get proper rest; they played and ran around till two o'clock at night. It was damp and cold in most of the tents as they had no fires at night and the children slept on caribou mats on the ground. Some of them had runny noses or colds and were also prone to ear infections, which led to draining ears and sometimes loss of hearing.

FEJES

It was Monday, the day the pilot had said he would try to land at Sheshalik. Although I wasn't sure he would take me, I had to be prepared, so I finished packing my things. Knowing bush pilots, I expected him to come quick as a flash out of nowhere and disappear just as fast.

About ten minutes later the Cessna appeared, landing on floats on the sea. Suddenly the pilot stepped out and I realized that I had not yet taken down my tent. Mary and Kanayak helped me pull up the stakes and pack the tent, and I ran to the float ship.

The women sat on the beach, holding jars and cans of fresh muktuk and watching the loading operations. The sea looked rough and the small plane wobbled in the water.

The pilot said: "The load is too heavy."

For a minute I thought he wasn't going to take me, but finally he said: "C'mon, get in," and threw my bags into the plane, hesitating over the tent but then deciding to take it. There was no room for the jars of muktuk and the women sat mutely holding them.

The women and I looked at one another, then embraced. Waving good-bye, I climbed into the float ship beside the pilot.

The pilot gunned the motor and in spite of our load we lifted higher and higher. As we turned toward the mountains it seemed to me that the one white mountain in the distance was shaped like a whale. I looked down at Sheshalik; small white tents were all I could see along the seashore; there were no other signs of life. I shall never forget these people, I promised silently.

The pilot kept muttering beside me: "Those Eskimos, they have no idea what a heavy load is!"

When we arrived at Kivalina, the villagers were out to meet the plane. One of the Eskimos wanted to know how many beluga they had killed at Sheshalik. "About eighty so far," I answered. The Kivalina hunters had shot ten that morning.

There was a large white schoolhouse but the rest were

sod and small frame houses. The whole village seemed no larger than about six city blocks and faced the sea. We made only a five-minute stop. After the pilot had unloaded the mail, he called out: "Ready to go now," and so we took off again, lighter by many pounds. Pointing downward to the sod houses of the villagers, he said: "They sure are strong." I thought he was referring to the construction, but he said: "No, the odor!" He said he couldn't approve of their way of life, but knowing that he had married an Eskimo girl, I answered, "One has to understand it." Unconsciously I assumed the viewpoint of an Eskimo.

We made a short stop at Noatak. A woman stood waiting there and from her face, and from the talk of the women at Sheshalik, I knew she must be Noyuk. I said hello to her and repeated regards from the women, apologizing for not having brought any muktuk. "We had too heavy a load," I said lamely from the window of the Cessna.

We left so quickly that all I could see of Noatak was the figure of Noyuk, a high river bank, and some wooden cabins. The motion of the plane was making me sick; I was becoming dizzy from the landings and startings. Finally we landed at Kotzebue and as I stepped from the plane, I vomited over the side of the door into the water. Wearing my high rubber boots I waded into shore, first leaning down to wash my face in Kotzebue Sound.

I had missed breakfast and made straight for Rotman's and a plate of ham and eggs. How good sliced white bread and butter tasted! It would be two hours before the plane left for Fairbanks, so I asked Mary Pilcher, who worked for the airline, if I could rest somewhere. She opened the back door of her office and led me to a huge bed with a wide mattress! I had almost forgotten about real beds and removing my boots and jacket, flung myself down and fell fast asleep. Ten minutes before the plane left, Mary wakened me. Men had stomped through the room in heavy boots and all manner of business had transpired in the office, but I hadn't heard a thing.

.   .   .   .   .

I arrived at Fairbanks airport in rubber boots, jeans covered with dirt, a red windbreaker, a kerchief over my hair, and with my face brown and healthy. My spirit had been nurtured by adventure. Whale oil permeated my clothes and skin and I wanted a bath desperately.

I carried beluga bones, plant specimens, driftwood, starfish, and hundreds of sketches in addition to my oils. Well-dressed women in high heels and furs passed me on the way to the southbound flight to Seattle. Joe and Mark took the duffel bags and assorted packages; Yola hugged me; Mama was home. My family looked well; they had managed without me and seemed to have eaten three meals a day.

"Oh, Mama, you sure smell funny," said Yola. "Why are you wearing your rubber boots? It's not raining here."

Our five-and-a-half-year-old had grown taller in my absence. She had missed me, of course, but she had been well cared for in my absence by our motherly Finnish neighbor who had two children of her own around Yola's age and she had gained weight as a result of my friend's superb cooking.

Mark, at twelve, was a self-reliant youngster busy with his many friends. He had helped Joe, taking care of the garden, doing chores around the house, and lending a hand at our store when shipments needed unpacking. He was learning to cook scrambled eggs. I need not have worried about the children. It was good to know that our family could function and progress without me; they needed me but could also stand on their own feet.

In my absence Joe had built a room in the basement for Mark so that he could have privacy; a room where his friends could visit and stay overnight, away from interference. His room had a separate entrance down the back stairs so that he and his friends would track mud and snow down that way instead of through the house. In addition to books, his room held his two passions, car engines and ski equipment.

He had begun to ski for the first time at Mount Mc-
Kinley when he was six. He had borrowed my skis and gone
down the slope in my boots, many sizes too large. Ever since
then he had loved the world of snow and skis. Now in August, with snow months away, he was already talking about
"Heads, Kneissls, and ski slopes."

"Mom, I think I'd like to be a ski bum when I grow
up!"

That evening the family enjoyed hearing about my adventures. They knew I was not outstanding at athletics and
feared husky dogs and the sight of blood.

In the short time I was at Sheshalik it was impossible
for me to get a fully rounded picture of Eskimo life. As an
artist, I had been given an abundance; I had not viewed
Sheshalik as an anthropologist or scientist but as a woman
and an artist. I had seen an idyllic picture of Eskimo camp
life, since it was Eskimo vacation time in a sense and everyone was enjoying the change of scene and abundance of
food.

There may have been undercurrents that I was not
fully aware of. I remember how once, for example, a man
came to his tent stumbling drunk and the people acted
ashamed. I had a feeling that the village was like most isolated Alaskan villages, broken up into factions. It looked as
though each group maintained an interdependence with
relatives and hunting partners within the group only, but I
couldn't be sure of my impressions.

They may have regarded me as an outsider or inter-
loper but I was not made aware of it, for they showed me
only courtesy and warmth.

Their direct simplicity and honesty demanded the same
response. Among isolated people every human being becomes significant and each incident is magnified. Eskimo
life strengthened my belief in the basic goodness of man—
and its indestructibility.

I had returned to a changed world. How tame house-
keeping seemed in comparison with the excitement of adventure. The silence of the Arctic was now replaced by the

idiocy of the radio; lack of speech by the overabundance of unnecessary words. The directness of Eskimo life and work was replaced by the pressures of commercial interchange, and I missed the vast spaces and the sea.

Joe and I talked it over that evening when the children were asleep. He needed my help in the store and the errands had to be done—yet if we hired a part-time worker and cut our expenses, it would save me half a day's precious time. If I organized my day and did the shopping and housework systematically, I might possibly have hours for myself.

Memories had stored up that begged to be released. A profusion of the colors and shapes of Eskimo life flooded my brain and pressed into consciousness. There was no order or plan to these thoughts, just an urgent necessity to paint, to create out of a chaos that threatened to overwhelm me.

With Joe's aid I prepared canvas and set up an easel in one corner of our living room, ending up with a cubicle of about six by eight feet. While the children were at school my time was my own. I simply began to paint, one canvas after another. I painted four-foot canvases as easily as if I had known how the end would be, yet in truth not knowing what the beginning was until I put my brush to canvas.

There was a great exultation within me. The compositions were strong, yet simple—brown outlined the forms where the sky met the ocher land; oranges, yellows, and blues set off the whiteness of the whales. Here was the primeval earth woman resting from her toil, standing in the blood of the animal. The men in the paintings stride and work, each movement purposeful, symbolic. The canvases seemed to have a life of their own.

I prepared meals for the family and cleaned the house, then entered the little work place and it became a place of worship. I could understand why Rouault painted in spotless white; I wanted to get down on my knees like that fourteenth-century Italian master who thought all artists should pray before painting because it was holy work.

I wanted to paint an illusion of light, an illumination

of the canvas so that it warmed and strengthened the on-looker, forcing him to catch his breath in response to a beauty his mind could never explain, only his senses understand. The painting should come out of its own ashes, as it were, out of one's own life and experiences.

Every minute seemed to be as precious droplets to be savored. In the past I had painted aimlessly, with restlessness and frustration. Now my vision encompassed a higher goal: I wanted to paint the Eskimos to show the spirit of love in man.

Thirty paintings of Sheshalik, of all sizes and colors, crowded the house, in various stages of drying; I decided to exhibit them at Thanksgiving time in Fairbanks. Opening day was crowded even though the temperature had dropped to thirty below zero. The American Association of University Women served coffee, and Alaskans, newcomers and old-timers, came to see the Sheshalik paintings. It was cold and dark outside, but in the inn where the paintings were hung, crowds in all sorts of winter furs and other attire were observing thirty large, brilliantly colored oils.

The paintings were subsequently shown in Anchorage, in Juneau, and brought me my first trip out of Alaska in ten years. I had not seen my family in New York in that time. An art teacher from the University of Washington, Ruth Pennington, had bought a little painting of mine five years before when she visited Fairbanks. When I mailed her slides of the Sheshalik paintings, she showed them to the Director of the Frye Art Museum in Seattle, who immediately wired that he wanted to exhibit my work.

Yola and I left for Seattle but we were not prepared for the crowds, the sudden attention and the publicity we received. It was unbelievable after painting for years in isolation and obscurity, and I could not feel I warranted all this notice. My first trip to a big city in ten years, plus the tension of the exhibit, was overwhelming.

Before the show closed at the Museum I left Seattle for

New York where I was born. All three of my sisters and their families were at the airport to meet us. We had suffered the loss of both parents in the interval.

I was the eldest of four sisters. We had always been a close-knit family and resembled one another a great deal. We all painted and each in a different style; no one was influenced by the others. My sisters had married artists. Joe, my husband, was the only one not in the field of visual art—he was a musician, a fine violinist. My sisters and their husbands painted and taught art, and their children also painted; their homes were crowded with paintings and sculpture. In the garden of my sister Elaine's house was my first stone carving, one entitled "Four Sisters."

Yola, happy with her new-found cousins, was the center of attention. She enjoyed most the warm air in March and played in the sunlight; Fairbanks was still cold, completing the cycle of another northern winter.

My father was born in a town called Lemberg, near Vienna. He spoke seven languages and read constantly; his overcoat pocket always bulged with books and newspapers. Father was volatile and sensitive. Mother, born in Warsaw, had been a beautiful woman, unassuming in her ways and of peaceful temperament.

Our home, although in a poor section of the Bronx, was always filled with books, music, and paintings. It was our father who took us to different museums on weekends.

The first place I visited with Yola was the Metropolitan Museum of Art. I had relied on reproductions for so long that now the real textures of paint were exciting to me. I wanted to touch the paintings, especially Gauguin's Tahitian works and Van Gogh's paintings of the Arles period. It seemed to me that each stroke of their brushes revealed the handwriting of their lives.

Jose de Creeft, with whom I had studied stone carving at the Art Students League, was chopping stone at his Greenwich Village studio when I surprised him with a visit; but Saul Baizerman was dead. Baizerman and his wife had taken me as a student when I was seventeen and they had encouraged me. I remembered the first time I saw Baizerman's sculpture at the Sculptors' Guild Show. At that time the Museum of Modern Art had not yet purchased his work. The four huge Rodin-like nude figures stood out among the eighty sculptures and I decided then that I would find out where he lived and ask him to accept me as a student. His hammered bronze figures even covered the ceiling of his studio and in the back was a tiny room where they lived.

I had one other teacher, Aaron Goodleman, a warm, inspiring teacher who instilled a strong feeling for form in my work.

When my thirty Sheshalik paintings opened in New York I received my first notice in *Arts Magazine*. To my pleasure it was a good review. Sidney Tillim wrote: "She puts one in mind of Gauguin (she has Hartleyish moments too) and certain Mexican art in her feeling for shape, . . . that communicates great strength in her understanding of her subject."

Back in Fairbanks, the trip to the States seemed unreal, like so much sugar candy disappearing when one eats it. Yet the trip had given me the confidence and the belief in my work that I needed. The main task still faced me at the easel. I felt full of vitality to be back in Alaska and could not wait to go to the Arctic again. The stories of Point Hope had only whetted my interest in that remote whaling village. Knud Rasmussen, who visited it in 1925, thought it was the most interesting village in Alaska.

I met a Point Hope Eskimo in Fairbanks. His name was Asatsiak Killigivuk and over a cup of coffee we spoke of his village. He gave me a letter for his wife asking her to let me stay in their house. A pilot going to Kotzebue offered me a ride in his Bonanza Beechcraft. "Okay," he said. "I can use you for ballast." He didn't know when he would be leaving —"Sometime next week." I packed bags and equipment and prepared food for the family, storing it in the freezer. It was almost a year since my Sheshalik visit, and mukluks that Okukchuk had made were now packed in my bag.

My work was at a standstill and I felt like a chained sled dog, ready to go. When the pilot postponed the trip another week, waiting one day more seemed unbearable, so I decided to leave by commercial flight for Kotzebue and then go to Point Hope by bush plane.

PART II

Point Hope

CHAPTER 6   *Tigara*

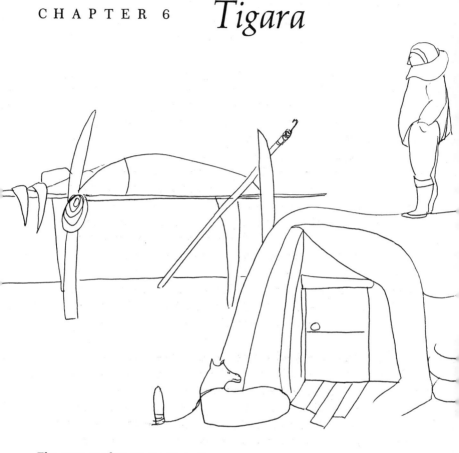

The great sea has set me in motion,
Set me adrift,
Moving me as the weed moves in a river.

QALAJAOG OF POINT HOPE
told this story to Knud Rasmussen:
"In long forgotten times, there were no lowlands here at
the foot of the mountains, and men lived on the summit of
the great Mount Irrisugssuk, southeast of Kotzebue Sound;

that was the only land which rose from the sea; and on its top may still be found skeletons of whales from these first men's hunting. And that was the time when men still walked on their hands, head downwards; so long ago it was.

"But one day the Raven, he who created heaven and earth, rowed out to sea in his kayak, far out to sea, and there he saw something dark moving and squelching on the surface of the water. He rowed out and harpooned it; blood flowed from the wound he had made. The Raven thought it must be a whale, but then saw that it was a huge dead mass without beginning or end. Slowly the life ebbed from it and he fastened his towline to it, and towed it to the foot of the hills south. Here he made it fast and on the following day when he went down to look at it, he saw that it was stiff; it had turned into land. And there among the old ruins of houses may still be seen a strange hole in the ground; that is the spot where the Raven harpooned Tigara. And that is how this land came."

According to Knud Rasmussen; the Tigara tribe of Point Hope was once a mighty people and there was a legend of a great battle fought by them on land and sea against the Noatak Eskimos at Cape Seppings.

Eskimos call their land Tikitaq (Tigara), meaning "index finger," because of its shape; it is a long narrow peninsula jutting out for about fifteen miles into the sea, naked to the wind. Yet it was the home of generations of Eskimos just because it caught every blast, driving the pack ice in and out from shore and making whale and seal hunting possible. The whale and seal were the people's staff of life, providing both fuel and food. Virgorous Eskimos, following the traditions and culture of their forefathers, struggled continually to harvest food, living in close harmony with the sea and land.

In addition to sea mammals, polar bears also followed the pack ice. A variety of wildlife allowed hunting all year round, for the land supported bands of caribou, Arctic wolves, foxes, squirrels, lemmings, and thousands of salmon, trout, and whitefish. Waterfowl such as murres, gulls, geese, and ducks swarmed into the Arctic in the spring, nesting in the rookeries on the sea cliffs and feeding at lakes, ponds, and rivers. In the winter owls, hawks, ravens, and ptarmigan remained in the North.

Although white men discovered Point Hope in 1826, it was another twenty-five years before constant, direct contact with the Eskimos was established. It was believed that the Russians began to trade at Anadyr in 1648 with the Eskimos, who exchanged furs and ivory for glass beads, iron, tobacco, and tea.

Point Hope was a hard three-day dog team ride from Kotzebue in winter and in summer a skin boat ride when the sea was open. In the past they had traded at Kotzebue with Noatak and other tribes who came down each summer to trade caribou fawnskins, fox, wolf, wolverine, and other furs, dried fish, jade, mammoth ivory, clothing, and utensils.

Nowadays, there was direct radio communication with Kotzebue. However, mechanical difficulties and bad weather frequently made it impossible for planes to fly and then the village was completely isolated.

From their permanent houses in Point Hope the people traveled hundreds of miles along the coast in search of food. Six miles east of Tigara on a narrow neck of land lay an abandoned settlement known as Jabbertown, which was established and named by American whalers who wintered there in the late nineteenth century.

Jabbertown was settled by deserters from whaling ships who were forced to spend the winter there. They taught the Eskimos how to make liquor and introduced venereal and other diseases, causing hardships and many deaths. The village lost half of its population within a few years from flu, measles, TB, and other diseases; unfortunately the Eskimos had no immunity to the white man's germs.

Liquor flowed all along the coast. The Eskimos still tell stories about the orgies during which they were cheated out

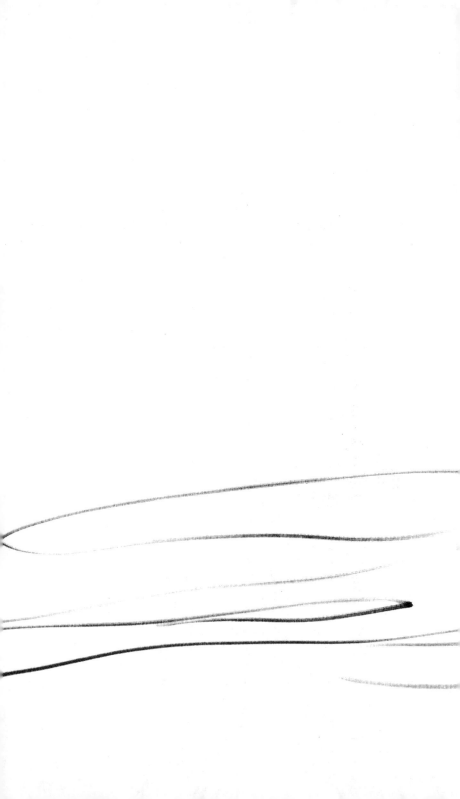

of their possessions and their women were sold by their husbands or fathers. Murder was not unknown.

Captains hired crews at Jabbertown, giving them the whale meat and taking the baleen. They also paid their crews in flour, black molasses, matches, cloth, tobacco, coffee, and tea. In 1906 a baleen substitute was found and whaling gradually declined.

The Noatak Eskimos also migrated to Jabbertown to work, then traveled to Sheshalik by boat when the whaling was over.

Along the north shore, east of the Episcopal Mission, was Ipiutak. Some scientists believe that several thousand years ago, before man walked in the Western Hemisphere, a land bridge connected the continents and Mongols from Asia migrated to Alaska. At Ipiutak the anthropologists Helge Larsen and Froelich G. Rainey discovered remains of an Arctic metropolis, dating around the first century A.D., where about three thousand Eskimos had lived in a highly developed culture.

Upon digging they uncovered thousands of artifacts, knives, snow goggles, arrowheads, animal carvings, elaborate instruments, and many unnamed objects. Most of the ivory and bone objects were covered with beautiful designs, delicately engraved with great skill. The most unusual finds were the skeletons. Some of the skulls had ivory eyes with jet-black pupils set in the sockets; others had ivory nose plugs carved in the form of birds with jet eyes.

Rainey and Larsen did not believe that the Ipiutak people were whale hunters like the present Point Hope Eskimos because of the complete absence of baleen and whaling harpoon heads in the ruins. The questions remain: Who were these people? Where did they come from? Why did they migrate? What became of them? Maybe some day these mysteries will be solved.

When I spoke with him in Fairbanks, Asatsiak Killigivuk had informed me that there was a Point Hope trading store where I could buy groceries, so I did not bring much food. When I asked what I could take his wife, he suggested, "Masterpiece." It was some time before I understood him— Masterpiece was her favorite chewing tobacco.

I flew to Kotzebue from Fairbanks and walked along the beach to Reverend Thomas's home. I had a warm reunion with Callie, the Reverend, and their five lovable young boys, who had been our neighbors in Fairbanks. The Reverend Thomas was "John" to everyone, and a more genuine, likable man would be hard to find. He had become immersed in his work with the Kotzebue Eskimos and labored with wholehearted understanding to help them. The Thomases lived in the basement of the church, with no running water or plumbing, but had plans to build another story the following year.

I spent the night in the basement home, sharing a bed with an Eskimo girl who lived there. By seven A.M. the fog had lifted and my plane was ready to leave for Point Hope. Quickly I washed and dressed in jeans, sweater, and rubber boots. A chunk of Callie's homemade bread was breakfast— there wasn't time for more. I thanked her for everything as she waved good-bye from the doorway of the church.

At the airport the pilot was fixing the door of an old Beechcraft. It would not close and I had visions of being sucked out into the Chuckchi Sea by the air currents. After a few kicks at the door and expressive words by the pilot, I was hoisted in with duffel bags and paint box. I was the only passenger; the door slammed shut.

The plane, which had two old bucket seats, was jammed with cases of milk, cartons, mail bags, and assorted boxes. The distinguishing features of an Alaskan bush plane were that it was rarely new and hardly, if ever, had a suitcase in it. Burlap sacks, crates, cartons, duffel bags, seal pokes, yes, but no suitcases.

It was June and we could see ice floes jamming the beaches as we flew over Sheshalik and then the village of Kivalina. We circled a small herd of caribou, then followed

the desolate coastline over large stretches of ice and ex-
panses of wind-driven snow broken by dark rocky peaks.
Chains of mountains rose in the distance, over lonely,
rugged, awesome country. I searched for beluga and saw
none, although Reverend Thomas had told of having seen
about a thousand beluga the day before on his flight homeward from Deering on the coast.

About one and a half hours later our plane lost altitude
in preparation for landing and we could see Point Hope
jutting out into the sea. The tundra was fawn-colored in
spots, and from the air it was hard to determine that this
was a village; but as we circled lower, small dots were revealed as low houses, all within a few miles. Most of them
were of sod and barely distinguishable from the surrounding tundra. Two large frame structures projected upward
from the flat terrain; later I learned they were the schoolhouse and the church.

Eskimos came rushing to meet the plane as we landed.
The first words I heard were "Have you seen a skin boat
along the coast? My brother left for Kotzebue by boat and
has not come back." A pleasant sunburned Eskimo ques-
tioned me. The pilot and I shook our heads.

The pilot unpacked cartons and mail for the village
while the Eskimo shouldered my duffel bag and asked,
"Where do you want to go?"

"To Killigivuk's house," I answered and lifting the paint
box and sketch pads, followed my guide.

Point Hope had the weathered ancient look of an older
civilization. The houses gave off a subtle seal oil smell, as if
they had withstood the worst of time and wear. The inhab-
itants wore clothing and footgear made from the pelts of
animals that wandered the barren stretches of land and sea.
The sod dwellings clung to the surface of the land, their
greater part under the frozen earth—the feeling of the place
was one of closeness and gravity.

High, white, bleached whalebones projected strangely
in the landscape. Georgia O'Keefe, the artist, would have
loved the bone architecture; bone instead of wood for walls,

clothesline supports, boat racks, grave markers, skin-drying racks, umiak racks, stakes for tying huskies, and for decoration. Some whale bones were twice as high as the dwellings next to them. The tundra was strewn with whale vertebrae, moss, lichen, small varicolored flowers, and other animal bones. We followed a twisted, well-worn path past vestiges of sunken sod houses which had been left to decay.

The people of Tigara walked as if the land and its tundra, the sea and its ice, belonged to them; as if by treading the earth they could absorb the earth's strength and knowledge, for indeed they must have had the knowledge of land and sea to have survived. In early days they believed they were the only people on the whole face of the earth and proudly called themselves the Inupiat, meaning the "Real People."

They looked proud, stoic, ready for humor, flexible beyond any people I had known. The land was strange, devoid of trees and flat in terrain, isolated for hundreds of miles. We had walked the length of the village to the last house and there were no people in sight.

Otoonah Killigivuk's house clung to the edge of the village, almost a part of the icy beach. The house seemed to have grown there; it was sunken and the sides were packed with sod. A strange tundra plant was this earth-sod-wood-bone house of the Arctic. At the doorsteps were large flat stones which must have been carried a long way. The bottom edge of the weathered door, created from the side of a wooden crate, was lower than the stones.

I ducked my head to walk through the small opening and blinked in the darkness. The Eskimo who carried my duffel bags entered behind me and pushed the second door open without knocking. A tiny wrinkled old woman, shoulders taut under her sweater, with scraggly hair arranged above small squinting eyes, peered up at my height and strangeness. This must be Otoonah, I thought. She turned around quickly with a rocking motion in noiseless mukluks and led us farther into the darkness.

We passed through the front storm porch, the natural

refrigerator, where all the hunting equipment and frozen meat was cached. A poke of seal oil was lying on one side of the door; on the other side was an enamel bucket with a wooden cover, the family toilet. We walked through the narrow passageway with our heads bent low to miss the ceiling and came to another door. This opened into the main room, large as an average kitchen, light and cozy. A big oil stove dominated the room and a worn red rug covered cracked green and white flowered linoleum. (The rug had formerly belonged to the church.)

I handed the old woman her husband's letter, but she could not read it, so the Eskimo translated it. Asatsiak had not notified her of his invitation to me. . . . Well, such arrangements are not uncommon, her duffel bags are already in the house—where else can she go, this strange tall white woman with blue eyes? What shall I feed her? There is nothing in the house but seal meat. . . . All this I saw struggling on Otoonah's face and on her quick tongue as they continued to size me up, talking to each other in Eskimo. What could they do?

"Okay, you stay here," said the Eskimo, translating for Otoonah.

Otoonah opened a small door off the main room, one step higher than the kitchen, revealing a room a little larger than a closet with just space enough for a small cot and a table.

"Just fine," I said as I moved my gear into it and thanked them both. There was a table made of packing crates with drawer space under it, and on this I placed my paint box. The cot sagged in the middle until it almost touched the floor, so I arranged my sleeping bags to compensate for the huge indentation. I would sleep hammock style.

After unpacking all of the groceries on the kitchen table, I gave Otoonah the packages of Masterpiece which her husband told me she liked to chew.

The house was about sixty years old. At the time it was

built, Fairbanks camp had not been founded yet, so the original lumber was brought in by whaling ships, probably from San Francisco.

In the kitchen area a serviceable homemade table held a short-wave radio, and against the walls were a cupboard, two chairs, and two cots. The wall behind the large oil stove had a small window through which the activities of the villagers could be seen.

Two years prior to my visit, electricity was first put into the village houses by soldiers stationed nearby who had given the town a generator. Electricity was turned on in the afternoon and turned off at night at a time decreed by the town council. I could visualize the coming of electric lights to Otoonah at the age of seventy-two. How utterly amazed she must have been at pulling a string to light up a bulb after a lifetime of using seal-oil stone lamps and later kerosene lamps!

Otoonah also had an electric hot plate, an electric iron, and a fancy gold scrollwork electric clock from Sears Roebuck. The tag claimed for it "charm, novelty, and accuracy," but the clock was never accurate unless it was reset to breach the hours when the electric power was shut off.

Two guns, a fishing pole, and two ulus hung on the wall near three calendars, one of them from Brower's Trading Post of Point Barrow, Alaska.

Otoonah poured me a cup of tea and as I had not eaten since that morning, I opened a can of spaghetti and meatballs and we shared it—all without a word since we spoke no common language. How to tell her that I wanted to go to the toilet? I finally had to pantomime the act of pulling down the zipper on my jeans. Otoonah then brought me a clean enamel pot with a lid. The common bathroom out on the cold storm porch was right near the main entrance and anyone could and did walk in. Now I would have privacy, a great luxury in an Eskimo home.

I later learned that the Killigivuk home was one of the better ones in the village and that Otoonah had a reputation for being an exceptionally clean housekeeper. While we drank tea, the house filled with some of her relatives who came to look me over. Otoonah instructed one of the younger boys to pull out a carpet sweeper from an attic space in the roof, and he demonstrated it with dignity and obvious pride while everyone watched to see my reaction.

After the formalities of our meeting, I offered to buy some stove oil. Otoonah showed me the direction of the native store and I started out, eager to explore the village.

There were two Eskimo-managed trade stores, the native store run by the Alaska Native Co-op and managed by John Oktolik; the other run privately by Andrew Frankson. The stores were supplied by the boat that arrived yearly in August, so groceries had to be ordered a year in advance. The native store was originally named the Point Hope Reindeer and Trading Company, but in 1920 it separated from the Reindeer Company because trading in goods rather than reindeer was more profitable.

The native store was a frame building with a corrugated-metal exterior. A large front room contained the merchandise for sale and a smaller room in back provided storage and the manager's living quarters. Three separate warehouses made up the rest of the store buildings. Oil space heaters burning constantly during the winter kept the merchandise from freezing.

The store had the atmosphere of a country store, Eskimo style. A potbelly stove squatted in the middle and several Eskimo men, hands in their pockets, leaned around it. Food lined the shelves to the right and hardware items to the left. Canned peaches, beans, cigarettes, dried apricots, raisins, milk, pilot bread, coffee, pans, jeans, axes, flour, shirts, bolts of calico, candy, oil, gas, fishing poles, chamber pots, and other paraphernalia jammed the shelves and available floor space.

For sale were whalebone masks, fine carved ivory, birds, ulus, Eskimo women's needle cases, and an extraordi-

Women in Native Store

nary whaling ship carved completely of ivory. Dark ivory pegs inserted into holes drilled in the light ivory held the beautiful ship and masts together and the ship's "rope" was made of black whale baleen. It was a meticulous work that must have taken months to create. Also made of baleen was a local product, a closely meshed basket made only here or at Point Barrow where the large black whale was hunted. The baskets had simple shapes and carved ivory animals on the lids, and inscribed on the ivory base was the name of the artist, Omnik.

The store bought whalebone masks and carvings on consignment from the villagers, giving credit for groceries in exchange. The villagers also traded sealskin and other pelts for food. A sign on the wall stated that fifty cents would be paid for caribou jaws. As late as 1950 the store shipped to Seattle by the annual supply ship forty drums of whale and seal oil for the manufacture of candles and soap; however, such shipments proved unprofitable and were discontinued.

After introducing myself to John Oktolik, the manager, I bought some flour, sugar, tea, stove oil, cans of food, and cookies. No eggs, potatoes, or even onions were for sale and I had not expected to find any.

The manager efficiently totaled up my purchases on an adding machine and in answer to my inquiry told me there were about three hundred and thirty-six people living in the village. Families were large, five or more in a house. "Most of the people are camping out at Jabbertown," Oktolik said.

"What are they hunting now?" I asked.

"Mostly seal and fish, some caribou," he told me.

On the way home I munched some dried apricots that were surprisingly soft and fresh after a year on the shelf.

I awakened to the sound of wind and rain lashing the house; my room was icy. The sky was gray and over the sea hung thick soupy fog. In the far distance, spray from the beach was hitting the banks. Otoonah had gone off for water. I did not understand her Eskimo when she put her head into my room and spoke, but I thought she meant she was leaving to get water. Choosy, the dog, followed her and I could see her walking to the beach, parka billowing in the wind and head bent. Her tiny figure rocked from side to side as she stepped over uneven tundra, getting smaller and smaller to my eye. She was carrying nothing and it was hard to guess why she went for water without a container!

The fire was burning in the stove so I quickly got up and washed, pouring hot water into the washbasin. When I turned the radio on, I heard a French short-wave broadcast, and then changing the station, could have sworn I heard Chinese!

Otoonah had cooked some sourdough hotcakes and left them on top of the stove. They were the size of a large frying pan and cold, but the coffee was hot. By the time I had washed the dishes, Otoonah was back carrying a huge chunk of ice for our drinking water which she dropped in the water container a few feet from the house.

As she came indoors, she struggled out of her parka, pulling it over her head. Never idle, she began to sweep the floor with the broom, then washed out a few clothes in the basin. It was difficult to be so neat when each bucketful of water was carried in from the ocean.

Otoonah had a disdain for chairs and was more comfortable on the floor. She worked with her feet stretched toward the stove, her little tin sewing box handy under the table. The box held needles, buttons, thread, sinew, thimble, and her favorite scraper which she used to scrape the back of skins to soften them. Hidden in a corner of the room was a lovely oval wooden bowl with a design carved around the top that must have been her mother's.

It was amazing how few words we needed to get along. While the wind howled, I drank tea, wrote home, and then helped Otoonah bake bread.

My first acquaintance was a lovely young woman named Ikkaheena.

"What does 'Ikkaheena' mean?" I asked.

"It means something about washing clothes. I like to wash clothes," she answered, laughing.

She carried her three-month-old baby in the back of her parka, jiggling it up and down as she walked beside me over the rough tundra. Ikkaheena had moist olive skin and wore her hair parted in the middle. Softly molded lips shaped gentle words as she accompanied me the length of the village. She invited me to visit her mother-in-law, who lived near the Killigivuks.

Their house was one of the ancient dwellings, large patches of earth sod having been staked to build the igloo which from a distance resembled a low moss-covered mound.

A long hook leaned on the entranceway and near the house a sealskin was stretched between stakes set in the tundra. Four dogs near the doorway did not bark at me, but I gave them a wide berth as I entered the side entrance, bumping my head hard on the low doorway. With bent heads we entered an underground passageway. The icy walls were formed of whale jawbones, so ancient that they were mossy green, making the tunnel resemble an undersea grotto. The overhead window made of walrus intestine emitted a faint light. Long ago the windows were made of animal membranes such as walrus intestines, but it was too dim to see what type of window this was. Frozen meat and chunks of ice filled a large washtub, and assorted hunting tools rested on the whalebone wall.

Ikkaheena maneuvered the baby on her back as we continued to walk in a stooped position shutting one door and entering another tunnel completely black. I held on to her cotton parka because I could not see a thing while we stooped even lower to go through another low doorway. I felt a bit like Alice in Wonderland.

The tiny room we finally entered was dimly lit, and contained a small stove for burning blubber, a table, and two small cots along the wall. Extra clothing hung on the wall and was draped over the cots. My first impression was that I was on a ship, for the curved walls were once the bow section of an old whaling vessel that wrecked at Point Hope. The whole room, crowded and small as it was, had one advantage: it was warm in winter. My imagination worked hard to comprehend that six human beings lived there, including young Ikkaheena, her husband, and their baby.

In one corner crouched one of the other occupants of the room. Ikkaheena's sister-in-law, small, shrunken, her hair unkempt, turned away in terror, cowering against the

Ikkaheena

wall. I smiled at her but, unusued to strangers, especially white people, she hid under the caribou skins. It was then I discerned that she was badly crippled with a deformed back.

On the cot nearby sat two teen-agers in jeans and plaid shirts, two boys with shiny faces and neatly combed hair swinging their legs under the cot. The whole room seemed transformed with their bright smiles when suddenly, start-lingly, music blared out, deafening in its rawness! In the dimness I located the outlines of a record player. The singer was Ricky Nelson! The room swayed with rock'n'roll rhythm and the boys tapped their feet as they told me they attended school at Mt. Edgecumbe in Sitka.

The taller boy was Horace, Ikkaheena's husband, a slender young man in his late teens who had no employment but hunting, no chance to earn money since he was un-skilled, and no way to buy lumber to build a home for his wife. He informed me that he planned to join the army as soon as they would take him. At least he would receive three square meals a day and see the world, while Ik-kaheena could save his allotment checks for the future. He also had to help his old mother and his crippled sister.

"We will move into a tent on the beach when it gets warmer," Horace said.

It was hard to ignore the human figure on the floor near us, for her trembling had not subsided. Ikkaheena asked if I would like to visit her mother's house, so we left the same way we came. This time the tunnels were not so dark and strange, for echoing down the passageway were the throes of Ricky Nelson.

Ikkaheena's mother was a short, stubby, smiling woman whose name was "Sunshine." Her quickness and agility belied her weight. I recalled the story Reverend Thomas told me about their first meeting at Point Hope. He had landed his plane in the rain, and the first person he met was Ikkaheena's mother who greeted him with: "It's raining out, but I'm Sunshine!"

Ikkaheena's father was an alert old man named Mr. Tuckfield; he was related to Joe Tuckfield, one of the white whalers who settled near Point Hope in the nineteenth century. One of their grandchildren lay sick on the bed and when I touched his forehead it was hot. Sunshine commented: "I think it is his bad teeth."

Ikkaheena put her baby on the floor and gave her a bird wing to chew on while we drank coffee and chatted about the price of food. Coffee, for instance, was seventy-five cents a pound in Fairbanks but a dollar and eighty cents here, more than double the price! The store was supposed to be a co-operative. But it seemed to me that paying airfreight on groceries from Fairbanks would be cheaper than paying for once-a-year delivery by boat. The problem was that most of the people could not pay cash but were given credit at the store in exchange for sealskins and other local products.

I walked back on the old beaten path across the rusty barrel bridge to the end of the village and Otoonah's home. Smoke swirled from the chimney and her white dog Choosy was barking.

The weather was windy, wet, and cold, and had I slept in my small tent as I did at Sheshalik, I would have had a hard time keeping warm. It was good to come home to hot soup and homemade bread. Otoonah watched me eat the caribou soup and chuckled as she muttered to herself pantomining my fast walk, rapidly swinging her arms. Rushing or walking fast was ridiculous to her, especially my long-legged stride. She had been watching the stranger walk in the village as had the others from behind their windows. What was my business? Why the hurry? I laughed hard with her at the person who walked so fast, then took off my wrist watch and left it off for the remainder of the trip—for, day or night, what's the difference, what's the rush, it's always light in June at Tigara!

.   .   .   .   .

It was a clear sharp day, still windy and cold. Ice in strange
animal shapes piled high in pressure ridges all along the
shore, casting green shadows. I could have ventured far out
on the ice but it was dangerous, for breakup time was approaching. Sea gulls and other birds perched on top of the
ice structures before diving for fish. I waded into the shallow water with my boots just to feel its iciness. When I put
my hands into the water the fish swam away but the birds
took no notice. Never had I seen so many birds and fish at
one time. Were there thousands? The sky and sea were full
of moving life. White birds blurred against the blue sky as
they darted against the greenish water and floating ice.
Small fishes flashed beneath the ice! Had they been there all
winter or did they just arrive? I picked up a starfish; I had
thought Arctic waters would be different, yet here and at
Sheshalik were starfish similar to those found on Atlantic
and Pacific beaches. Remote as we were, we had a kinship
with the rest of the world. Someday an Eskimo child from
Point Hope might pick up a starfish near some far-off ocean
and poignantly think of home.

A hunter threw a weighted hook attached to a rope into
the open water between the ice floes to catch a seal. No
luck. He tried again, pulling slowly, but did not land the
animal although the water was red with blood. I noticed
that several families were camped in tents along the beach,
enjoying the change from their leaking sod houses.

A ragged boy, his coat torn and his shoes several sizes
too large, aimed a slingshot at a sea gull. He coughed and
wiped his runny nose on his torn sleeve. He was Koahk, the
son of Ahksivvokrook, the seal hunter who was having bad
luck.

Ahksivvokrook's wife, Nathlook, scooped up the fresh
water on top of the sea ice to fill a teakettle. The other
source of drinking water was a lake five miles out. Sea ice
becomes fresh water, but many polar explorers did not believe Vilhjalmur Stefansson when he related this fact. Sea

Otoonah

Clare Fejes

water becomes fresh during the period between the formation of the ice and the end of the first summer thereafter.
Koahk's mother had an agile, sturdy body and a placid face.
Her husband gave up trying to get the seal and came toward
me, looking skeptical when I smiled. They continued down
the beach carrying the teakettle casually between them.

Koahk and I walked together past the old sunken sod
houses with their whalebone remnants jutting upward. We
discovered the shoulder and back of a mammoth animal as I
stumbled over a vertebrae. A massive whalebone about
three feet in diameter and far too heavy to move lay in our
path; it had a sculptural curvature that would have made a
perfect seat. I would have loved to set it in our garden
surrounded by tall irises.

Koahk walked the whale's length to show me how long
it had been and gestured to indictate how high it was as it
lay there on the beach after the killing. He made all sorts of
movements to describe the hunting of a whale. In Fairbanks
Joe and the miners told bear or fish stories but here the
whale story was the thing. I could imagine an Eskimo
describing the whale that got away.

We passed birds with fledglings nesting low among the
sparse tundra flowers. Sandpipers and another bird with
reddish head and a white spot on the breast calmly hopped
close to us. They seemed unaware of human beings and I
had to restrain Koahk from using his rock and slingshot.

He said scornfully, "How else we going to learn to
hunt if we don't shoot birds?"

Other children had joined us as we explored the tundra.
The boys all carried slingshots, made of heavy gum bands
with a piece of caribou skin handy for placing the stone, and
they aimed at every bird, even a flock of terns flying high
overhead. They showed me a snowbird's nest in an abandoned sod house. Snow and ice had fallen through the window on top and on the long yellowed grasses inside lay six
small blue speckled eggs. The boys wanted to destroy
them.

"Let's leave them, the mother will feel bad when she finds them gone," I said.

Koahk quickly remarked: "Father comes, not mother."

However, they reluctantly put the bird's eggs down and aimed at other birds, curving the rocks expertly.

"Let's leave the bird's nest or there won't be many left," I urged.

"We have to play—if there's no birds, we kill fish!" they answered.

One boy gently said, "Jesus says, love birds," but while quoting the missionaries he took sharp aim with his rock at a passing wee mouse!

Koahk pointed to a bird flying toward us. "It's the father," he instructed me. I could see nothing yet, but the boy's sharp eyes had sighted the bird and he could tell whether it was male or female. As if to settle the matter and to justify the situation before he took careful aim, Koahk said: "If I don't shoot bird, how will I learn to hunt—what will I eat?" I was silent.

Koahk's elbows jutted out of his coat and when the wind blew, his joints were exposed like skinny bird wings. He followed me back to the house, looking feverish, his face unnaturally red. Otoonah took one look at him and let loose a barrage of Eskimo, while he stood there shamefacedly, wiping his runny nose with his sleeve. He took off his ragged coat and handed it to Otoonah, and she pretended to be mad, chattering to herself as she sewed the huge rents. She brought him some canned milk diluted with bread and water, putting it on the floor before him as if to feed a puppy dog.

Koahk ate hungrily, then sat back in awe of Otoonah as she continued to sew up the impossible holes. She belabored him in Eskimo about his condition, no doubt blaming his mother. When she finished the coat, she started to work an odd-shaped tool over some scrap of fur she had dug out from under the cot. I did not recognize the fur and she could not tell me what it was when I asked her, except in

Eskimo. It was a small skin with rather short hair. Koahk
could not tell me the name of the fur either, but he offered
to draw me a picture of it. This was no help, however, for it
looked like a seal from the shape of the head, and he said,
"No, it isn't a seal." I found out later it was a marmot, or
siksikpuk.

Ikkaheena's mother-in-law, Ahnah (meaning grandmother),
brought Otoonah a tubful of dried seal meat, which was
black and tasted like dried jerky. Otoonah stored it in the
cache in the front part of the house. I went to bed while the
two old ahnahs chatted a long time in Eskimo. I wondered
what they said.

CHAPTER 7

Baleen, Ivory, and Whalebone

Bring hither your wooden hair ornament,
I will deck myself with it. . . .

TIGLUK AND ANAHKALOKTUK came
to visit us. Anahkaloktuk, who was Otoonah's daughter,
towered over her mother and was at least three times her

girth. She did not have her mother's spryness and I thought I knew why, although it was hard to tell whether she was pregnant under her huge black calico parka. She hardly resembled her mother, and Asatsiak was not her father. Although she was in her early thirties, she had borne seven children; her oldest boy was fifteen and the youngest was four.

Elizabeth, the youngest, sat unsmiling, refusing to recognize my existence except to sit and glare silently at me with a stoical expression. Dark impenetrable eyes, fixed like a hawk's on their prey, watched my every movement as she tightly clutched her mother's knee. Her dress was too long, sagging in the front, and her hair had been cut slantwise, which gave her crooked bangs and hid half her face. Her cheeks puffed out and hung heavily, so that she resembled a little squirrel with nuts stuffed in his mouth. I offered her bubble gum, but bribery did not work; her little button of a nose turned away until her mother had to accept it for her.

Her father, Tigluk, observed me between heavy brows as he tilted his chair back to accommodate his long legs. According to what I had read the Tigara people were supposed to be short, but he was taller than most white men, being well over six feet. I asked him if he had been born at Point Hope.

"No, a place north of here."

With the wind storming outside, it was cozy to sit indoors around Otoonah's stove. Finally Tigluk reached into his pocket and showed me a small whalebone carving he had made of a walrus with ivory tusks inserted in the bone. Tigluk carved mainly for income, yet this animal was different from the usual whalebone mask. I showed him a book on the Canadian Eskimo carvings and he was interested.

Anahkaloktuk and Elizabeth quietly watched me while Otoonah sat on the floor scraping skin for Asatsiak's parka. The fire was warm, the light was right, and my oil paints were handy. I was itching to paint but reluctant to ask. Finally, after an hour, I asked Tigluk if he would pose.

He said agreeably: "I have nothing to do today," and draped his legs around the chair facing me.

All eyes watched me squeeze the juicy bright oranges, yellows, greens, and blues onto the palette. When the white would not open, I asked Tigluk for a lighted match and held the flame under the cap. I took a white canvas and set it on the chair in front of me, assuming a casual pose to cover up my nervousness, and began to paint slowly but forcefully, outlining the bold structure of his proud bony face and black piercing eyes.

Tigluk had a fascinating face; his features reminded me of the natural shapes of rocks and crags. The color of his skin pulsed with life and brightness; I could almost sense and see the blood coursing under his skin as over hills and valleys. He had a controlled, ready expression, although it must have been difficult for him to maintain such poise with a white woman observing him so closely. No doubt some foolishness on her part! Yet he sat quietly, rather like a king distributing his largesse. His look was regal, rather sophisticated, in fact amused.

The balance between us was delicate but finely maintained. If he had shown signs of being bored or tired I would have stopped, and if he had been unwilling in spirit I would not have been able to paint him. Luckily he did not tire; he seemed interested, and we achieved the rapport necessary for me to finish the painting. I had captured all I needed: the force of his fierce personality, the strong set of his bones, and the bright red shirt against the warm umbers of his skin.

The storm had not abated; it howled and blew around the house. Otoonah made another pot of coffee and fed us biscuits, while Anahkaloktuk took her turn as a model. I sketched her with a black laundry-marking pen which I had brought for quick sketching. I drew Anahkaloktuk's face swiftly, as she was tired and I hated to impose on her. The few lines depicted the hair straggling over her forehead and her mouth slack with her own thoughts.

Tigluk and Anahkaloktuk showed little interest in my

paintings. They had no frame of reference with which to compare it—it was simply out of their scope of experience. That really helped immensely—the fact that they did not care a bit—I had only my own standards to meet.

Many children came to Otoonah's house on some pretext or other, mainly to look the stranger over and to report back to their parents what they had seen. They showed curiosity over my drawing and painting, sitting on Otoonah's floor with all their heavy clothing on and watching every motion I made.

Soon they were spread out on the floor drawing their own pictures; the boys specialized in ships and planes and seals and whales, and the girls drew more domestic scenes of people in brightly colored fur parkas. The children were on their best behavior; it was a treat to be in Otoonah's house because she gave them bread and milk to eat.

Koahk also sketched, still wearing his ragged coat, a shock of black hair falling over one eye and causing him to hold his head to one side and squint. He coughed, flushed, glad to be out of the rain and wind. I felt his head and it was hot.

"My brother is in TB hospital."

Before I came to Point Hope, I knew that I might contract the disease, but I decided to take my chances. A Fairbanks nurse had told me that TB had been present at one time in almost every house at Tigara but that it was under control now. The only precaution I took was to drink coffee holding the cup handle turned to the left, which presumed that most people were right-handed. It gave me small assurance, but I had a natural immunity to depend on which probably was greater than that of most Eskimos.

When Otoonah was through with her sewing, she got out an old deck of cards and started to play solitare, which her husband had probably taught her. "One, two, three," she counted to herself in English. We all got the idea, and sitting on the red rug near her we played cassino. Koahk's

Anahtaloktuk

younger brother kept winning. Tiring of cassino, I tried to teach them to play rummy, but it was a flop; Koahk caught on to the game but no one else did. I did not do too well myself, not having played the game for years.

The children would have stayed all night, but I went to bed. Otoonah stayed up and played solitaire, counting, "One, two, three," to an empty room.

I was interested in the work of the village artists and enlisted Oktolik, the storekeeper, to take me to the leading mask-maker's house. I had bought his whalebone mask at the store, an unusual carving made with the tongue sticking out.

Attungorah, the carver of the mask, lived in an underground sod igloo of the old type. He was of the generation which had not succumbed to the "new" houses built above the earth where wind and weather blew through their thin walls. His walls were thick sod pieces piled like brick, one upon another, with whale ribs, jawbones, and shoulder blades reinforcing the construction. The grassy side of the sod was faced to the weather and each sod piece was approximately one foot square and about six inches thick.

We entered the long low hallway which warmed the frigid air before it entered the igloo. In addition to the front entrance, there was another opening in the roof, with a short ladder leading down into the entranceway. This entrance was necessary in the winter because heavy blizzards sometimes buried the ground-level entrance.

Flowered linoleum covered the floor and a neat wooden bed, crude table, kitchen cupboard and shelves made the inside of the igloo neat, compact, and warm.

The ceiling was low and over the bed was a clothesline with socks drying. A gas lantern hung in one corner. The house appeared empty but it contained everything needful, so few are the true needs of men.

Seal hunting and mask carving netted Attungorah extra money to trade at the store for flour or an occasional bit of cheese or tobacco. The carver spoke very little English but his greeting was warm when Oktolik explained that I had admired his carving and wished to see more.

Attungorah was working on a new mask; he sat on the floor carving with his handmade steel adze, roughly blocking out the whalebone. He showed me his tools, most of which he had adapted or changed from the store variety. He worked with two kinds of whalebone—the vertebrae, which were soft and easy to carve, and the knuckle bone, which was harder—rubbing the finished mask with crude oil. This mask had a place below the lip for an ivory labret.

In ancient days when a boy reached puberty, he acquired the privilege of wearing a labret. An older man would hold his head steady while another "expert" drove a sharpened stone point right through the skin with one quick blow. The hole was filled with a round or oblong labret made of stone or wood. As the boy grew older, he wore a bigger and bigger labret, sometimes made of ivory or jade. Asatsiak had shown me one made from an unusual green stone the size of a half-dollar. No one wore labrets anymore.

Attungorah was descended from the famous whaling captain of the same name. Attungorah's grave, marked by two gigantic whale jawbones, dominated the village graveyard. It was set apart from the other graves, each of which was marked by a single, upward-jutting whale jawbone, forming one of the most unusual graveyards in the world.

He had been greatly feared in his lifetime, according to Charlie Brower in *Fifty Below Zero*. "The people were convinced that he had the power to kill anyone by devil driving." According to Brower, who lived at Point Barrow but went whaling off Point Hope, "Attungorah was a surly, thickset brute with cunning eyes."

He was supposed to have been a good shaman until the Jabbertown whalers brought alcohol to Point Hope and taught him how to brew whiskey. Killigivuk told me that at one time Attungorah had tried to make war on Brower and the Point Barrow Eskimos. Brower recalled that Attungorah had shown him several graves of the men he had murdered. "He ruled Tigara," Brower said, "with terror and his hands were supposed to be red with the blood of his people."

As the story goes, according to Brower, "one night when he was drunk sleeping in an igloo with the gut window foolishly uncovered, he received a mysterious bullet which paralyzed him so that he could not move. One of his many wives squared a debt for long years of mistreatment. She crept up to him as he lay asleep and slashed him to death with her ulu."

When I asked the carver about his ancestor, he disclaimed any knowledge of the stories and reputation of Attungorah, saying only, "He was not mean, he was good." The carver bore no resemblance except in name to Attungorah as described by Brower. His strong peaceful face was framed by gray hair and he walked with dignity.

I hoped that I had not offended him by repeating what I had read about his ancestor. On the way out of his igloo I banged my head hard on the low entranceway; if I had offended him he was avenged.

A village artist who made use of baleen was Omnik, the Eskimo whose baskets I had admired in the native store. Each black basket was tightly woven and had a close-fitting lid embellished with a white ivory carving of a bear—highly professional work. The baskets were priced at twenty-five dollars apiece.

As I entered Omnik's home he was working on an ivory harpoon head gripped in a vise at a long table. His wife and sons rested on bunks around the small room. Omnik was a solid round-faced man with inscrutable oriental eyes and an industrious manner.

Baleen, the stringy black bone from the inside of the whale's mouth was formerly used for corset stays. Omnik cut ten-foot-long pieces of baleen about three quarters of an inch thick into strips and wove them into baskets. Some craftsmen at Nome made jewelry out of baleen, sometimes with ivory inserts, but at Point Hope it was not used for jewelry.

Omnik's ivory carvings were simlar to the animal carvings done on St. Lawrence Island; one showed a seal in the bear's mouth. In the early days carving was as important as hunting, since without ivory tusks brought in by the hunter there could be no ivory carving and without carvings to trade there could be no guns or ammunition.

The head of one animal in another animal's mouth is a common motif in Alaskan Eskimo carving. Either the bear has a seal in his mouth or the seal has a fish. Animals are depicted in many positions, the newest of which was inspired by the construction workers of the DEW line. They had ordered the Eskimos to make them a "six-legged bear" —a bear mounted on a bear. Point Hopers as well as other villagers were selling *oosuks,* or the bone within the walrus penis, which afforded them no end of amusement. The demand for these had begun on St. Lawrence, where soldiers suggested to the carvers that they cut out animal heads on both ends of the well-polished bone. Eskimo carvers could not understand why white men wanted them, but they gladly took the price offered. Some Eskimo families had a mask in process constantly; it hung on a nail and brother or mother would chip at it a little until the mask was done, whereupon they took it to the store to trade. Some of the women carved crude dancers and drummers out of whalebone, or a group of hunters in a bone with baleen paddles.

The people earned extra money making masks, weaving baleen baskets and carving ivory. The women especially made money by digging up artifacts from the old ruins. The women's most artistic products were the beautiful fur clothing, the border designs on their parkas or mukluks, and their everyday garments of calico trimmed with row on row of colored rickrack twisted into geometric designs. Some more ambitious women also designed intricate beadwork bands to apply on their mukluks.

CHAPTER 8

Summertime

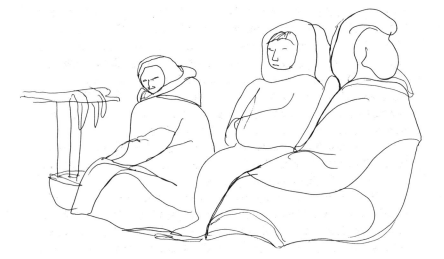

Whither is my soul gone?
Let me fetch thee, let me fetch thee!
It is gone to the southward of those
Who live to the southward of us.
Let me fetch thee,
Let me fetch thee!

FOURTH OF JULY, 1959,
and a historic day for Point Hope.

David Frankson, the postmaster, flew the forty-nine-star American flag over the post office building for the first time since Alaska achieved statehood. The post office, which housed David's family and the family of his son, was located in the center of the village in a nondescript weatherbeaten frame house. The inner passageway had the unmistakable scent of seal oil. The post office was a small cubicle of a room, where all the villagers came to transact the business of mailing and receiving letters and packages, their main contact with the outside world.

David was a head shorter than his wife, Dinah, and wore spectacles; he was sallow-faced and thin because he led a rather sedentary life due to his work. Well read and shrewd, he carried on much of the villagers' government dealings and typed many letters of correspondence. Dinah was as gay and fun-loving as David was sober-faced. The sadness of the whole village was reflected on David's face; when there was a death, David sorrowed—he was the conscience and barometer of the whole village.

The new flag waving in the wind gave us all a feeling of pride. None of us knew what changes statehood would make in the lives of Alaskans everywhere.

The church bells announced the beginning of a triple celebration: the Fourth of July and signing of the Declaration of Independence; the founding of the St. Thomas mission of the Episcopal church at Point Hope sixty-nine years before; and the flying of the new forty-nine-star flag, signifying statehood.

At the sound of the bells, parka-clad figures moved slowly across the village toward the large parish hall.

The church, Point Hope's finest building, was painted bright green with a neat white trim and rose higher than any other edifice. The parish hall, the missionary's residence, and the church formed a cluster of buildings at the northeast end of the village. Eskimo underground sod homes were warm, of practical design, and made use of natural building materials; but since the school, church, and store were of lumber, sod houses were becoming a relic of the past.

Gradually the rectangular parish hall filled with villagers who sat down on the benches facing the huge stove. The celebration had been set for two o'clock but late comers were still arriving at four. Meantime mothers were busy in the church kitchen making coffee and frying dozens of Eskimo doughnuts in seal oil.

Infants slept in the backs of their mothers' parkas and when baby became restless, the mother jiggled up and down to soothe it. If this did not succeed, she squirmed and shifted until she slid the baby around to her breast to suckle.

Mothers had little false modesty about breast feeding; in the early days it was the custom to take off all the fur clothing in the igloo because it became very warm. Mostly the women did nothing to bind their breasts; to the older women brassieres were unknown. Two- and three-year-olds sat astride their mothers' knees and suckled. Sometimes the baby was taken out of the parka to play on the wooden floor and then, when it became sleepy, the mother picked it up and, leaning over, slid it up under her parka, tying a belt under the baby's buttocks and over the top of her breasts in front. The baby would be completely covered and gave its mother a hump-like silhouette. When a mother became pregnant, she eventually had a large bulge in back from carrying a one-year-old and a protruding bulge in front from the baby-to-be.

The younger set roamed at will, playing hide and seek with no interference from the elders as they raced up and down the hall.

Finally, at five o'clock, coffee and doughnuts were passed around, everyone using his own coffee cup. Then the games began, missionary games—not the types of games Eskimos played before the church was established, but games picnickers play on the Fourth of July.

The women lined up, had their feet tied in potato sacks, and raced across the hall. I had heard about Eskimo games of strength in which men and women tested their muscles to see who was the strongest. In one of the more strenuous games of the past a sharp double-pointed stick was held between two men, a pointed end beneath the upper lip of each. The men pushed against each other to see who could withstand the pain the longest. Some of the games, such as this one, were sadistic and blood flowed, which is evidently why the missionaries stopped them.

The celebrants moved out of doors to see who could jump the farthest. Two white men conducting an aerial survey of Point Hope had joined in the jumping game and one of them jumped too hard and fell, pulling a tendon.

Then came the game of baseball as satirized by the villagers. An old man wearing mukluks got up to bat and a group of lively matrons jumped up to take over the bases. The old man squared his chin and shoulders, imitating an Eskimo version of Casey at the bat, while Dinah, the postmaster's wife and clown of the bunch, mimicked the old man. The crowd roared its approval and egged on the players.

I sat in an unobtrusive corner with a sketch pad on my lap and tried to sketch through a wall of youngsters. Otoonah chewed her Masterpiece snuff and talked to an older friend who had three ancient tatoo marks on her chin and was smoking a cigarette. No doubt I came in for a good share of the conversation.

I wondered what statehood would mean to these people. The teen-agers traveled out of the village to school, many of the men worked in Fairbanks on summer jobs, and a few received newspapers or magazines; but for many it would be hard to fathom a world outside their village. It was the fortunate ones of the young generation receiving education who would reap the fruits of Alaskan statehood. Statehood meant that I and every Alaskan citizen, which included every Point Hoper of voting age, would be able to vote for President in the next election.

The wind wafted the fragrant wild sweet pea, forget-me-not, and other wild-flower scents. One could see for miles over the flat village, and the homes became small risings on the horizon. The tundra was so thickly strewn with flowers that one trampled them underfoot with each step;

the colors gleamed more brilliantly than any I had ever
seen. I filled my lungs again and again, never had air
smelled so fresh and pure.

The sun in the bright blue atmosphere never set at all.
It was light at three o'clock in the morning and teen-agers
played ball across the roofs of wooden dwellings.

The Assembly of God minister and his young assistant, who
had arrived by fiber-glass boat from Kotzebue en route to
their Point Barrow mission, invited me to dinner. Koahk had
shot and winged a sea gull with his slingshot in front of the
minister's tent and he followed me, the half-dead gull
docile, its white head still and wounded wing dragging.

I asked Koahk: "What are you going to do with it?"

He answered what he thought I'd like to hear, "I will
keep it for a pet."

I made several sketches of the immobile bird while the
men cooked a delicious dinner on a two-burner stove consisting of canned salmon, corn, potatoes, cocoa, and hardtack with jam. They had plenty of rations with them, even
bacon and eggs which were not for sale at Point Hope.

The minister was a blond man, tall, rather like a simple
fisherman, which he told me he originally had been until he
had the call to come north and preach. He talked of Oral
Roberts and other Pentecostal matters in a slow drawl. In
addition to his regular mission at Point Barrow, he was seeking to establish one at Point Hope.

The Episcopal church was established at Point Hope in
1890. Since it was a remote village of only about three hundred and fifty souls, one church had more than sufficed. In
the early days the church had also supplied the first schooling for the children in addition to religious instruction and
had built missions at Kivalina and Point Lay.

The Friends church established at Kotzebue in 1898
branched out into the Kobuk area and Noatak. The Catho-
lics settled in Kotzebue and Holy Cross, Nome, Barrow, and

Diomede Island; and the Swedish Covenant church was first at Nome and Unalakleet. By 1959 Nome had fifteen churches and Kotzebue five.

The Seventh-Day Adventists had come into villages which had already established churches and caused confusion. At one village the natives were told by the Adventists not to work on Saturday and were commanded by the other church to rest on Sundays, thereby being constrained to miss two good days of necessary hunting. It was a case of feel damned or go hungry and in any event was confusing. Moreover, the Friends commanded the Eskimos not to dance, while their Episcopalian relatives at Point Hope could dance all they wished.

However the Friends seemed to have the most influence among Eskimos, according to one minister of another faith. Except for the white minister at Kotzebue, the Friends' missionaries were Eskimos serving their own people. A translator was unnecessary and this made their ideas more acceptable.

Eskimos at Point Hope accepted the religious beliefs of the Episcopalian church, yet mixed them with their old beliefs retaining some of their ancient ceremonies such as the whale feast. The roots of a deeply felt belief are not easily torn out.

It is interesting to note that the Eskimo language lacks words for general or abstract ideas. Missionaries had a hard time finding the Eskimo equivalent for God.

The mysterious force that played so great a part in Eskimo fate was called "Sila." Sila was a mighty spirit with many meanings; it meant the universe, or wisdom, or the weather, snow, rain, the fury of the sea, all forces of nature. As far as I could determine in talking to the older people, Sila meant a greater force in the beyond.

In the old days the angatkok was the interpreter who served to define the rules and taboos between Sila and mankind. It was essential not to offend the "powers" lest Sila should retaliate. Food had to be treated with respect, hence the drink of water for the seal and the whale. Man had to obey the taboos or evil would come to him.

At Point Hope they also had a moon god called Alignuk. He was the man in the moon whose face they could sometimes see and who helped them in their hunting, especially whale hunting.

In the belief of the early Eskimos, Alignuk was somehow equated with God. While I was at Sheshalik I had heard a legend about a male figure named Alignuk who controlled the sea mammals and now at Tigara I heard the same legend:

"A long time ago, Alignuk and his sister, Suqunuq, once lived in Tigara. Each lived alone in a house near the center of the village. One autumn, when the *qalegis* were lighted, a man came to Suqunuq's house and slept with her. It was dark and she could not recognize him. The next night he came again. She was curious about him; the third night she marked his face under the left eye with soot. If he were a man and not a spirit she would recognize him the next day. The following evening when she peeked in through the skylight of one of the *qalegis* she discovered the tell-tale mark on her brother Alignuk. Upset by this affair, she returned home and cleaned out a wooden tub into which she defecated and urinated. She cut off her left breast so that it bled into the tub and then stirred the blood into the earlier contents. She carried this mess to the *qalegi*. Placing it before her brother Alignuk, she said, "If you really love me, eat this, it is from me." He did not answer, but she insisted; finally he picked up his tool box and walked out. Together they walked round and round the entrance of the *qalegi*. The people watching them saw that they gradually rose higher and higher into the air until they disappeared from sight. Alignuk said, "You go to the sun where it is always warm and I will go to the moon where it is always cold."

"The Tikeramiut say that you can still see Alignuk in the moon carrying his tool bag and when the sun sets you can see blood from Suqunuq's breast in the sky."

The Eskimos had to struggle in life for everything; they searched day and night for animals in the hills and on the land and under the sea. They believed in reincarnation; they worshipped birds and animals and wore lucky talismans. They even saw a "little people" similar to elves. One man said he saw the little people traveling to Point Hope. "They wore parkas of caribou hair and played outdoors. They looked like little babies. But the dogs ate them."

Froelich G. Rainey summed up the religious attitudes of the Eskimos in *The Whale Hunters of Tigara*: "In spite of the teachings of Christianity, there was and is now no doubt among them that men can fly to the moon, that they can restore themselves and others to life within a four- or five-day period, heal the sick, eliminate a mortal wound in an instant, pluck out their own eyes and replace them, kill men and animals at any distance, control the weather, halt the movements of ice, bring or send away the animals (famine was always due to an angry *angatkok*)."

And an old Eskimo angatkok named Igjugarjuk told Knud Rasmussen, "All true wisdom is only to be learned far from the dwellings of men, out in the great solitudes; and is only to be attained through suffering. Privation and suffering are the only things than can open the mind of man to those things which are hidden from others."

CHAPTER 9

The People

The arch of sky and mightiness of storms
Have moved the spirit within me,
Till I am carried away
Trembling with joy.

THE WORD WAS PASSED QUICKLY
through the village from house to igloo that the new minister would hold a meeting. That afternoon the tent was put up, huge and billowing in the wind. The villagers looked forward to the meeting all day as if it were a circus; great

excitement filled the air; they were curious to hear what the new minister would say.

The whole village, including the Episcopal minister, his wife, and myself, squeezed into the tent which was so packed it was hard to find a place to sit.

The minister and his assistant began the program by singing a hymn in Eskimo to guitar accompaniment. Then he began to speak without an interpreter in English using simple common words and speaking slowly so that all could understand. He alluded to the hunters, how hard they must hunt, how cold they must get, and how much they must love God. He painted a verbal picture of Christ on the cross and his voice broke as he cried: "And the blood that you hunters are familiar with every day came from our Lord." Afterwards the two men sang together in Eskimo and taught the simple words of the song to everyone. The air was charged with emotion; the singing and guitar music was novel and satisfying. The people coughed, the children's noses ran, and the ground was cold to sit on.

Sunday, Otoonah and I dressed in our finery and walked the long distance to the Episcopal church for services. Otoonah's finery was her best pink parka with a huge three-toned fur hood, while I wore my parka and white kerchief. I followed her single file along the narrow trail worn deep into the tundra by many footsteps, trying to avoid the dogs staked on either side of us.

The church was full when we arrived and I followed Otoonah up to the front wooden benches. The walls were a lovely old red and the altar held many lighted candles; in the middle of the back wall hung a faded religious painting in a dull gold frame. Eskimos in white robes assisted at the altar and the minister gave the ritual with his interpreter translating each sentence into Eskimo.

I recalled that in every home I had visited a cross hung on the door, some of wood, ivory or metal. The Eskimos had depended on charms in the past and they had not prayed, for why should they beg anything from spirits they believed they could command?

All around us the children whispered and wiggled, and there was the usual coughing and stirring. When the babies were hungry, their mothers nursed them. The minister introduced the two men conducting the aerial survey and they stood up in acknowledgment; one of them was still limping from his Fourth of July accident.

The Episcopal ministers at Point Hope were usually rotated every two or three years and a new young man-and-wife team was sent in. The new minister would be inexperienced in Arctic and Eskimo ways and had a difficult adjustment to make, especially if he was not athletically inclined and unused to cold and lack of material comforts. Many ministers had never seen an Eskimo before and most regarded him as a "heathen object." It took many months for a minister to become acquainted with the Eskimo way of life. At the same time, the Eskimo was under a handicap with each change—he had to instruct the new minister in the rigors of dog team travel, in cutting ice for water consumption, and in the mysteries of Arctic plumbing (or lack of it). If the minister wanted to get from one village to another he had to fly or hire an Eskimo or else learn to raise and drive a dog team. If he did not learn to hunt or fish, he had to pay for fish and seal meat for his dogs out of his meager salary.

All this was relatively simple compared to his wife's initiation into Arctic living. If she tried to keep house according to her usual standards, she would soon find it difficult. In addition to cooking on an oil stove she had to learn to bake bread or do without it. She had to acquire a taste for native game, relying heavily on caribou and duck, and on canned vegetables as fresh vegetables had to be flown in from Fairbanks or Kotzebue. During spring breakup there was no way to avoid dragging mud through the house, and puppies and their excrement were always underfoot. Water was rationed out and had to be used sparingly. If she was pregnant, she managed as best she could, traveling by plane to Fairbanks in time for the baby's birth, as the Kotzebue Hospital was for natives only.

The only other white woman in the whole village usually was the schoolmistress. The teacher I met was an unassuming unmarried woman in her late thirties, dreadfully tired after the school year. Her house had the finest toilet at Point Hope, an ordinary toilet but with no pipes leading outward. It was a chemical model that had to be lifted out and emptied by the school janitor. The bathtub had to be filled with tubs of water as there was no running water.

When I called on the teacher, I invited one of the mothers to come with me; it was her first visit to the teacher's quarters although the building had been there for some time. She asked what that white box was so the teacher opened it and showed her the refrigerator, then the bathroom, displaying the shiny tub and toilet accommodations.

We toured the schoolroom, and one carefully printed paper displayed on the wall attracted my interest. It was entitled "The Wind": "On January first the wind started, the wind blowed harder and harder. It blowed the kids towards the beach. The wind blew me and let me bump the whale bones. When I didn't cry I called myself Champ. But when I say I was Champ I cry. It was hurting a lot. I cry one second. The wind wasn't good to me."

Living close to the Minister's home were Billy and Alice Weber, a young couple who combined the best of the old and new ways of Eskimo life. Alice, a few years older than Billy, had studied at the Mt. Edgecumbe School of Nursing and was the village public health nurse. Billy, who had an open likable personality, made union laborer's wages in Fairbanks doing summer construction work and in the winter hunted at Point Hope. The Webers had lived in Fairbanks one summer but found that the rent and other expenses made it impossible for them to save for the winter.

"We liked meat for breakfast," Billy said, breaking into a grin, "the kind that costs a dollar fifty a pound."

Their home was a large Quonset hut neatly arranged with comfortable beds and other furniture. Billy had made

the large stove out of iron. The walls needed insulation and
he had the choice of buying modern insulation for cash in
Fairbanks and paying high freight costs or cutting up the
turfed earth and piling bricks of it against the house in old-
time style. The old method was laborious and the sod had to
be cut in the summer before the earth became frozen and
snow covered.

"Cara, Cara." The children ran excitedly to meet me.

"Cara, you are my *atka*," said a little girl whose parka
sleeves covered her hands completely.

Little Rosa whispered: "That means you have the same
name she has."

Men and animals had souls, the Eskimos believed. The
name was also a kind of soul. It stayed with a person when
he died, but left him when a child was named after him.
The child was supposed to inherit the namesake's qualities
and was even considered to be the reborn person himself.
Little Clara, my *atka*, or namesake, claimed a strong kinship
with me and set about teaching me Eskimo words.

"*Ahpah*—father! *Ahkah*—mother. *Alapah* means it's
cold outside." Brother is *Ahpee-yeak*, and *Punnick* is daughter." Laughing, the children prompted me. They heard Eskimo at home and conveyed their thoughts in a mixture of
English and Eskimo. My English had become very simple
and I found myself using shorter sentences and speaking
more slowly; if I spoke too fast I was sometimes not understood. The children were very shy, but their eyes were eloquent wells, so I learned to read their eyes when their lips
were still. Their love was unmistakable, however, and my
heart went out to them.

I became especially attached to Rosa and Elmer, two of
Ah-gaik's children. Their cheeks were burnished red-copper
from the wind and they had their mother's fine bones and
sensitive expression. They looked loved and their clothes
and furs were neat and clean. They followed me everywhere, as did the other children.

Ahpara eehseekseeruk aiviq! shouted my little atka, running to the beach. "Her father is bringing in a walrus," translated Rosa.

Five hunters had just returned in a skin boat with a bull walrus, the first of the year and a large one according to David Frankson. A crowd had gathered around the five men cutting the meat.

The walrus' bloody head lay cut off and ferocious, his eyes bulging out, one tusk broken off; even his whiskers protested the indignity of death and quivered in the wind. Evidently he was an old bull. Two men were stripping and dividing the main carcass, cutting the flippers first. The other hunters watched to see that the portions were fair; and their stoic wives sat in the background, waiting with sharpened ulus to complete the butchering.

Usually the walrus hide was used to make skin boat or umiak coverings, but this one was not to be used that way. Ah-gaik, with her son on her back inside her parka, told me: "The hide is good to eat."

The other women had their great fur hoods up around their faces to shut out the wind. They sat huddled together, making a fantastic design in their bright purple, red, and pink parkas against the blue and white ice background. The whole scene was one of incredible beauty.

Evidently one of the young boys had shot his first walrus, and now he leaped and jumped for joy over the carcass. How he danced over that bloody beast! Graceful, free, and wild, throwing back his handsome head, tossing his long black hair and laughing, proud to be among the group of seasoned hunters.

"Twenty shots it took to kill him," he said. "We saw a group of ten walruses sitting on the ice. When we shot, they all scattered, many wounded got away, but we got this one."

After the men cut and divided the meat in equal portions, their wives stepped up and cut it in smaller sections. According to ancient ritual, more walrus was given to the one who owned the boat and to the one who shot it. The hunters now stood proudly, watching for the choice parts, and their children watched carefully too. Everyone was in high spirits.

A young boy rolled on the beach nuzzling a husky puppy and when a three-year-old girl came over, he bussed her affectionately. One of the young girls of marriageable age watched him shyly. When I asked her if she could cut walrus, she replied: "Not yet, but I will know when the time comes."

David Frankson, leaned on a gaffing hook used for hooking game from the sea. His bulky fur parka bulged over his pants and although the hood was down, a small portion of his black hair could be seen over the top. Fur mukluks came up to his knees and were tied around his legs in a graceful pattern.

I whipped out my pencil and pad and did a swift sketch of his back. Before I could finish it, though, he moved, breaking off in the middle of a conversation with a hunter, and with one swift motion grabbed his gun, leaned on one knee, and shot up into a flock of ducks, killing two. I saw them fall, one dropping into the sea too far away to retrieve. The whole action had taken place before I grasped the situation; I had not even been aware of the flight of ducks.

The ice floes along the shore were littered with hundreds of birds, among them murres and gulls. The children aimed at the birds constantly with their slingshots, applauding one another when one was hit far out at sea. One of the men told me: "Those slingshots made in Point Hope factory." Koahk shot another sea gull and proudly claimed it.

Farther up on the beach two men were sewing a walrus skin onto a driftwood frame to complete an umiak. Every once in a while I saw something that evoked memories. As the men bent over their work, I knew I had seen this before; it reminded me of scenes at Sheshalik when the women bent and kneeled over their smudge fires.

The fur-clad hunters punched a hole through the

bleached white skin, then lashed it to the wooden frame with a lacing of sinew. Fur hoods hid their faces as they bent over the umiak, one man pushing a needle through the tough skin and the other pulling it out the other side. At one place the skin was too short to cover the frame and they patched it with another piece of skin. The needle holes would shrink when the umiak hit the sea and become water-tight.

Rosa and the other children had been watching me sketch and when I asked them if they would like to draw a large picture, they shouted, "yes!"

David Frankson said we could use the council house and so we rolled some white butcher's paper out on the floor for the children to crayon on. They drew a mural of Point Hope, including its sod houses, parka-clad people, and walruses, and for background they painted in a blue ice ridge filled with birds. When they could not think of any-thing else to draw, they ran to the door and surveyed the scene.

"How can I draw a house?" they would ask.

I said, "Go look out at your house and then you show me."

When they had finished the mural, we carried it down to the native store and John Oktolik, the storekeeper, hung it over the door. The children and I stood back proudly to look at it; although it was the first crude attempt at painting for many of these little ones, their strokes were bold and sure.

Koahk's sister posed for me. She was about fourteen, with long black braids framing her sensuous face, her body lithe and budding, without self-consciousness. Childish words excitedly poured out of her, half in English and half in Eskimo. I finally understood that her mother had ordered new slacks for her from Sears.

Childlike, yet woman-wise, she lived, ate, and slept in

one small room with her five brothers and mother and father.

I invited her to eat supper with me as Otoonah was out visiting. "Big sister, big sister," she cried, jumping up and down.

When I began to cook rice with raisins in it, make cocoa, and set out cookies, she could hardly contain herself. In great excitement she threw her arms around me, and then I knew it must have been party fare for her, quite a change from a seal-meat diet. We added canned milk, sugar and cinnamon over the rice, and it was a feast for me also.

It rained for days on end; the sky was gray and forboding. Otoonah and I stayed close to the fire. The children dropped in to see us and when I gave them paint and paper, we played "art school" while Otoonah mended or chewed mukluks. I sketched the children while sitting on the floor wearing the calico dress that Okukchuk had sent me. I used the black laundry-marking pen that did not need a refill; its bold simple lines were just what I wanted.

Around our cosy fire came Anahkaloktuk and her little girl, bringing the ingredients for two cakes. One cake was to be for Elizabeth's birthday and the other for Tigluk. She came early to use her mother's stove, for it was better than hers, and she spent the day baking bread and cake, making the kitchen fragrant. Otoonah boiled coffee and two whole unpeeled potatoes on top of the stove while bread baked in the oven.

Koahk came, still feverish and coughing, and Otoonah fed him hot canned milk mixed with water. I began to realize that he came to Otoonah for warmth and food. He had just gotten out of bed, his house was cold without a fire, and he was sick.

When the cakes were done, we watched Anahkaloktuk decorate one cake with raisins, slice it, and put it on plates. The other cake was laboriously packed into a cardboard box for Tigluk, who was leaving on an egg-hunting trip to the cliffs forty miles away.

We sang "Happy Birthday" to Elizabeth, who was wearing her best dress and a bow in her hair, and everyone had a generous piece of cake. Elizabeth could not be coaxed to smile even though an old man, a close relative, came and gave her a dollar bill for a present. She was still painfully shy and her face was red and hot, her black eyes expressionless, as she hid behind her mother's calico with one foot digging into the other one. I gave her a head scarf and added candy and cookies to the feast. Otoonah singled out the old man to receive one boiled potato as a special treat along with his coffee and cake.

Killigivuk had mailed the potatoes to Otoonah from Fairbanks. The old man ate his lovingly, without any adornment or salt, but simply as one eats a rare delicacy, savoring each bite, cutting each piece with his knife, and preferring it to the cake. The children and I glanced at him, relishing it with him.

Tigluk came by to pick up his cake, warmly dressed for the long boat trip he and another hunter were making. He was always complaining about his gun. "It won't shoot straight." "Something is wrong with it," or "It's too old," he would say. However, he whistled happily as he left.

Hundreds of thousands of murres, called crowbills by the Eskimos, migrated to nest on the cliffs of Cape Lisburne about forty miles northeast of Point Hope. Murres flew in formation with eider ducks, which migrated at the same time and nested around damp marshy ponds while the murres followed an instinctive pattern and nested on certain cliffs, ignoring others. In the past the Eskimos had used murre skins to make warm lightweight parkas.

The meat of the murre was eaten but it was not a favorite food, whereas the eggs were a great delicacy and were either eaten right away, raw or were boiled, peeled, and stored in pokes of seal oil. Each murre laid only one egg a year; the colors were a beautiful light blue-green mottled with brown. Each egg was twice as large as a chicken egg and had a thicker shell. The murres did not build nests but laid their eggs on the long bare ledges on the face of the high jagged cliffs; the pear-shaped construction of the egg causes it to roll in a small arc instead of falling.

Tigluk told me that he took the eggs from the cliff and put them in his parka pockets. Sometimes the murres swooped down at great speed, just missing the heads of the pickers, and if a man threw up his hands to chase them away, he might lose hold of the cliff and fall to his death. The birds have also been known to attack planes that were flying too close.

When their pockets bulged with eggs and perhaps some young birds warm from their nests, the men climbed down and stored them in barrels. They repeated the process until the skin boat could hold no more. Perhaps a thousand eggs were collected this way on one trip. The men climbed without ropes on the wet, slippery cliffs; one slip and they could be dashed against the cliffs. Perhaps, being men, they enjoyed the danger, knowing that the large fresh eggs would mean a change of diet for their families.

I thought of Tigluk and his trip in the rain and how lovingly his wife had baked the cake for him and how happy her face looked when she handled it to him. I imagined him and his friend resting beside a fire, their work done, and after a dinner of boiled fresh murre eggs and tea, opening the cardboard box with the raisin cake in it. How satisfying would be the knowledge of a dangerous job done and the eggs safely in the skin boat ready to take home. Perhaps he would take his hunting knife and cut the cake for his friend and himself, savoring it near the icy shore. Perhaps he would sip hot tea and look up at the cliffs and the birds winging around in the lonely night and think of home.

CHAPTER 10 *Journey*

I will take care not to go towards the dark.
I will go towards the day.

THE DOG TEAMS traveled over the green tundra and it seemed strange not to see them on ice and snow as in winter. These huskies were used to hard work and heavy loads, and they pulled the heavily laden sledges over the rough terrain. The hunters from Jabbertown brought in five caribou and some ugruk; and as they drove by, everyone ran out to see what meat was piled on their sleds. Much seal was needed to feed the dog teams and not much meat had been shot lately. The dogs seemed terribly thin and scrawny; they were hungry and mean.

The ice had been sweeping out to sea so gradually that I was not aware of it. Soon the shore would be free of ice and the yearly ship able to come in with fresh supplies. Unfortunately I wouldn't see the ship, for I was going home. I looked out and saw gulls by the hundreds lined up on the shore. The beach was gravelly and the great numbers of starfish and shells smelled strongly of seal oil when I sniffed them. Was it because seals had been butchered on them? Hundreds of tiny baby tomcod fishes a few inches long were plainly visible in the ocean water.

David and Dinah Frankson had been walking along the beach to watch the sea gulls and the shore ice moving out.

"That place there," David said, pointing, "is where we have *nalukatuk*, the whale feast."

"Half of us on one side of the beach and the other half of the village on the other side," said Dinah, laughing.

David explained, "Something like Republicans and Democrats."

"Over here is where we have walrus blanket toss," Dinah said. "Here is where we raise the flag." She pointed to a group of tall whale jawbones on a bare windswept beach. But in my imagination I could see the villagers in colorful clothes celebrating the whale feast among the whalebones.

Dinah's eyes lit up. "You must come, Clara; we women cook good food for feast, lots of muktuk, plenty to eat. You must come back, you would like it."

"Come back, Clara, come back," echoed David.

That evening I stopped in at some of the sod houses to say good-bye and hug the children. Looking out at the barren windswept coast, I felt a strong pull to remain; to share these people's lives, the hardiness and depth of their struggle.

The trip had been satisfying; my sketch pad was full of drawings, ideas, and watercolors. Otoonah had cared for me as a mother cares for her child, yet we could not speak each other's tongue; it was amazing that we understood each other so well. It was by intuition, anticipating each other's wants, and by simple pantomime that we got along. I do not know what she thought of my outlandish clothes, for I wore slacks and sweaters around the house when most of the other women dressed in calicos. Only lately had I begun to wear the calico Eskimo dress that revealed nothing of a woman's figure.

Electricity had changed Point Hope life, and it was a shock to see power lines leading into some of the sod igloos. Civilization had also brought the church, phonographs, some washing machines, electric irons, carpet sweepers, and corn flakes.

Olanaktuna is the Point Hope way to say good-bye or the equivalent of "I am going away." I had my last cup of coffee with Otoonah. The water had begun to taste very salty from the sea; the coffee was brackish and undrinkable.

When I asked her what her message to her husband in Fairbanks was, she stood up, clicked her heels together, and bowed from the waist. In English she repeated: "How do you do, Jimmy; how do you do, Jimmy; how do you do, Jimmy." (Jimmy is Asatsiak's American name.) She bent over double with laughter, then giggling like a young girl sat on the cot to pry off a piece of chewing gum that Koahk had probably left under the edge.

Olanaktuna, I repeated to Otoonah, then I bent my head and walked out of her doorway. But I choked when the time came to say it at the plane. The plane, the same old Beechcraft I had flown in on, came too soon, much too soon. Little Rosa, Koahk's sister, and other children came with the women to see me off. When the motor started, I looked out and saw their faces, especially Rosa's close to tears; her eyes and heart were as heavy as mine.

The pilot flew to Cape Lisburne, farther north, because

he had to drop off a soldier stationed there. We had to circle to land after hugging the coast for forty miles, and the runway was fogged in when we landed at Cape Lisburne, a military radar installation. Miles of cliffs bordered the base; it certainly looked like a God-forsaken place. It felt strange standing on the beach, knowing I was the only woman for miles. One of the G.I.'s complained bitterly to me about having nothing to do, the loneliness, and the miserable weather. He said: "We saw two natives in a skin boat go by," and I thought they must have been Tigluk and his friend.

The pilot looked anxiously about as the rain fell and visibility grew dense. Before we took off, I said to him: "Maybe we should wait till the fog lifts and the wind stops."

"No, it will be all right," he answered tensely.

The plane rose into the air and we were instantly enshrouded in fog. I was the only passenger so I sat next to the pilot, who nervously fiddled with the controls while the rain thrashed the plane and the engine sputtered. The old plane was patched inside and the bucket seats rattled beside us. After five minutes in thick soupy fog, I hesitatingly asked: "Are we all right?" I knew we must be flying near the bird cliffs.

"Uh huh," murmured the pilot, trying to get a radio position.

Although I was warmly dressed in heavy parka, mukluks, and kerchief, I was shivering. Glancing out the window I saw that the antenna had ice crystals on it, and that shook me because I had read of planes going down because of ice on the wings. I could hardly see the end of the wings for the fog. I looked at the pilot for reassurance but he looked bleakly ahead, probably thinking of the cliffs all around us. Later it turned out that this was his first run in this part of the Arctic; he was substituting for the regular pilot!

Nervously he put a cigarette in his mouth but could not find a match for he was concentrating hard, so I offered to get a match and lit his cigarette for him.

I had heard of pilots lost in fog who went into tight spirals and crashed into the ground or a nearby mountain. They lost their sense of gravity and could not tell whether they were flying right-side up or upside down.

The murres were known to launch themselves when an airplane passed over the cliffs, diving off into space to gain flying speed, beating their wings like flails, and crashing into the plane.

The pilot took out a large map and I thought: My God, is he lost?

I was afraid, thinking this was the end, and trying to remain calm I began to pray. Finally, about forty-five minutes later, we saw the earth below and the beautiful open sky. The fog was gone and the pilot had found his way out. With a sigh of relief I took the cigarette he offered me, although I do not usually smoke. The rest of the flight was routine, except that as we flew over Sheshalik I asked him to dip his wings.

I overheard the pilot and a group of men talking together after the Beechcraft landed; my pilot shook his head and said, "Never again."

At Kotzebue I stopped in to say hello to Mary Pilcher, who gave me two lovely kittens, one white and one black. "The huskies would only kill them here," she said. "Take them for your little girl." Eventually Yola named the kittens Kotzy and Boo. I also bought a jar of muktuk from an old woman to take to my Eskimo friends in Fairbanks.

I rushed to the airport and transferred to a modern plane, an F-27, which happened to be on its inaugural public flight from Kotzebue to Fairbanks. I tenderly placed the jar of muktuk on the floor of the plane near my feet and the kittens were in a carton. Starfish, ugruk bones, and whale discs were wrapped in my sleeping bag in the baggage section.

In the plane, which flew at three hundred miles an hour, was the Wien Airlines' regular mail pilot to Point Hope and Lisburne who was traveling as passenger to Fairbanks.

He told me that they called the flight to Cape Lisburne the "beer run" because of all the beer they delivered there. He said: "Cape Lisburne is the worst place to land because the runway is in front of a three-thousand-foot cliff and high winds make it dangerous. Added rain and fog are absolutely hazardous," he said flatly. We could easily have crashed into the cliffs.

I was the only passenger dressed in jeans and a parka; the rest were summer tourists. I sat in the rear by myself, utterly drained, reacting to my narrow escape. Tears ran down my face; I sniffed and bawled like a baby.

PART III

Nalukatuk

CHAPTER 11

Jade Adze

And I think over again
My small adventures
When with a shore wind I drifted out
In my kayak
And thought I was in danger.
My fears,
Those small ones
That I thought so big
For all the vital things
I had to get and to reach.
And yet, there is only one great thing,
The only thing:
To live to see in huts and on journeys
The great day that dawns,
And the light that fills the world.

FROM MEMORY I PAINTED the people
of Point Hope clustered in groups near the ocean, their faces
and bodies expressive, motionless against the windswept

landscape. One stage was over and now came the hard work, the real test after a beginning. There was no welling up of the creative springs as after Sheshalik. I had many doubts.

I came to the realization that among Eskimos nature and life were closely aligned. The rhythm of life was apparent, the cycle from the sea and land to the people. If the Eskimo was at the primal source, the heart of nature, I as an artist should experience this essence in order to paint it. Eskimos were never far from my mind and many letters back and forth bound me closer to them.

From Ah-gaik and Alec Frankson came a gift wrapped in a crushed brown paper bag: a priceless jade adze! The jade cutting edge was dull from years of use and the handle was made of whale rib with indentations for fingers. Sinew bound the whole together, a useful, beautiful object from ancient times.

I had become a part of the endless Alaskan snow and bitter cold. I had developed a directness like an Eskimo's because it is the basic, essential things that count, for survival and everyday life. It is not easy to simplify one's life. What is not naturally me gets cast away. The hard part is to cast off continually the excess of things one accumulates, not only the excess words, but the material comforts, false gestures and relationships. I wanted to be truly myself so that when I wrote or painted I could get directly to the core of what I was trying to express without any tricks or artificiality or my own ego in the way. I'd rather be plain than fancy; deep than shallow. I liked the Jiménez poem which says:

> Let my words be
> the thing itself
> created by my soul anew.

The pull to the north was very strong, especially at Christmas time. My whole family shared in the wrapping of gifts for the Point Hope and Noatak families. One special package with Masterpiece chewing tobacco and warm clothing was for Otoonah; it also contained shirts, coffee, nuts, and magazines for Asatsiak. Yola helped me pack, giving up many of her dolls for the packages, and Mark tied up the cartons. Joe and I hauled them to the airport to be delivered by Wien Airline for Christmas in the Arctic.

When we chopped down our holiday spruce tree in the woods, I thought of treeless Point Hope; and when we decorated our tall spruce with bright globes and cranberries, I wondered if the minister would have a tree delivered by plane.

On the coast the weather was forty-four below zero and wind and storm raged through the village. At Christmas it was thirty-eight below zero in Fairbanks, but because of the surrounding hills we had little wind which made the bitter cold bearable. A thick crust of ice crystals coated the inside of our windows and heavy ice fog pressed the chimney smoke down over the town. Frost rimmed our fur hoods and our breath was steamy about our faces, yet everyone went to work, the stores were open, and the children did not miss a day of school.

The birches surrounding our home were beautiful, each twig covered with ice patterns; they seemed an answer in itself. Tuned to the silence and continual snowfall, we had slowed our pace.

We passed from a long, desperately dark winter to the beginning of May before the snow melted and brought us to the mud season in Fairbanks. The Chena River ice jammed and then broke loose, overflowing our banks, and with that flooding some tight bonds within us broke.

In early June the earth became dry and warm enough for the planting of seeds. The chokecherry tree in our garden, which had been piled high with snow a short time before, now leaved, budded, and broke into riotous perfumed flowers all in the space of one week. It was light twenty-four hours a day; there was no more darkness. Bluebells, daisies, and delphiniums were coming up and the grass was green.

In spite of the green and the sun, I left Fairbanks and flew north. When I landed in Kotzebue, the wind was blowing air fresh from the ocean and ice patches still covered the withered brown tundra in many places. The town hummed with hopeful excitement and a careless freedom filled the air. Eskimos sauntered, hands in pockets, their fur garments replaced by lighter, brighter coverings. The wind tore at the women's loose black hair, unbound from winter's fur hoods. Hunters scanned the distant waters for the white whale's spouting.

I walked down the sea front and stopped to visit a family I had met on my previous visit. The father was a tall blond from Illinois and the part-Eskimo mother, was a beautiful serene woman. They had five girls, all of whom had a grace and vigor that comes of eating choice whale and seal meat in addition to eggs and carrots—the best of the Eskimo and Western diets.

The mother, a good cook, always prepared plenty to allow for the unexpected wayfarer such as myself. A huge baked salmon, homemade bread, and coffee were set down on the table. Pregnant with her sixth child, the woman moved with grace. How she managed to keep placid in their small quarters with little one's underfoot, without plumbing, and with continual diapers to wash, was a mystery to me. Her life seemed to move smoothly past the wet diapers to some inward vision few of us achieve. She talked tenderly and softly and laughed much; no sign of strain marred her olive face.

Her oldest daughter had her exquisite skin coloring and her face glowed with golden undertones. I painted her in an orange sweater which was just the right shade for her.

An Eskimo girl with a long straight nose lived with them to help with the housework. Her parents, who cared for her baby, lived in a tent at the reindeer camp miles from Kotzebue. They came to visit while I was there, entering the house timidly, warmly dressed from the trip. The baby had fat ruddy red cheeks and two eye slits peeping out from her fur hood. She showed no emotion at seeing her mother but the girl pressed her close. The parents sat shyly, speaking in Eskimo while they sipped coffee. The warmth must have felt good to the old couple for their cheeks were wind burned. They sat with their work-hardened hands held loosely on their laps, watching the baby suck a lollipop. The girl shook her head when they asked if she wanted to go back to the reindeer camp with them; she was used to an easier, softer life now.

Quavuk was living at Kotzebue instead of Sheshalik because her husband had a carpentry job. Their tent faced Sheshalik and was a few feet from the sea. The skin of a loon lay outside the open flap while a broth bubbled on the camp stove. Quavuk quickly put some coffee to boil, the inevitable sign of hospitality in the North.

As we drank coffee, Quavuk met my glance again and again, measuring me according to her standards, and I prayed I was not lacking.

When I told her I was going to the nalukatuk at Point Hope, she looked at my clothes and said I would not be warm enough. She insisted that I wear her muskrat parka with the wolverine hood trimmed with a black and white fur border and ermine tails set in below the shoulders. She was about a size forty-four and I was a thirty-six but I was grateful to have a real, warm Eskimo parka. I didn't own a fur coat and with anything but Eskimo clothes I would have been conspicuous.

For my one-night stay over I had rented a room at Rotman's Hotel which faced the sea. It had a bathtub and plumbing. Most of the plumbing in Kotzebue consisted of a porcelain pot located in one corner of the room. Occasionally the pot sat on the outer storm porch; sometimes the facility was an outhouse, or honey bucket, the name given a chemical toilet. Except for the hospital, school, hotel, oil company, Federal Aviation Agency, and a few private homes, real plumbing was a rarity. Most of the women washed clothes with rainwater and paid two dollars a barrel for drinking water.

The next afternoon I took the bush flight to Point Hope in the antiquated Beechcraft. There was another passenger, a soldier, going to Cape Lisburne. As we flew over the desolate Arctic coast, I became happier and he sadder.

At Point Hope David Frankson was there to receive the mail sacks, while Asatsiak and Dinah Frankson helped me carry my stuff to the Killigivuk house.

Otoonah must have seen us approaching, for she stood at the doorway, greeting us with a bashful bow and leading the way to the warm kitchen. The women were shy at first, observing me as if I had just dropped in from Mars, but the parka was the object of much talk and handling.

"It's Quavuk's," I explained. They examined the stitches closely and looked at the fancy border design. It was rather large on me, and only when I returned home and saw photos of myself did I realize how large it was and how polite the women had been not to say so.

Children came trooping in to say hello, and the gift contents of the boxes disappeared quickly as we tasted the homemade fruitcake I had brought for Otoonah with tea.

My little room was ready; all I needed to do was put my sleeping bag on the bunk and set down the paint box. That evening I wandered around to visit several families who were living in summer tents.

The flatness of the terrain forced me to become completely reoriented. I had been used to the shelter of trees but here I was exposed to the elements, stripped, alienated. The sky was so close; it seemd right on top of us. Upon this land man fused with nature, his was the moving shape on the landscape. All sense of perspective was gone; the flatness of vast distances dominated the eye.

The earth had not yet turned green; there was no sign of flowers. Barren ground, ravaged and cracked, showed signs of winter. I unwound slowly, my speech became softer and my actions unhurried. Time again became a lost thing, nothing was of importance except the now—the Eskimos and me.

Soon the children surrounded me—"Hi, Cara; hi, Cara"—Rosa and her brother Elmer, Koahk and his brothers and other children shouting and laughing. And so my days at Point Hope began with their happy welcome.

CHAPTER 12

Asatsiak

I call to mind
And think of the early coming of spring
As I knew it
In my younger days.
Was I ever such a hunter!

OTOONAH'S HUSBAND, Asatsiak, was born in 1891 at Point Hope. He was an *umelik,* the captain of a whaling crew, a position of great prestige in the village. His father and his grandfather before him had been umeliks, hunters of substance and strength. Asatsiak carried on this tradition, but now he had no son willing or capable of continuing the family heritage.

Asatsiak had no children by Otoonah, but she had three children by another man who was now dead. Asatsiak had been married to another woman who bore him six children, three boys and three girls, of whom three were living. One son was a bookkeeper in Seattle, the other son had spent most of his life in a hospital, and the daughter lived in southeastern Alaska.

When the mother of Asatsiak's children died he mourned her greatly. For three years he did not sing, compose songs, or beat the drum at dances, or even smoke his pipe which was his greatest pleasure. He had gone through the village saying: "I guess I'm never going to hunt whales again." That was the worst thing that can befall an umelik; he was lost and inconsolable without her.

Finally one day the men of the village came to ask him to play the drum and sing for the dance, saying: "It's time enough," and so he broke mourning.

They needed him, as he was the leader of their dances and composed most of the songs. Songs were valuable to a hunter and men would pay for songs to be composed about them, for they could bring luck in hunting. A song would last; a song could be passed on from generation to generation.

"My father always followed old rules for hunting. Songs were the most important. Not many hunters have songs," Asatsiak stated firmly. "My father died in 1925 and I took his place. He died of appendix; no doctor in those days.

"If a man wants to kill me he can sing songs and I can die, just crushed like paper." He made motions with his hands as if crumbling paper. The songs were so powerful that it was believed merely singing them could break the bowstring of an enemy attempting to shoot, or force an animal to return if sung over his tracks.

"Some songs very strong, make die. Each crew have

own song. Never sell song or tell secret whaling song. Only sing when whale is struck and before, for luck. "Young people not care about songs any more, not listen to old people."

Asatsiak's songs were famous up and down the coast from Kotzebue to Point Barrow. He had many relatives in other villages, but as far as I knew only he and his brother bore the last name of Killigivuk. I asked him, "Ahpah, how did you get the name of Killigivuk? What does it mean?"

"It mean elephant, *punnik*."

"Oh, you mean old-time mammoth?"

"Yes, that's it."

"When a little boy is born they give it a woman's name. When a girl is born they give it man's name because father or uncle names her. They try to name the child same name as someone from another village," he explained to me. "When a man is grown up he goes travel to another village. People want to kill, but if his name is like another of that village, they won't kill him."

"My namesake, Asatsiak, was an *angatkok*. You call it medicine man. When he went to the Siberian side they got my name from an angatkok there. They know Asatsiak very well," he said proudly. "Protects me."

Eskimo names in addition to being a man or woman's name could mean "old woman"; Howard Rock, Eskimo newspaper editor originally from Point Hope, used actually to be called "Mother." Some names have developed by taking the first name of an older relative, usually the father, and adding "son" to it. Hence the name of Frankson.

Killigivuk's face lit up with a smile. "My mother's name was Nikuwanna. She was always nice, always invited people to come and eat. Always food in my house. Children, men and women always welcome. She liked people.

"My mother taught me songs, my father taught me to hunt. My mother knew how to help people if they were hurt. When Attungorah's wife was hurt, my mother wrapped ermine skins around her head and it stopped the blood. No doctor in those days."

Killigivuk had wide experience with all kinds of white

people, from the early whaling captains, the traders, explorers, and missionaries, to an artist like myself. He tried to understand them but came to the conclusion, "White people not same as Eskimos. Eskimos think different, not use many words. White people can make airplanes, lots of things, real smart."

The Eskimos often say that I must be part Eskimo. Asatsiak, rooted in the old Eskimo belief in reincarnation even though he is a Christian said, "Oh sure, you might have once been Eskimo. Human—two parts—soul and body. Everyone when he's dead, go up and look down for his mother. Always look for mother to be born. Maybe you pick Eskimo, maybe white, maybe black."

Asatsiak and his son had lived with us in Fairbanks for a short time when Eugene was released from the hospital in Anchorage. Asatsiak was not used to the strange variety of food, especially my Hungarian specialties, lentils and kolbase, or stuffed cabbage. He gamely ate them but what he really enjoyed were eggs, store white bread, and ice cream.

Yola called him Grandpa and watched TV leaning against his mukluk'd legs. TV fascinated him and he absorbed it with dignity as one does a pleasure one cannot always enjoy. Most of all he enjoyed walking downtown and standing in front of the main drug store to greet all the Eskimos passing by and exchange news of other villages. Sometimes he took a cab and got off in front of the drug store and I think he liked that best of all.

I called the Department of Rehabilitation of the Bureau of Indian Affairs in Fairbanks to try to find a job for thirty-year-old Eugene but it was impossible. He had been ill for years with tuberculosis and epilepsy and had spent most of his life in hospitals, where he had learned the trade of retouching photographs. He could draw reasonably well but he had not practiced much. He would have to go back to his native village.

At Point Hope, Asatsiak looked younger than when I had seen him in Fairbanks. His skin was tanned, hairless, and unwrinkled. He wore glasses over his heavy-lidded eyes and bushy eyebrows and was short of stature. He seemed happier at home, his movements unrestrained.

In 1946 he had been ill with TB of the bone and had spent eleven months at the Mt. Edgecumbe Hospital. In later years he rarely saw a doctor except for yearly check-ups. He said he felt fine but his legs bowed out and he had difficulty walking. A doctor who saw him said that he must be in dreadful pain, but he denied it.

"I feel fine," Asatsiak said. "My legs don't hurt. Otoonah and me never get sick."

Nothing prevented him from hunting in all kinds of weather. Yet sometimes I saw his face twitch and his mouth move to one side in a small gesture of covered-up pain.

There was a quietness in him, a peace. I always recognized him as he left to go hunting in the early dawn with a gun and his *neekohowtuk*, a short three-legged stool used to sit on ice, strapped to his back, walking awkwardly on his bent legs, his arms free and his body moving from side to side.

He was a good shot: "Hunter can see animal's backbone clearly when he hunts." Asatsiak remembered paddling in his father's umiak during the whale hunt. "My father show me how to throw harpoon to strike whale. My father used a darting gun to kill whale; before that they used flint or jade harpoon head, after that a metal point."

He had his father's eagle feather on his seal poke for identification when the whale was struck. The other hunters used a hawk or loon feather, and most of them engraved the harpoon shaft with a private symbol.

"My father's house had four lamps burning, one in each corner of the room." The lamps burned whale oil.

His father's house was built underground. "It was plenty warm and light. We could cook our food, get light and heat from the whale oil lamp. Now Eskimos getting lazy, burning store oil. We used to get driftwood on the shore when I was young."

6

Asatsiak reminisced. "In my grandfather's house lived three sons, the wife, wife's mother and husband. When the sons got married they stayed with wives and children. Maybe eight or ten people slept on bench.

"In those days parents tell son: 'You'd better marry relative; if you do not, someone else marry. When war comes your wife won't tell you what happens. Wife protected man if relative, otherwise not. I could marry my father's first cousin's daughter—best kind of marriage—but not father's brother's daughter!

"When someone dies we put his whale hunting things in his grave, spear, sled, anything, but not skin boat with him. Same thing for woman, her things buried with her. We sometimes put seal meat in grave."

During the past century there had been six *qalegis*, or meeting houses, in Tigara, but by the early 1900's there were only two left, the Qaqmaktok and the Ungasiksikaq. When Asatsiak was old enough to shoot an arrow he joined his father's qalegi, the Ungasiksikaq.

The qalegis were Tigara's largest underground structures. The roof, floor, and walls were made of driftwood and the entrance frame of whalebone jaws. Sod blocks covered the outside and the qalegi was lighted through a gut window in the roof.

During the day the men in the qalegis worked on their hunting equipment making harpoons, nets, spears, or umiaks. The women brought food to the men in wooden bowls. In the evening the men told stories, mostly about hunting or nature to instruct the younger boys. A hunter might tell about the movement of the pack ice or what to do when lost on the ice. They also told stories about their ancestors and folk tales.

An old man told me one such tale, called "*Koomuk*, the Flea."

"Alone in an igloo lived a lonesome *koomuk*. Every day and every night he stayed in the old igloo. After he had his last meal in the middle of the night he went to sleep.

"One night after his last meal he fix up his bed. While fixing up his bed he heard a dog team come to his old home. So he fixed up some meal for his guests. For a long time they unharnessed their dogs. Then all the people went inside his igloo. They ate what the koomuk, a little bug, a flea, that live on human head, had fixed up. They stop eating and stretch their sleeping bags and went to sleep. The little house was filled from wall to wall.

"When everyone was asleep, koomuk went down in one of the caribou sleeping bags that someone was sleeping in and he went down until he reach the toe.

"When morning came, everyone woke up and ate, then they packed up. Koomuk was still in the caribou sleeping bag. It was warm and ticklish inside the caribou bag. The owner of the bag let the hair come out of the bag. Koomuk held on hard, but he slipped and fell to the floor.

"Koomuk was alone again in the house. Everyone was gone except poor koomuk. Koomuk have no brains at all. He sat on the floor for an hour, then suddenly he had an idea.

"The next day early in the morning he start his trip to the door. It took him days to get out of the igloo. He followed tracks for hours. The next day he saw a tree; the tracks led upward, so he waited. The next day he did not wake up, he was frozen. The tree was only a grass. Koomuk had a good time in his life, but he went the wrong way. He should have stayed home."

In those days great feasts and games were held in the qalegis. At these clebrations the families dressed in the manner of animals associated with them. They wore, for example, parts of a polar bear skin, or the skin of a loon or other animal.

In the qalegis were held dances, angatkok seances, and games of competitive skill. These games were tests of endurance and often quite bloody. A man had to endure a whipping with rawhide lines or perhaps a pointed stick pushed against his upper lip.

"Another practice at this time was called *suliruk*." According to Rainey, "a man who had a partner in another *qalegi* sent him a gift, a fine wolverine skin or a skin full of oil, requesting a specified exchange." On one such occasion the partner was asked for the "smell of his flesh being sawed, like the smell of wood. . . ." So he cut off his leg and sent it to him!

The church had stopped this practice a long time ago. Today the qalegis are gone at Tigara, washed away by the erosion of sea and ice, but the two rival groups remain. During the nalukatuk, however, the division of the whaling groups into Qaqmaktok and Ungasiksikaq was retained.

In Fairbanks we had taken Asatsiak to visit some friends one evening. At Point Hope the women were quiet, deferring to the men, their masters. The women never gave their opinions or talked as boldly as I seemed to that evening.

When we went home, I asked Asatsiak, "I suppose you think women here in Fairbanks talk a lot compared to women at Point Hope?"

He replied: "I'll tell you a story. An old woman at Point Hope many years ago had two sons. Every day she brought food to the qalegi. First she took one son to help her carry the food, then the other son. She talked a lot. Finally the men couldn't stand it. One man jumped on her and held both hands and her feet and took out a big knife and cut off her tongue. He cut her mouth all around. The sons sat there and watched and never said a word. The woman got up and went home. Her mouth healed but she never said another word; she went around the village with her arm covering up her mouth. She never showed her mouth, always hide it. We tell that story to our women; they never talk much now."

The mystery of the medicine men, the shamans or angatkoks, of old had always fascinated me. The rituals, the trances, the magic, the healing they were supposed to perform were part of a primitive life our generation could only read about. The angatkok had power and sway over the people to be used for good or evil.

Killigivuk had known many medicine men in his lifetime and he told me about them. Angatkoks had the power to kill, cripple, or blind. They could do anything, even fly through space to another village. They could even fly to the moon! They could cure the sick, set bones, and find food during a famine.

An angatkok dressed in skin clothing with appendages of animal claws and other charms. When he held a seance, he dulled the seal-oil lamps, darkening the room in the qalegi, then proceeded to beat his drum and go into a trance, making strange sounds, twisting his legs and body into contortions and rolling his eyes, while he communed "with the spirits."

"Point Hope people give angatkok presents of sinew or skin, or ugruk bottoms for mukluks," Asatsiak said. They tell him, 'You should find food for us.' From a hole in the floor he pulled up a bag full of tomcod, throwing them to the hunters and saying, 'You should get plenty fish tomorrow.' "

Ahyerik was the oldest angatkok at Point Hope whom Asatsiak remembers. Twewhalcheluk was second oldest; Anahkaloktuk, after whom Otoonah's daughter was named, was third, Ahjoonik, fourth; Shevowna, a woman, fifth; Choobuk sixth, and then Kayoutuk.

Kayoutuk was the Eskimo name that Ah-gaik and Sunshine gave me; it meant literally "big dipper" or berry picker. They had named me after Ah-gaik's grandmother.

Kayoutuk, the angatkok, was the same age as Attungorah but lived most of his life on the outskirts of Point Hope and Kivalina. He was an umelik, hunting whales and polar bear. Asatsiak remembered that he made his own teeth from walrus ivory.

"I see Ahyerik, the angatkok, myself. He was a good one; when he heard someone was sick, he tried to cure them," said Asatsiak. "He sat in front of the door with his skin raincoat covering his legs and called the spirit of his own dead father." Here Asatsiak put his hands to his mouth and imitated the angatkok calling.

" 'Bad weather, sick people,' I heard his father's spirit answer," said Asatsiak. " 'Feed sick people seal meat, ocean animal, fish, or whale. Do not eat inland animal with ocean animal together or they will die.'

"Twewhalcheluk helped my mother and father," Asatsiak went on.

" 'What's going on in hunting?' they asked Twewhalcheluk before whaling started. 'We want to get a whale this spring!' My father gave him some ugruk."

"Twewhalcheluk got his drum and shut out the skylight, all dark, no light. After when it quiet, spirit goes to whale place. After few minutes, sees something in mouth, caught between teeth. Twewhalcheluk said: 'I'm marking your whale with my teeth.' He caught whale fluke with teeth. 'When you catch your whale you'll see my tooth marks.'

"When spring is come, my father got whale. He cut it and saw this mark on the whale fluke. Man's teeth cut into whale muktuk!" said Asatsiak emphatically.

By the time I visited them, Point Hopers rarely spoke of their past angatkok history. The church had made them ashamed and confused, yet vestiges of the old beliefs were sometimes evident. Ancient beliefs were not so easily forgotten and it seemed wise to pacify old spirits as well as new.

In the old days an animal effigy, or *kikituk*, carved from wood was believed to have the power to kill a person. Such a kikituk with sharp teeth was found by Rainey in the old houses in 1939. I learned that some of the people of Tigara still believed it had magical powers. When a schoolteacher sought to have them carve a kikituk in whalebone for tourist sale, it was quickly suppressed by the church.

The old people of Tigara were believed to have power to control another person's life and for this reason were treated with great kindness in the village. It was believed that they could prevent a hunter from killing game, so the hunters made sure that a little of the meat they killed went into the old people's pots. The custom of the aged's exposing themselves to die when they had become useless, as practiced in other Eskimo villages, was never done at Tigara, according to Rainey.

CHAPTER 13

Stefansson, Jenness, and Asatsiak

And an old man, seeking strength in his youth
Loves most to think of the deeds whereby he gained renown.

IN THE EVENINGS Asatsiak, Otoonah, and I drank coffee. Sometimes I played two-handed pinochle with Asatsiak while Otoonah sewed, patching her old furs, her head bent low over her work. Asatsiak reminisced about his youth. "I learned to play pinochle on a whaling ship." He crossed his mukluk'd legs and leaned back on one arm. "One year we struck twenty whales. A black man was the harpooner. We used to save the baleen and throw away the meat.

"I met Stefansson on the *Karluk,* used to be a whaling ship," said Asatsiak as I looked up in surprise. "I met Stefansson in 1909. In July *Karluk* is come. I go. Left my wife." Asatsiak took a long sip of coffee and put away the worn deck of cards.

"Stefansson like me. He talk Eskimo." He paused significantly. "Stefansson know everything. Everything about Eskimo. Eat. Talk. Eskimo. He never wore undershirt, just fawn shirt.

"In 1913 on *Karluk* we woke up to find the ship surround by ice. Bartlett was the captain. I looked from crow's nest and saw mountains far away with snow on them. When ship is stuck, no move, captain is mad. Freeze up, ice. No move any more. We wait maybe two weeks, then hunted sea seal with kayak.

"One day Stefansson told me: 'Asatsiak, we try to go hunting caribou.' We go six of us together. We have two teams. One sled have nine dogs—eighteen altogether. We go out leave ship. We could not make it—too rough ice. We camp on ice all night."

The *Karluk* was hemmed in with ice between Point Barrow and the Mackenzie River. It lay there helpless, unable to move either forward or back, even under full steam.

In the *Friendly Arctic* Vilhjalmur Stefansson explained what happened. There were two main views of Arctic ice naviagation, the bold Atlantic policy of "keep away from the land, face the ice and take your chances," or the cautious Alaska one of ". . . hug the coast, play safe, . . . I decided for what a friendly person would call the bolder course. But whoever prefers to be truthful rather than kind must say I chose the wrong alternative."

Gradually the ice pressed against the ship's sides until she groaned and quivered with the strain. "Drifting in the pack is a tense game. In the beginning you have a certain amount of discretion in chosing your berth. After that it is luck upon which the life of your ship depends," wrote Stefansson.

Each day the weather grew colder, the ice more solid, until it seemed certain that the *Karluk* would remain there all winter. When Stefansson decided to hunt caribou, he left the ship with two sleds and a rifle, taking with him five men, Wilkins, McConnell, Jenness, and two Eskimos, one of whom was Asatsiak, the other Pauyurak who was Attungorah's son. They expected to be gone a week or two and then return to the *Karluk* laden with fresh meat.

A strong wind had been blowing all night and the gale increased until it became the worst storm of the season. Stefansson wrote: "I was scarcely willing to believe my own eyes when I saw her [the *Karluk*] moving to the eastwards —against the wind, against the current, and against any theory which I could formulate. . . ."

A blizzard had opened up a dark land of water and the ice seemed to be drifting with a dark spot that looked like the *Karluk!* The men stood transfixed, watching that dark spot on the horizon.

When it cleared to seaward, the *Karluk* was gone. Stefansson decided there was no sense in searching for her by sled for there was more water than ice, so they went on to the mainland. They never saw the *Karluk* again!

Whether the vessel had freed itself from the ice, or whether, still imprisioned, it had been carried away by the ice, they could not know. In any case it was gone, leaving the hunting party of six men marooned and surrounded by thin ice and open water.

"This was a night of high tension, although free from that deepest of uncomfortable feelings that what was happening could have been prevented." Wrote Stefansson: ". . . the *Karluk* was at the mercy of the ordinary forces of nature and of the laws of chance, at least until the coming spring."

Asatsiak told me in his simple way what happened. "We woke up to find the *Karluk* surrounded by ice, every-

thing on boat—other men, dog team, umiak, grub—all lost!
When the ice broke off and carried *Karluk* out, we stayed
and make big fire. Ship didn't see us. Next day we sleep on
ice. We followed the coast, then move inland. We camp.
Next day Stefansson, me, and Pauyurak go hunting for caribou. We never found anything. Stefansson go hunting, tried
to see caribou inland. He looked with his *keenurooutic.*
Means 'looking close with binoculars.'

"We go back to camp. Sleep in two tents. Men talk
which way we go. Ice broke off. We build a fire, smoke,
drink tea. We sleep all night. In morning Stefansson decide
to go Point Barrow."

Stefansson wrote in *The Friendly Arctic:* ". . . we had a
rather narrow escape from a serious mishap, for in the attempt to make shore . . . [we] found ourselves on ice that
owing to its extreme . . . mushiness had upon it black
patches of damp snow. It was partly a matter of luck that
we did make shore without losing sledges or lives."

Diamond Jenness, in *Dawn in Arctic Alaska*, noted:
". . . our food supply was beginning to run low. Where were
we to go? There were no signs of habitation in the vicinity,
no one to ask about the *Karluk.* . . ."

Taking another sip of coffee, Asatsiak continued, "Next
morn we start. Afternoon we see small island, Oloouklutk
Point. We stay overnight. Keep going North."

Jenness wrote: "We headed therefore to Barrow. The
dogs, though on short rations, moved steadily forward over
the smooth ice offshore at the rate of about three miles per
hour. We knew from our chart that high mountains lay
south of us behind the narrow coastal plain, but the haze
that always blankets the land in early winter hid them from
view. So low and featureless was the shore that from a short
distance it was impossible to tell where the sea ended and
the land began. Every now and then we sighted a seal bask-
ing on the surface of the ice near a crack or breathing hole,
and we halted while Stefansson or one of the Eskimos went
off to stalk it; but there was so little cover that the animal

invariably took alarm and dived out of sight before the hunter could approach within gunshot."

Jenness went on: "On the third day, near noon, we passed two sand bars known as the 'Point Hope Islands' because many years before a war party of Point Hope natives had perished from starvation there after the local Eskimos had stolen their boats. Then, a mile or two farther on, we sighted a tent and a wooden platform on the shore line. Here, surely, were people. . . . We pointed our sleds in their direction."

Asatsiak had this to add concerning the remains of the Point Hope "war party": "We saw tracks, man track. Funny sled, no dogs. Towards Barrow we come to Big Island and see whale boat. Long time ago Attungorah wanted to make war on Charlie Brower at Point Barrow. We find the place. We used to have lots war. When Eskimos drink in strange place, he always used dipper because he couldn't bend down head. Careful always. Fight in dark, afraid to fight in daylight. We had to watch for enemies. A long time ago, war between Eskimos. Now no war."

Stefansson wrote: "The next day we were traveling along in the general direction of Halkeet when one of the Eskimos said he could smell smoke. None of the rest of us could, but I was willing to rely on the Eskimo, for my experience is that while in eyesight, hearing, and every other natural facility he is about the same as the rest of us, he does seem to excel in the sense of smell."

Asatsiak told me: "Next morning Stefansson ask me, 'Which way we go?' I tell him, 'People up ahead.' We camp on big lagoon on ice. Had little pemmican which we use for dog food.

"We camp on ice again near coast. Next day we saw a family, Colville River people, man, wife, and little girls. They had no flour, nothing except frozen fish and whale oil. We eat frozen fish. Stefansson liked seal oil, told his men: 'You better eat frozen fish with oil. If you don't eat, you starve.' Next day we take fish from them and promise to pay.

We camp, me and Stefansson and Pauyurak, in one tent and the other men in other tent.

"Nobody else around coast. Next day we make another camp. Stefansson promised people he would send them something from Barrow in exchange for grub. We go to Point Barrow next day. Borrowed flour, sugar, coffee, rolled oats. We make bread. We all got sick. Sore feet. Sick from running behind sled for five days."

At Point Barrow Stefansson decided to leave Jenness at Cape Halkeet, where he could winter among Eskimos and learn the language, while he and the rest of the party proceeded to Collinson Point. He purchased dogs, skin clothing, and sledges to carry on the work of the expedition, *Karluk* or no *Karluk*. Charlie Brower was helpful in outfitting him and his party and was optimistic about the outcome of the *Karluk* which was reported to have been seen off the coast of Barrow by Eskimos.

"After a few days I go with Jenness with one team to the first family we met, the Colville River people. We fishing a lot, something like grayling. Stefansson came to get me one day. Ask me go to coast with him. I tell Stefansson I quit.

" 'Why?' ask Stefansson.

" 'I don't know,' I say.

" 'Do you want more money for wages?' He was paying me two hundred dollars a year and room and board. I say no. Stefansson liked me to lead dogs, help him. Good runner, never get tired, run in front of dogs. Speak English too. I run an hour, lead dogs, then Stefansson. But I stay with Alaocoq, the Colville River man, and his family. I did not tell Stefansson. The reason I stay is Alaocoq told me there was gold in the river. That's why."

"How could you know there was gold in the river if it was frozen in the winter?" I asked, interrupting him and wondering if the Nome gold fever had reached that far north.

"Alaocoq tell me wait till spring, plenty of gold. I listen him," said Asatsiak, scratching his head. "All winter we fish, then we trap foxes. Alaocoq caught lots of white foxes. I caught ten all winter. Gave him five because they were his traps. Five skins I get thirty-five dollars apiece. Spent all the money in Barrow. Later I was sorry I didn't go with Stefansson."

Stefansson wrote that Asatsiak left the party because of a woman, but Asatsiak maintained it was because of "gold." Asatsiak spent the winter with Jenness and Alaocoq hunting and trapping foxes; there was no sign of gold in the spring.

Jenness took a liking to Asatsiak and wrote down his songs. One of them appears with a photograph with the caption "Jimmy" in *Dawn in Arctic Alaska*.

Four months later in 1914 the *Karluk* finally was demolished by pack ice pressure. It had drifted south until it was about one hundred and ten miles northeast of Wrangell Island near the coast of Siberia.

Stefansson and his original party were all safe, although Stefansson had been believed dead by the outside world. Of the entire ship's company of twenty-five, only Captain Bartlett and an Eskimo named Katsaktovik, reached the Siberian shore. One sailor had died of self-inflicted gunshot wounds, two men had died of nephritis (due to the pemmican's lacking oil, Stefansson believed), and eight men who left the ship were never heard from again. The rest of the men, headed by an Englishman named Hadley, were found on Wrangell Island existing on fish and seal meat and were rescued.

Asatsiak made his way back to Point Hope and Stefansson went far into the Canadian Arctic, exploring new territory with Eskimo methods and staking his life on the belief that if Eskimos could survive in the Arctic he could too, provided he lived as they did.

Asatsiak picked up the pinochle deck and said in his old man's voice, "I wish I could see Stefansson once more before I die. I'd like to go hunting with him. He never sat in sled, run like Eskimos, sometimes fifty miles a day if good ice."

Asatsiak never got his wish. Stefansson died in 1962 at the age of eighty-two.

CHAPTER 14

Preparations

I rise up from rest,
Moving swiftly as the raven's wing
I rise up to meet the day—

OTOONAH WOKE ME at ten A.M.
I had slept deeply. "Coffee, coffee," she whispered.

I washed up and had oatmeal, bread, and coffee with
the Killigivuks. On the cot were two pairs of beautiful new
white calfskin mukluks with red beaded designs worked
around the tops in tiny stitches. Asatsiak and Otoonah
urged me to try them—"Your new nalukatuk mukluks." The

nalukatuk, or whale feast, was to begin in a few days. Unfortunately Otoonah had forgotten how big my feet were—try as I might, I couldn't get them on. Asatsiak then sat on the floor with a long thick stick and tried to enlarge them, wetting the bottoms and jabbing with all his strength to make them longer, but they still didn't fit. No Cinderella I.

Mukluks are not mass produced like shoes; they have to be made to fit the individual. It seemed it was the custom for everyone to have new mukluks for the whale feast!

Sunshine Tuckfield had also made me a pair of mukluks but they were too large. Finally I put on my regular shoes and walked over to the post office to see if there was any mail.

Dinah and David Frankson invited me in to see the treadle sewing machine that I had been instrumental in procuring for them. A Fairbanks businessman I knew had traded a secondhand machine for a pair of men's mukluks sewn by Dinah.

When David saw that I wore no mukluks, he asked Dinah to get a pair of his and have me try them on. They were made of white calfskin, with an intricate three-inch-wide colored bead border around the cuff.

"Put them on, Clara," Dinah pressed.

"They are not very good," David insisted.

They fitted perfectly. I protested weakly, "But I couldn't take them."

"Take them, Clara; I have other pairs," said David.

They looked so elegant I couldn't refuse. Now I wore mukluks and a parka, an outfit fit for a feast, like a proper Eskimo.

David's brother Alec lived in the next house so I visited him, proudly wearing the new mukluks. Alec, his wife Ahgaik, their children, their married daughter, her husband, and their newborn baby lived in two rooms.

Their wooden house had sod banked all around the sides. The entranceway, or storm cache, housed frozen meat, hunting implements, toilet facilities, and the whale-bone vertebrae Alec used for carving masks.

I had known their children, Rosa and Elmer, from my last trip to Point Hope, and Ah-gaik and I had become better acquainted through correspondence. Ah-gaik wrote English well and spoke it better than Alec.

I sought her face eagerly as I entered the house, and when she came forward out of the darkness, her face was illuminated by a light that seemed inexhaustible. Her bearing was shy, yet warm, her nose curved in delicate swirls around her nostrils, her skin color was pale and her teeth white, and black hair hung in a knot at the base of her neck. Dressed in a printed black calico parka, she bent over the stove at the back of the room to make coffee.

Her married daughter stooped over a bowl on the floor, mixing doughnut batter, or *maporuks*. Off the main room was a smaller bedroom where Ah-gaik and Alec slept. Unless the children were small like Silas, the youngest, they did not sleep on the bed but on caribou skins rolled out on the floor.

The youthful married daughter seemed very fragile, listless, with delicate joints. When her baby cried, she picked him up and placed him in the hood of her parka and continued to roll the maporuks. After she shaped them with holes in the center, she placed them in hot seal oil where they quickly browned on both sides.

Silas, Ah-gaik's three-year-old, was a healthy sloe-eyed boy who hung onto her skirt demanding attention and eyed me with suspicion. I remembered how possessively he had nursed from Ah-gaik the year before.

In Ah-gaik's background was the blood of a Portuguese whaler who had stayed over at Jabbertown, which might have explained the bony structure of her face. Her life was given over to Alec and the children, and she was the kind of mother who seldom demanded but usually gave.

The golden light of June streamed through the windows as she sewed her children's parkas for the feast, put-

ting intricate rickrack trim along the cotton ruffles. She reminded me of the Vermeer painting of a woman sewing as
she laboriously turned the handle of the sewing machine
with one hand, guiding the print material under the needle
with the other. We chatted while she sewed and I asked if I
could paint her as she worked. Before long all of the children were drawing with me on the floor.

Alec came into the cozy atmosphere beaming good-
naturedly. "What does your husband look like?" he asked. I
asked him to guess. "Short and fat," was his retort, and the
insinuation was, of course, that a man who let his wife
wander around the country must be short and fat.

"He's tall and thin," I answered, laughing, "and very
handsome."

Ah-gaik interrupted apologeticaly, "He doesn't mean to
tease you."

Ah-gaik hardly ever left the house, but worked constantly at caring for her home and children. She had never
gone into the only establishment in the village where for ten
cents she could sit and have a cup of coffee by herself; it
would have been too open and immodest to do so. Even
when she and the other women danced, they kept their eyes
lowered.

I asked Alec: "Who is your best friend at Point Hope?"
having in mind to find out who his hunting partner was.

Without hesitation he looked at Ah-gaik as she sewed
and said: "My wife is my best friend." Ah-gaik looked up at
him and her eyes shone. Alec looked like a young man; his
skin was smooth and his cheeks were round and unshaven.

Their married daughter lay down to nurse the baby on
a mattress on the floor. She looked exhausted; her lovely
skin was flushed and her eyes had dark stains beneath them.
(Six months later her condition was diagnosed as TB and
she left for the Anchorage Hospital.) When little Silas saw
her nursing, he promptly demanded his rights and grabbed
hold of Ah-gaik's breast to suck as she used the sewing
machine. He stood there, plump and domineering, with his

two feet braced on the floor, his mouth puckered up and pulling at her nipple while Ah-gaik nonchalantly went on with her sewing.

"One of the scientists here want to take Elmer to the States with him when he leave," said Ah-gaik." They want to bring him up with their own son. He can go to a good school."

"Elmer plays chess with their son and he beats him even though he just learned the game," added Rosa.

"Are you going to let him go?" I asked.

"I don't know," Alec said. "He is too young to leave home. We'll wait. We love him."

"How are Rosa and Elmer doing in school here?" I asked.

"Elmer gets good grades. Rosa gets A's," said Ah-gaik, showing me her school papers. For a fourth grader, her work was excellent, her handwriting fine. I detected a superior rather than average intelligence in Ah-gaik's children.

Little Rosa's cheeks constantly glowed with two bright spots of red and her eyes were bright. Her sweet face was lit by a seriousness and depth of expression. Her devotion was touching and I loved her dearly. She insisted upon carrying my pad and when she called on me at the Killigivuks', she stood in the doorway waiting politely until Otoonah bade her welcome.

I painted her portrait in my tiny room, squinting to get a feeling of distance and depicting her in warm reds and greens with loose strokes that showed vibrant colors coming through underneath. Her dark eyes were huge, full of tragic implications. Her cheekbones protruded; there wasn't any fat to spare on her bones. Young and lovely, about the same age as our Yola. I tried to paint the yearning and aspirations etched on her face, without knowing what they expressed but feeling with her that wonder and mystery about the world in which she lived.

A woman ran in front of the dog team carrying her baby inside her parka while her husband stood leisurely on the runners. They were on their way to where the old sod dwellings used to be, the place where the old women dig to dredge up what the anthropologists left behind, such as old arrowheads, scrapers, and other ivory remains.

The Eskimos also used these frozen ice caves as refrigerators and this family had come for some meat. I watched as the man let himself down to the bottom of the cave where chunks of beluga, caribou, and other wild meats were stored.

The woman and I sat down at the top of the cave. "If anyone in village asks for food, we have to give it until there is no more," she said, rocking and bouncing the baby on her back.

"Why?" I asked.

"You know, our native custom is that we feed other people too! We got no food at home, only store food," the woman said, shifting the baby, who peeped out of his hiding place and stared at me unblinkingly. "When we eat white man's food, we still hungry. When we eat white man's food, too soft, we get tired of it. We are still hungry for our own meat."

Her husband climbed up, his arms laden. "Some of the young people don't like to eat Eskimo food," he said. "Change. When I was young, everyone go hunting; now they have money and buy in store, not go out hunting."

"You still hunt, don't you?" I asked.

Laughing, the hunter said, "Sure, I guess I always will."

The wife smiled good-naturedly. "Sometimes the young meet here at night; then the boys sometimes come down for a piece of meat for their girl. Sometimes a man is too lazy to hunt, they come to ask us for meat and we have it so we have to give it away."

The couple got up to leave, packing the hind leg of a caribou and some chunks of seal meat on the sled. The baby was leaning on his mother's shoulder, nodding with her movements as he slept. Following a harsh command from the man, the dogs sped toward the village. The meat would be plunked down in the front shed to keep it frozen and away from the dogs until the wife needed some for dinner; then a piece would be chopped or sawed off and put into a pot of boiling water with rice or macaroni, or sometimes an onion or potato if they were available. Mustard was also enjoyed with meat.

Most families had one large meal a day, served when the hunters came home at night. The women and children had a light breakfast and lunch; and the men had only coffee with bannock left over from yesterday's meal. Often the family had little else with coffee if hunting was poor. They preferred meat in the pot for dinner, but if the hunter came home empty-handed, then biscuits made with flour and water had to suffice.

Some of the families were able to subsist by hunting and by trading sealskins and whalebone masks at the store for goods they needed. Many of the younger and married men worked for wages at Kotzebue, and a few came to Fairbanks in the summer months to earn money as laborers or carpenters. Steady salaries in the village were earned by the school janitor, the postmaster, the store manager and his assistant, and the members of the National Guard unit. Helping to unload the *North Star,* the ship that came once a year, provided most men and boys with extra money, as did other small chores like hauling wood and water.

More and more Eskimos lived on pensions and welfare funds. Such money came to the sick, widowed, old, and those without husbandly support for an illegitimate child.

Meals at the Killigivuks' consisted of a little bit of Eskimo food and a little bit of white man's food; for breakfast we ate mush or sourdough hotcakes and coffee and for dinner whatever native meat was available.

I offered to make the mush one morning and served it to Otoonah, then ate my own bowlful, thinking the water had a strange taste. Otoonah made a horrible grimace and getting up to investigate the pot, pointed to a little plastic bag from which I had taken the salt. I tasted it. Instead of salt it contained soap powder. Evidently it agreed with me for I had no ill effects, but Otoonah had a good laugh on me.

I ruined some other food by accident that week. The children had a habit of coming to Otoonah's for breakfast. No matter when they awoke, they entered quietly and leaned on the door, silently rubbing the sleep out of their eyes. For each one Otoonah usually put a piece of paper on the floor by the door, then placed a bowl of canned milk and water and a thick slice of homemade bread upon it.

Anahkaloktuk's oldest son came in one day while Otoonah was out. There was a bowl of sourdough batter on the top of the stove and thinking it was ready to use, I made pancakes with a bit of lard in the frying pan. They wouldn't brown and looked rubbery, even though the stove was hot, but the boy ate them uncomplaining. Later I realized why they wouldn't brown: I had used the starter batter which contained the yeast, flour, and water mixture only, without the salt and baking soda for leavening!

In the evening Asatsiak and I played pinochle. Otoonah was out visiting her cronies and Eugene looked on from his bed. After Asatsiak won and we had had coffee with Eugene, Asatsiak translated a hunting song he had composed called "The Polar Bear Song:

> "When I throw the sling
> For the white bear
> It's like cash money
> It's like flying like a duck;
>
> "How can I get cash money
> Unless I hunt?
> Trapping fox, trapping lynx,
> And shooting polar bear?
>
> "If I get a skin, I get few dollars;
> If I get nothing, no cash money,
> Cash money go fly by like sling.
> If I trade red fox, lynx,
> And polar bear, then I get cash money!"

Asatsiak and I worked together to get the translation just right. I especially liked the line, "Cash money go fly by like sling." No longer could Asatsiak or the others live by hunting alone; cash was needed to buy store food and guns. Yet Asatsiak would not take any money for my stay at his house; he considered me his guest.

Before getting into bed I hung my new mukluks up on a nail and rubbed my instep; my arches ached from walking around on flat uneven ground without the support of shoes.

The ceremony of the whaling boats, or umiaks, marked the beginning of the nalukatuk. Early in the morning after breakfast, Asatsiak led me about half a mile from his house to the north beach. The ceremony was for men only, but Asatsiak said it would be all right for me to see it.

In the spring of this year four great bowhead whales had been killed at Point Hope. The larders in the underground caches were full of whalemeat. By June the whales had passed Point Hope and pools of water had appeared on the ice. The pack ice had begun to break up and ponds had opened close to shore.

The umeliks decided it was time to put the boats away and begin the spring whaling-feast. Only the umeliks and crews who had struck whales lifted their umiaks on their shoulders and carried them to their traditional places on the beach. The umeliks who had not made first strikes at the whales left their boats on ice piles at the shore.

Each of the four umeliks who had struck a whale that year placed his skin boat on a pile of whalebones. One of the umelik's pronounced a prayer over the teakettle, assorted tools, and equipment used in the hunt. With dignity and silence the umeliks put all the paddles upright in the umiak, then placed an American flag in the bow. Then the four umeliks, or whaling captains, stood alone in front of their umiaks.

Afterwards all the men sat down near a pile of whale

bones and then, as if on signal, the women appeared in bright calicos. I had not seen them before, but now they came walking proudly, bearing large pots and carved wooden bowls full of special whale meat.

Micheaq, the whale delicacy, had been cut in strips and soured near the heat of the stove. The women served it wearing strips of spotless white cloth around their hands in lieu of gloves. They dipped their hands into the pots, lifted out the *micheaq*, dripping with red-black juices, and handed it to hunters.

Evidently this was one of the highlights of the whale feast and the men really relished the sour meat, tilting back their dark heads to drip the meat into their open mouths, savoring it with their eyes closed. Asatsiak handed me a piece on his knife and I tasted it. It had a pickled sweet-sour taste. The women came around with seconds, putting their hands into the bowls and dripping the black slippery meat to the hunters again. I asked, "Why is it not put on a plate like the other meats?"

"It is an honor to the hunter to drip it to him," said one woman. I had another piece, even though it was rich for my palate.

Asatsiak and I sat in the sun on the tundra chewing micheaq. "When I was a young man, I walked thirty miles to hunt polar bear," he told me. "No food. No breakfast. No dogs. Just spear and warm furs."

"What kind of clothing did you wear?" I asked.

"Young fawn, caribou undershirt, fur pants, warm mukluks," he replied. "Then I walk back late at night drag polar bear skin all way. Nowadays," Asatsiak scoffed, "hunter takes dog team and white hunter takes plane to hunt polar bear."

A bright, clear, flawlessly blue sky met my eyes, sunny and with an immensity of reach. I was aware of the earth and sky meeting in all directions.

Close to the ground pink clusters of flowers were up a

few inches even before the wild grasses had turned green. They clung stubbornly to the face of the earth in spite of strong winds, the roots intermeshed and as tenacious as the people who inhabited Point Hope.

Lots of husky pups rolled and played near by, their short bodies enjoying the brief playtime before a lifetime of hard labor. The dogs were hungry at this time of year and several had died. I witnessed a pup, who had been bitten and wounded by the others, crying and yelping helplessly. The next day he was gone and the children told me the other huskies had eaten him. There wasn't a trace of him left.

A plane landed, bringing Okukchuk and others to the whale feast, which would go on for several days. Okukchuk, wearing a new blue velveteen parka with a dramatic white fox hood, was as surprised to see me there as I was to see her get off the plane. I asked for news of the other families and of her husband. She was staying with the Webers, who were her cousins, so I walked her to her destination.

When I got home that night, Asatsiak, Otoonah, and Eugene were sound asleep, Otoonah on one cot, Eugene on the other, and Asatsiak on the floor in front of my door. I climbed as best I could over his bedroll and went to bed, thinking that I must find a place to sleep so that he wouldn't have to give up his bed for me.

It was Otoonah who slept on the floor, I found out the next morning—not Asatsiak! When I called Eugene to task, he replied: "She likes it and she is comfortable."

I said: "You're kidding!" his favorite expression.

He said with a serious face, "You're kidding me."

When I thought it over, I realized that Otoonah had probably, like most Eskimo children, spent the greater part of her life sleeping on a caribou mat on the floor.

She and Asatsiak sat on the floor for nearly every task. Only Eugene and I sat on chairs. Otoonah made bread, baked doughnuts, sewed, and performed other tasks sitting on the floor, so I put my watercolors down and got down to her level and the difference was astounding. I painted so much more freely—perhaps the Oriental painters were right. We think chairs are a necessity, yet to the Eskimos they are not basic.

I bumped into Kinnerveak, the whaling captain, at the native store and he said a friendly "hello." He was a big brawny man, earning good wages as a carpenter in the summer at Kotzebue. By Point Hope standards he was a well-to-do umelik.

He invited me to visit his home so I followed him to a large house near by and entered the warm kitchen. The big table was heaped with food and utensils and opposite was the largest oil stove I had ever seen. In addition to the table, the outer room had a couch, captain's chairs, and a general air of comfort.

Kinnerveak's wife was cooking all manner of feast food with the help of visitors from Noatak and Kotzebue. She dashed from table to stove, stirring, cooking, tasting. She welcomed me with a tinkling laugh, "Come in, Clara, come in."

Okukchuk was grinding dried meat, and another woman was cutting a wolverine hide for a parka ruff. Kinnerveak played a tape recording from Noatak which ended with "God bless you all" in English. His sister-in-law, her face rosy from the heat, sat on the floor beating tallow in a large basin with her hand to make *akootuk,* or Eskimo ice cream. I watched the swirling motion of her hand as it swung around and around and the caribou tallow became frothy. A woman came in with a bag of frozen blueberries which she tossed into the bowl along with a handful of sugar. The mixture turned pink, then purple; it looked like whipped cream. The woman switched hands just as I ached empathically for an electric mixer.

In another corner the grandmother mixed a batch of tallow which would contain meat instead of berries. I asked Kinnerveak if I could do my work, hoping to paint the girl mixing tallow with her strong hands, but he looked unhappy at my suggestion so I helped Okukchuk cut up caribou meat instead. She ground it fine and then put it in the grand-mother's bowl, which gave caribou meat flecks to the white tallow. The women added chunks of whale meat to huge pots of boiling water while batch after batch of hot sour-dough biscuits baked in the oven. The good cooking aroma and the camaraderie of the women, along with the Eskimo religious songs now playing on the recorder, were reminis-cent of Thanksgiving; instead of pumpkin pie we were mak-ing whale delicacies and caribou-tallow ice cream. The spirit reminded me of a painting by Grandma Moses of New Englanders gathered around a big coal stove. This was thanksgiving, nalukatuk Eskimo-style, for bountiful whale received.

Back home Asatsiak was fixing his drum in preparation for the dance. Nalukatuk literally means "dancing in the air." He stretched a new whale liver membrane across the top for a drumhead, giving me the old worn-out walrus intestine drumhead. The frame of his drum had an ivory handle carved with an intricate face and had belonged to his father, who had also owned the large stone lamp that was kept under the table. The lamp, which was more than three feet long, must have given off plenty of light when the whale oil was burning.

I sketched Asatsiak as he worked on his drum and Ikkaheena, who had come to visit, as she nursed her baby, her lovely neck poised over the little one's dark head. Later Asatsiak and I played pinochle; he was two hundred points head of me. Even though we were not playing for money, we acted as through we were playing for high stakes.

CHAPTER 15   *Whale Flukes*

And I thrust the harpoon into its side,
and the hunting float bounded over the water.
But it kept coming up again
. . . trying to tear the hunting float to pieces.
In vain it spent its utmost strength, . . .
. . . and when it drew back, blowing viciously,
to gather strength again,
I rowed up and stabbed it
With my lance.

OTOONAH MADE NO BREAKFAST
nor did any of the other women; they knew the day would
later be given over to feasting. Families began to walk out

from their homes to the tundra where the celebration would begin. Otoonah carried her mother's old wooden bowl and plates and spoons.

The women wore colorful new parka coverings, bright kerchiefs, and new mukluks. Most of the mukluks had row upon row of rickrack trim in the geometric pattern distinctive of that region, which favored the colors red, white, and black.

Ah-gaik had made matching denim tops for all her girls' mukluks and their faces were shiny and clean and their hair combed neatly. Instead of mukluks Otoonah wore a brand-new pair of black and white sneakers bought after much deliberation from Sears Roebuck. For her they had a special prestige, a unique, even exotic flavor, since they were not homemade but had cost hard-earned money.

I wore Quavuk's oversize muskrat parka, which certainly gave me an exotic flavor, and on my big feet I proudly wore David Frankson's white calf mukluks, which gave me the doubtful distinction of being the only woman in man's mukluks.

The village lay in fog; grayed skies made visibility difficult. Small planes were arriving for the feast and although they had a hard time landing, the Reverend Thomas and his wife Callie arrived safely in his Cessna, bringing two other Kotzebue Eskimos.

An American flag flew in the center of the feast area, surrounded by high, curved whale jawbones from past whale hunts. About four thousand whale jawbones had been counted in the village.

Canvases held up by wooden paddles were set up in a semi-circle to act as windbreaks. In the center was a skin boat turned on its side; and a sledge covered with caribou skins, the seat of honor for drummers, special guests, or umeliks, was placed in front of it.

According to Froelich G. Rainey, the anthropologist who spent a year at Point Hope, the Tigara people used to be divided into two main groups, the *qongoaktuktuk* and the *irniroaktuktuk*. "One who is of the *qongoaktuktuk* has charms which 'work with things of dead people,' while one who is of the *irniroaktuktuk* has charms that 'work with things of a woman at childbirth,' " Rainey noted. In the past those umeliks who worked with objects of the dead placed their boats so that they touched one another, while those who worked with things of women after childbirth placed theirs so that they did not touch.

Moreover the property of the dead was *kiruq*, or taboo, to anyone of the other group. Rainey wrote in *The Whale Hunters of Tigara*, "One whose charms are derived from the property of the dead would be unsuccessful on a whale hunt if a menstruating woman had sewed his whale boat skins." The taboo system was dangerous if one did the wrong thing.

Until as late as 1940 "the bodies of the dead were deposited on scaffolds along the slough. . . . As the bodies disintegrated, decomposed remains washed into the water . . . and thus, naturally, it became violently *kiruq* to persons of the *irniroaktuktuk*. . . ." To drink the water was fatal, but to the group whose dead had been laid there ". . . it was like a healing spring . . . and rendered them impervious to danger. . . . What was one man's drink was literally another man's poison. As Rainey tells it, the people who worked with things of the dead "went so far as to drink this *kiruq* [or taboo] water from human skulls."

Many people in the olden days used charms to assist them in hunting and to rescue them from danger. Rainey discovered an old man called Qoqoq in 1940 who wore a dried ermine, rabbit tail, wolverine tail, a sea gull, an ermine skin, wing feathers from a sea bird, a blue bead, and a fragment of coarse grass. Qoqoq was *qongoaktuktuk*, one whose *angoaks*, or charms "work with things of the dead."

Today there are two qalegi groups still active, the *Qaqmaktok* and the *Ungasiksikaq*. Existing mostly for social and competitive purposes, these groups sat on two separate sides of the beach for the nalukatuk, one facing east and one west. Asatsiak's group had killed one whale that year and the other group three whales. Mark Kinnerveak, Nicholas Hank, Daniel Lisbourne, and Larry Kingik were the honored umeliks this year. All men were over forty, sturdy, and bronzed. They were honored as the leading hunters for killing the whales which provided 70 per cent of the food for the village.

The women had brought cooking stoves from home and set them up in front of the canvas windbreaks. Four camp stoves burning whale oil were going, as well as a few small gasoline Coleman stoves. What a cookout! Otoonah was boiling whale meat in a big pot. Ikkaheena was browning doughnuts and I offered to help her mix the dough, which she rolled around in her hands and popped into the hot whale oil. Some of the other women were making artfull twists and oval shapes out of dough and one girl decorated her batch with thumbnail marks.

The men had cut frozen whale flukes, or tail sections, into thick slices that looked like huge steaks, their black rims startling against the white centers. Mrs. Kingik, the umelik's wife, stood in front of the whole village in her best furs and called out each member of her husband's crew, then the names of their relatives, to come up and get their muktuk. I heard Asatsiak's name, then Eugene's.

Bursts of hilarious laughter greeted some of the men as they walked up to Mrs. Kingik, who jokingly berated them in Eskimo for attempting to kiss a woman during the whale hunt. Then she called all strangers and visitors to come up to receive meat. Asatsiak poked me, so I went up with the Kotzebue and Noatak Eskimos and Reverend Thomas.

Next the Kinnerveaks took their places to distribute the whale flukes. Mrs. Kinnerveak in her new muskrat parka held the center of every eye while she handed out the meat. This time I distinctly heard the name "Clara" among the Eskimo names she called. I looked around to see if there was

Three Women at Whale Feast

an Eskimo named Clara, but when Otoonah pushed me to get up, I knew she meant me and proudly took my share. She called the minister, the schoolteachers, the scientists, and all visitors. Last one called was the white man in the village who had been building an umiak to use for the next year's whale hunting.

I could see why Otoonah needed her large bowl to take all the meat home. My share of the muktuk was heavy. The Killigivuks insisted that I keep it all instead of adding it to their larder, and I planned to share it with Quavuk and my Fairbanks Eskimo friends.

Blueberry and caribou akootuk was passed to everyone. Since it was mostly pure tallow it was very rich, so I had only a small portion of each flavor.

The walrus nalukatuk skin was set up for the "dancing in the air." The large hide had throng handgrips along the edge. About fifty people held the grips to keep the walrus hide at waist-high level as Mrs. Kingik, the umelik's wife, prepared to jump.

For a woman of forty-five she showed surprising agility as she was tossed into the air and then landed on her feet on the walrus skin. The crowd, shouting in unison, tossed her up again and again. Once while aloft she took some things from her pockets and threw them into the air. The old women scrambled onto the tundra and Otoonah came back, grinning her toothless smile, and showed me her hand, which contained seven pieces of bubble gum. In the past the umelik himself had distributed gifts of baleen, boot soles, or skins.

Dinah Frankson, full of grace and always in the middle of the fun, was next up on the blanket. The year before, she had been the champion baseball player and she proved her athletic prowess again, jumping higher and higher and landing each time on her feet without a tumble. She got off the hide modestly too. It looked tempting but I declined an invitation to try it; it seemed a good way to break a leg.

Billy Weber went up next, spinning around in the air and shrieking a deep-throated male shout of joy. The sound was electrifying but impossible to transcribe. The young girls squealed and the other hunters answered his call exuberantly. With perfect balance, like an arrow, Billy rose to greater heights each time he jumped, revolving around in the air as he came down. Reverend Thomas tried next and sprained his ankle badly.

Many people think that the purpose of the blanket toss is for hunters to spot game a long distance away, but it is mostly for fun.

The little children held the hide next and took turns jumping on it, imitating their elders while everyone enjoyed their antics.

Fog was settling heavily over the village and it had begun to drizzle. It was cold sitting on the tundra even on a muskrat parka, so I shifted to a caribou hide. The crowd was completely relaxed; some of the men were playing cards in the shelter of the skin boat, drinking coffee and eating whatever their wives brought them. They and everyone else ate all day long—a choice bit of whale meat, a doughnut, biscuits, red Jello, coffee, and of course akootuk.

Many women reclined, most with a baby inside their parkas. Sometimes the baby was pulled around to nurse and then it was covered by the parka, leaving only a bulge to denote its presence. Some of the women were cooking, while others rocked their babies on their backs like mechanical rocking chairs. A youngster came to be fed a tidbit or to have his nose wiped. There didn't seem to be any coquetry among the girls; most of them were helping with the food and if one slipped away for a walk with her sweetheart, she was hardly noticed.

One attractive woman had changed from her traditional fur parka to modern clothes, consisting of slacks and a short red jacket over her blouse. When her baby cried, she automatically put him on her back and began to rock him as she sat on the tundra. The short jacket was inadequate and she had to support the baby's buttocks with her hand, leaving his naked feet exposed.

The drummers began slowly to beat out a rhythm while

several men danced on the walrus hide which had been laid on the ground and converted to a dance floor. The dancers faced the drummers who sat in front of the umiaks. The drizzling cold rain dulled the enthusiasm of the crowd and when no one volunteered to dance, the drummers finally stopped beating and put away their instruments. Families began to straggle homeward and the Killigivuks and I followed them.

Eugene was moody and restless that evening, resenting our pinochle game. With several ribs gone as the result of various operations, he had little stamina and the cold had probably tired him. He rarely left his cot these days, only occasionally going into town to get the mail.

He woke us in the middle of the night with the groans and writhings of a seizure. Finally he quieted down; perhaps the games and rich foods of the feast had upset him. He stayed in bed the next day.

On the second day of the feast, two separate camps were set up on one side of the beach. Camp stoves were smoking and the cooking was beginning. Otoonah made a campfire with whale bone sockets, using them as rocks to enclose a fire, and instead of wood for fuel she used whale blubber which burned long and brightly. She filled a five-gallon can with water, threw in chunks of whale meat, and set the can in the fire to boil. Some other women were plucking the feathers from ducks. They cut up the birds and threw them, heads, feet, and all, into a large pot on one of the stoves.

With her ulu, Nathlook sliced unpeeled potatoes and three onions into boiling water, then added a handful of rice and large pieces of frozen caribou. The concoction turned out to be the best caribou soup I ever ate; unskimmed with floating caribou hairs—no matter, it was good.

The women cut the cooked whale meat into dainty chunks with their ulus, eating neatly with their fingers so as not to soil their clothing. Okukchuk taught me how to cut raw muktuk into slivers with her ulu so that the base remained whole but the top was easy to bite.

"Remember when you eat beluga heart soup at Sheshalik, Clara?" Okukchuk said, offering me pieces of whale heart and tongue. "We miss most at Noatak the whale's tongue."

"Delicious!" I answered as I ate piece after piece.

Otoonah and Sunshine called me over to show how the whale's heart had been prepared. The tongue, stomach, and other choice delicacies had been placed into the cut-open heart of the huge whale and left to freeze until today, when it had been cut into sections and boiled. The tongue tasted like beef tongue, only sweeter and more tender.

My sketch pad remained idle in my pocket. It was good to sit behind the stove and watch the children eating well; sometimes they went hungry when food was not so plentiful.

The great whale symbolized all that was good to the people. The skull of the whale had been returned to the sea, "to give the crabs a share"; some said it contained the whale's *inyua,* or soul. The baleen and ribs were to be used for tools, the jawbones as grave monuments or for storage racks, the skin of the liver and lungs for drumheads, the vertebrae for carving masks; the rest of the viscera was eaten by the dogs. Every part had its use for the entire village.

The umelik began to cut the ugruk hide from his umiak as was the custom, offering it to the woman to make soles for mukluks. The women of Tigara stepped aside politely to let the visiting Noatak and Kotzebue women have the skin. The umiak was strong, in good condition, but since it was thought the whale liked new umiak skins a new one was made for the whale hunt in the spring. Okukchuk and the other women took home the ugruk skin and plenty of whale meat which they stored in the seal pokes they had brought with them for the occasion.

CHAPTER 16   *Nalukatuk Dance*

Now is abundance
With us once more,
Days of feasting
To hold us together
aja'—ja'—japape!

THE NALUKATUK DANCE was scheduled
for nine that night but did not begin until ten thirty. The
parish hall filled up slowly; first came the children, heavily

clad in warm parkas, who ran excitedly in and out without supervision; then the elders walked in, a few at a time, in their best clothes. No one was left home; even the tiniest baby was carried on the back of his sister or mother. Families huddled together in groups, the eldest on benches, the children on the floor at their feet. I sat down on a bench among the older folks while a group of women singers took their places on the floor at the back of the hall with a child or two snuggled up among them. Then the drummers took their places in front of the women singers, Asatsiak first, since he was the leader, then the other elders; leisurely they sprinkled water from a can onto their skin drums to wet and tune them. (The water loosens the drumheads and lowers the tone.)

Asatsiak, waiting until the children settled down and everyone was seated, sounded the first drum beat, his head to one side, and shouted, "Aja, aja, aja, ja ja ja aaa." He beat several times slowly, then faster, increasing the tempo; then the four drummers joined him, beating firmly and swiftly and singing in a minor key. Behind them the women's voices rose in pitch, their bodies jerking to the pulse of the drum.

Old Tingook began the dance. As he slowly moved his caribou-mukluk'd feet, he drew on white canvas gloves. It was the custom to cover the hands when dancing but no one knew why.

Tingook lifted his head, tossing back his gray hair and immediately focusing everyone's attention on his rapt face. Eyes closed, he seemed to be in a trance, lost in his own thoughts. Slowly bending his strong legs, he stamped on the wooden floor, making movements with his outstretched arms, his feet, hands, and head turning, bending downward then upward, every part of his body working in harmony and unison. The audience bent closer to watch each motion; Tingook's timing was dramatic. Oblivious to all but his own inner rhythms and feelings, he portrayed the spirit of his ancestors.

Every motion of his bent body was vigorous and expressed courage and joy in life. He began to dance faster and faster to the music's beat, stamping and bending low, the muscles of his back and legs pulled tightly, then bending backward with his elbows bent. No surplus flesh showed, for even at eighty he was agile. This was his own dance, drawn from his hunting experiences in which he depicted a hunter and a seal, then waved his arms to pantomine the hunter's motions and the gun and the sliding motions of the seal. Asatsiak, his friend, had composed the song for him.

> A medicine man was hunting north,
> When the days grew long in spring;
> As he walked along he heard a voice sing
> Behind a big ice ridge.
> It sounded like a man singing a song
> And here is the song that he sung:
> > "I am sitting here
> > Enjoying the sun
> > Where it is warm
> > On the lee of the ridge."
> When the song was done
> The medicine man went around the ridge of ice
> And there, there was no man at all;
> A seal slipped down quickly into the sea.

Tingook's skill as a dancer was known up and down the Arctic coast. His face was beautiful that night, and his joy was reflected on all our faces; his rapture was infectious, lifting our spirits. His dance expressed the freedom, the ecstasy of the hunt, the strength, aliveness, and alertness an Eskimo must have to every aspect of life. As the height of pure dance and artless emotional response, it was an eloquent performance, a dance I shall never forget. Tingook's dance was inseparable from the life of his people; they were woven into one fabric: the hunter a dancer, the dance his experience, and the music and song composed for him alone yet universally understood.

Two younger men, Billy Weber and Howard Stone,

friends and hunting partners, performed next. Drawing on gloves, they began to mimic a walrus and polar-bear hunt. Facing each other with hands on hips, the two men bent their knees and moved their heads and torsos from side to side, stretching their necks, then drawing back their heads. Weaving close, then apart, they leaped and stamped, ever wilder, until the dance reached its climax, the drums throbbing. The men then faced all directions with bent knees, stamping in rhythm, never losing a beat, sometimes bending one knee to the floor, sometimes slashing the air with an arm, looking up and down and sideways, juxtaposing their movements together and apart in a magnificent design. Then they stopped abruptly.

The old women danced in a dignified manner, with proud faces, their eyes cast down modestly. Their heads turned in an oriental movement, their arms swung rhythmically in arcs, and their mukluk'd feet made little movements, as their knees bent and their bodies rocked from side to side and from back to front, their torsos twisting and their heads moving in opposite directions. The fur tails on their parkas swung in time, accentuating the primitive beat. The old women's faces assumed a mobile cast, making them look mysteriously young and agile. The womens' chorus continued its everlasting refrain, "Aja, ja, aja, ja ja!"

The beat of the common dance began and some twenty men and women crowded the floor space, each one joining when he pleased. There was no set pattern, and anyone who felt like it could dance. No couples danced together; arms and legs moved in all directions, each dancer independent of the others. Since teen-agers and young children alike were dancing along with the older people, I got up to dance too, thinking I could be lost in the crowd during this free-for-all.

I tried it for one dance and then sat down. It was too confusing. I watched the minister dance and realized how inbred the dance is for an Eskimo. When the minister danced, he danced the outward forms only; since he had no long association with hunting and Eskimo life, the inner meaning was lost. The people enjoyed watching him dance, and by his participation he showed his own approval.

Asatsiak closed his eyes and leaned his head back in ecstasy, beating his drum and singing loudly, perhaps envisioning his youthful days. The women's high shrill accompaniment contrasted with the men's somber tones. The music, words, and dance movements were a single unity, depicting the Eskimo at his most exalted and giving insight into his deepest thoughts.

The chorus of women now sang about the raven while a male dancer imitated the bird marvelously.

Otoonah got up to dance, looking like a young girl in her pink calico, her hair falling on her wrinkled cheeks. She swung gracefully, sedately, her body moving only above the hips and her arms and hands waving in stylized gestures. When she turned her back to me, she looked like a sixteen-year-old. Her face had an expression of restrained mischievousness; she must have been a wild youngster, full of fun.

The younger married men then took the places of the older drummers—Asatsiak gave his place to Billy Weber—assuring that old dance customs and songs would be carried on to the newer generation. The elder drummers clapped their encouragement as the young men drummed and sang.

They sang well but they made some mistakes in drumming and everyone laughed sympathetically. The younger men danced with great shows of strength and muscular sequences. Their pullings and stampings pleased everyone, especially the old women, who chuckled appreciatively and applauded loudly. Asatsiak had translated an Eskimo woman's love song and I remembered it as I watched the women dance.

> Here I am sitting
> And I am sitting still
> And I see two kayaks coming;

Here I am sitting
I am sitting still
And two men are coming
To court me
And here I am a ne'er-do-well
And not very good-looking.

Several boys under five danced, stamping their feet in manly imitation and drawing loud applause.

Halfway through the evening a washtub filled with frozen chunks of whale muktuk was brought in and passed around. The meat tasted sweet and cool in the hot room. The minister passed around treats of candy and filberts.

Mothers began to nurse their young and the children ran noisily around as the hour grew late. The dance went on, growing wilder and wilder to the insistent rhythms of the drums. The women egged me on to dance again but I shook my head.

Everyone was tired and it was almost four in the morning when the Killigivuks and I walked home in the bright daylight.

On the last day of the nalukatuk the drizzle of cold rain stopped, but the sky was overcast and a gray fog hung over the flat village. From the window of Killigivuk's house we could see tiny figures on the tundra and hear the sound of drums. We left the house to join the crowd and although it was June, we were all warmly dressed and wore woolen mittens.

We could see that the blanket toss had begun again, for a small figure was in the air. The people tossed the figure up again and then looked down as the figure, gone awry, fell not on the walrus hide as intended but onto the hard tundra. The shock of it struck us as we hurried toward the scene and saw the crowd gathered in a circle to enclose the body of a young girl.

It was Nina Frankson, Ah-gaik's niece, who lay there.

The force of falling about twenty-five feet had knocked her unconscious; she moaned and someone covered her with a caribou hide. A conference was held as to the best way to move her, since it was thought she might have broken her back or pelvis. Finally the men cut the ugruk hide from a skin boat, slit holes for handles along the edge, and carried her home on the makeshift stretcher.

Her father, Andrew, hovered near, touching her hair and murmuring, "Nina, our daughter."

Alice Weber, the nurse, who administered penicillin and aspirin, spoke over the radio band to the Kotzebue doctor, "Doctor, a girl has fallen twenty feet and is in shock, unconscious. What shall I do?"

It was decided that a plane would have to be chartered to come from Kotzebue to Point Hope to take Nina to the Kotzebue Native Hospital.

When I entered the Frankson house to see how Nina was, she was lying on her ugruk skin stretcher on the floor, covered with furs. She was still unconscious and her usually cheerful face was white and drained; she had bitten her tongue when she fell and it protruded swollenly. Her mother, her face red and tear stained, held Nina's hand as if to give her strength. Nearby other women watched and her old grandfather sat on the bed, his gray head bent in prayer with a child's simplicity.

The roar of a motor eventually signaled the arrival of the plane from Kotzebue. The men gently lifted Nina and carried her out to it. Other villagers joined us in the quiet procession until it assumed the proportions of a funeral march. She was put carefully in the back of the Beechcraft behind the pilot with her mother beside her.

All sorts of coins and bills were being passed into the mother's hand without her seeing the donors, and I also gave. The plane took off with everyone watching. Nina's father smiled and tried to laugh when I told him I hoped Nina would be all right. No matter how serious the outcome, he would accept it. "Well, it can't be helped. That's it."

CHAPTER 17 *Aftermath*

. . . Great grief overcame me
My sun quickly rose over it.
Great grief came over me.
The sea that was out there off our settlement
Was beautifully quiet—
And the great, dear paddlers
Were leaving out there—
Great grief came over me. . . .
        Rendered from the Eskimo
        by WILLIAM THALBITZER

SEVERAL CHILDREN and adults
became sick as the aftermath of too much whale meat,
akootuk, micheaq, and maporuks. In the Tuckfield tent
Ikkaheena was lying on her cot feeling miserable, Sunshine
was sorting out a box of tools from the diggings, and her
husband sat bent and quiet on the bed, not feeling very well

either. The baby was asleep, swinging from a hammock, a convenient place when floor space was at a premium.

When I told Sunshine that the parka I was wearing was Quavuk's, it turned out that she had cared for her when she was a baby. Overcome with emotion, she picked up the hem and kissed the fur that Quavuk had sewn. Since I was leaving soon she gave me a package of muktuk to give to her with love.

The church bells rang clearly in the cloudy morning. A mist hung low over the tundra, while far off gleamed the white whalebones in the ancient graveyard. Ice chunks remaining on land in isolated places were used for water and a boy with a pail scooped up some of the top snow ice and ran back into his house with it.

The church was filled with people. The deep red walls and the old polished wooden benches were a colorful relief from the drabness out of doors. Gold glittered from the crosses on the altar and one faded painting hung slightly off center; the new oil stove gave off a regular warmth. The church was luxurious, if not elegant, compared to the bare homes surrounding it.

I sat near the Noatak women with Otoonah on the other side. Eskimos sat simply on the wooden benches, their postures and attitudes depicting much of their lives. Even the old women moved with agility and dignity and the old men's worn hands were bent in prayer. One hunter sat cradling his head on his arms on the bench in front of him and I recognized Nina's father. We all prayed for Nina's recovery; she was uppermost in our thoughts.

The minister was very young and blond and had neither the simplicity nor the power to establish a strong hold on the people. Yet he sufficed, going through the rituals with Donald Oktolik translating the words into Eskimo, which really lessened their effectiveness because it gave the Eskimo, who towered over the minister, the more moving role. The Episcopal church always hired a translator for the sake of the old people who couldn't understand English.

The regular ritual of the church went on while babies were passed from one woman to another to keep them quiet. One could never tell who the mother might be, or the sister, or cousins, since everyone was related to everyone else, with a lineage so involved that it was better not to ask questions.

When it was time for the blessing and the taking of the sacrament, the people walked up to the altar and returned with lovely transformed faces.

After church I walked to one end of the new airfield where a large wooden building was used as a lodge. This was new since my visit the previous year and the propietors were a Fairbanks couple, Allen and Frances Rock, who had come back to their village of birth. They had spent many years at Fairbanks and with their savings had bought a house at Point Hope, converting it to a lodge for the white polar bear hunters to sleep and eat in. They had flown in beds, sheets and towels, and kitchen equipment; the freight from Fairbanks for this alone was eight hundred dollars, according to Mr. Rock.

The menu was posted: Eskimo Bar ice cream was thirty cents, coffee fifteen cents, and a hamburger one dollar twenty-five cents. The children could have Kool-Aid at five cents a cup. The kitchen had a counter bar and a few tables at which the men could play pinochle. The older Eskimo men were regular customers; they sat beneath a sign proclaiming "Point Hope Lodge" with a whale darting gun hung beneath it.

The plane brought eggs from Kotzebue at one dollar and eighty cents a dozen plus airfreight. Substituting for Mrs. Rock the day I visited was a neighbor who made me scrambled eggs. She probably had not made them before, for she put an ordinary saucepan on the stove and broke the eggs into it without grease. The women are used to boiling food instead of frying it, but the eggs turned out fine and I ate them with some of Mrs. Rock's homemade bread.

Ah-gaik joined me at the lodge for ice cream and coffee;

it was the first time she had eaten there and she behaved as
if it was a bold thing to do. I guessed that the polar-bear
hunters who lodged there drank and that the men did not
like their wives going there.

My plane was late in coming the next morning and Asatsiak
helped me carry my bags to the lodge where we had coffee.
He was loath to have me go and it warmed me; I had a
feeling I would be back. Ah-gaik came to see me off, her
children fluttering around her. Anahkaloktuk and little Elizabeth came and Elizabeth smiled at me for the first time. By
the time the plane finally swooped down, I had shaken
hands with practically everyone.

   With me on the plane were Okukchuk going back to
Noatak with her seal poke filled with muktuk. The pilot was
the same one who had flown me over the cliffs two years
before and he brought back unpleasant memories. I felt
uneasy looking down at ice floes and dotted lakes. Someone
shouted, "Walrus!" and we spotted them on the ice. It got
rough in the air and I held Okukchuk's hand tightly. At
Kotzebue, I changed planes for Fairbanks. The family was
waiting for me at the airport and I was happy to see them
and to be home again after a month's absence. The garden
at home with its bordering rock path had a wild profusion
that I liked, iris, daisies, forget-me-nots, buttercups, and
weeds! The lilacs were in bloom, unbelievable after the
Arctic. Taking off my Eskimo clothing I changed back into a
housewife once again, causing hardly a ripple; except for a
few friends and the family, of course, no one even knew I
had been gone. Some women went South for their vacations;
I had gone North!

   The Eskimo way of life had become so familiar that it
seemed normal to use whale blubber for fuel. I longed to
possess the inner knowledge I had seen in the old Eskimo
faces. The old people intrigued me but language was a bar-
rier in getting to know them. Their eyes spoke much but
that wasn't enough. Ah-gaik told me that her tongue seemed

tied when she spoke English, but behind her eyes lay a tested philosophy of life in a lonely land.

Several images remained with me strongly: Ah-gaik sewing with a hand on her wheel and her son nursing; Sunshine, the matriarch, presiding in her tent over the stove; Asatsiak with his bent legs walking alone on the tundra with his gun; Otoonah looking at me, her face perspiring, wondering about me; Nathlook making caribou soup; Nina lying on the floor surrounded by women, the scene transformed by their prayers.

I painted the Tigara people clustered at the nalukatuk and each brush stroke was a memory.

While I was gone, Joe had ripped out my old kitchen cupboards and replaced them with new ones of birch wood. A new dishwasher, wall oven, and sink had been installed— all the newfangled contraptions any woman would be proud to own. The kitchen cupboards had been so old they wouldn't close, yet I felt guilty having all these luxuries— especially running water. Whenever I used the running water I remembered how the Eskimo women had to dole out each precious drop.

Black Whale

CHAPTER 18 *Storm*

Joy bewitches
All about us,
Skin boats rise up
Out of their moorings,
Fastenings go with them,
Earth itself hovers
Loose in the air.

I RETURNED TO POINT HOPE the following April. I wanted desperately to see the whales and I had begun to think I would never make it, for I had struggled for two months with a terrible virus that left me so weak I could hardly lift a coffeepot—a calamity for me. I had been sick and dormant in the gray winter, watching the snow fall, unable to think or feel or even imagine vitality. I watched hundreds of birds chattering and feeding near my window.

The whale run started in April and ended in May, depending on weather and ice conditions. I had planned to meet Cyrus Norton in Kivalina and make the trip by dog team to Point Hope. I had hoped to see the country under deep snow cover, to reach and experience that "heart of silence," the real isolation. I had dreamed about the bird cliffs and the ice trail along the coast all winter, but that was out now for I felt too weak and the whales were coming close to Point Hope. It had become an obsession with me to see the whales; the symbolism of the whale as source of life, food, and fuel fascinated me. I pictured the black whale and the white snow.

When the doctor finally said that I could travel and that there was no danger of contagion, I prepared to leave. I called Tom Richards, Wien Airlines' Eskimo pilot, and he said, "The whales could come at any time now."

An Eskimo made me warm *tutiliks*, knee-length caribou mukluks, and caribou socks, and I borrowed a pair of sealskin pants and fur mittens, preparing for an indeterminate stay, depending on the run of whales.

Asatsiak had sent me a whalebone mask and a small, elegantly carved ivory whale. He wrote:

Dearest Papnikluatak Clara,

It is cold weather. Blizzard from north east wind. I know its the week the crews go out whaling. Yesterday the whales come by. I know you want to know. That only cold weather. Nobody frozen dead. Still life all the peoples here. They was very happy. They like to hunt whale. So happy I'll go too. I had own crews. If you like to come you stay at my house. No spend money, free home. I'll fix up your room. I expect you like a snow owl. Otoonah OK. She said wonderful to see you again to play cards.

Your ahpah,
J. A. Killigivuk

It was certainly a bad beginning. The F–27 returned to Fairbanks after only half an hour in the air due to an oil leak. The next day, after I said goodbye to the family for the second time, the F–27 had to stay over at Nome for four hours due to bad snowstorms and a snowed-in strip at Kotzebue. We had flown almost to Kotzebue before we turned back to Fairbanks because the landing field was completely snowed in and it was impossible to land. Four hours in the air only to be back where we had started, and I hate to fly! The family was surprised to see me home again but I was more determined than ever to go. This time Yola extracted a promise from me that I would be home for Mother's Day since she was having her first piano recital with her class on that day. I agreed, assuming that I would have seen and painted enough whales by then.

The next day, after a third good-bye to everyone, I boarded the F–27 once more with Tom Richards at the controls. When we landed at Nome again, it was snowing and we had to wait for the weather to clear. The Kotzebue airstrip was in the process of being cleared.

The worst storm of the winter had hit Nome; the snow-drifts were above my knees and had all but hidden the houses, making street passage impossible. People were shoveling out their homes and a bulldozer was clearing the streets.

Several hours later we flew to Kotzebue, landing carefully on the small snowy runway. The road along the beach was obliterated but the Wien Airline truck managed to get me to town from the airport by making a wide mark out on the ocean ice while going at full speed to avoid getting stuck. The driver drove the wild bronco of a truck over humps of drifted ice and snow. I held onto the ceiling with both hands so as not to get fatally jounced on the head.

Kotzebue was covered with snow and only the tips of the shacks showed, a pole sticking up to indicate a doorway or steps carved out of ice. Occasionally I could see a bent figure, its face covered by furs and averted from the gale.

Kotzebue, seen in a wintry April, was clean and beautiful; the fish entrails, cans, and beach debris were covered and thick white snow hid the leaning shacks, unifying the village. Now it looked picturesque, a white landscape, broken only by smoke pouring from the chimneys and a pure blue sky.

Reverend Thomas and his family were happy to see me and they fed me in the grand manner as if I had not eaten for a week, the Reverend himself frying thick caribou steaks over the oil range.

We talked and talked in the manner of friends who see each other by chance from time to time, yet act as if the last time were yesterday. Their warm loving faces flushed with pleasure as I drank up the news of Kotzebue and they the news of Fairbanks. They told me about a local white boy who had married a Noatak girl and started a chicken farm in Kotzebue, living in a basement and adding a top story for the chickens. All the Eskimos wondered how long he could keep five hundred chickens in the Arctic without sun, but he rigged up lights and the chickens survived. The old timers complained that the eggs tasted "funny"—they were used to the taste of months-old storage eggs shipped in from the outside. (Alaskans still refer to the rest of the U.S. as the outside!) Still others grumbled that the eggs tasted fishy! Here was the first agricultural venture in Kotzebue since Gene Joiner planted grass and raised lettuce in his front yard and the critics were already complaining.

Archie Ferguson was putting up a huge building near the beach, to be a combination post office, bank, grocery, restaurant, with poolrooms and movies in the back. He had recently married a young Mexican woman, his second wife, who was not more than half his age. He offered me a cup of coffee without charge as he energetically began to wipe the counter, then ran into the poolroom to fix the pinball machine.

Archie's first marriage had been to an Eskimo woman. He and his brother were aviation pioneers in northern

Alaska. They built a sawmill and a trading post, opened up a mink farm, and brought the first automobile, the first cow, the first motorcycle, and the first movie house to Alaska. A wealth of stories had grown up about him, mostly concerning his patched planes and his crackups.

The classic story about Archie was told by Jean Potter in *The Flying North*. He was reported as yelling one day to the Nome station, "Ya hear that noise? Christ, that ain't static; that's a bear!

Yeah, I gotta bear in the plane with me, jest a cub, I brought him to train as a pet, but he's broke loose. He's climbin' right up here beside me, growlin' 'n' showin' his teeth—big sharp teeth! Oh Geezus, he's tryin' ta eat up the fuselage! There's two of us up here now, but it looks like purty soon there's only gonna be one 'n' it ain't gonna be me! Stand by, I'll call ya every other minute!"

Narrow escapes were so routine with Archie that no one was surprised when he landed safely. Alaska laughed about this flight for weeks and rumor spread that the bear had been at the controls when the plane came down. "The best landing," someone wisecracked, "Archie ever made."

One year John Cross, a veteran pilot, had cracked up near the Kobuk Lake and called Kotzebue for help. He had a stretcher patient he had picked up on an emergency call from the village. Archie in Kotzebue heard his call for help and ran out in a hurry. The first plane he saw on the beach was a new one belonging to someone else. He hurriedly talked the pilot into lending him the plane for the emergency and took off although it was a type of plane he had never flown before. When he landed, John was waiting for him, but the patient, scared out of his wits had taken off across the tundra after the crash.

When they had recovered the patient and boarded the new plane Archie refused to fly it back, "Geezus John, I can't fly that new fangled plane you better take it back!"

Eight phones had just been installed in Kotzebue, all of them in pastel shades. The airport had a luminous yellow one and Archie's was bright blue. New phones but no wells, no sewers, no roads, no running water and hardly any plumbing. There was still no high school except the ones at Sitka and Wrangell for native children. Some teen-agers had to be flown out to Oregon for schooling. Hundreds of young people were deprived of a high school education for lack of schools.

The Thomases were sending their oldest son out to school next year. The grade school lagged behind because the Eskimo children had trouble with English. "The major difficulty," Emily Brown, Eskimo schoolteacher, told me, "is that it is hard to make the Eskimo children understand how important education is to their lives." Their parents lived by hunting and they did not understand how book learning could fill their stomachs.

Emily, who was born at Unalakeet, Alaska, had a degree from the University of Alaska. We had met while she was attending the university. She lived in comfortable modern quarters at Kotzebue and insited that I take her bed while she slept on the couch. We spent three days visiting and drinking huge quantities of strong coffee between meals, three days while I waited for the weather to clear so that I could fly to Point Hope.

Emily lent me more cold-weather gear, urging me to wear her full-length parka of muskrat skins. I was wearing my regular winter parka with the fur inside and cloth outside but Emily's was much warmer. She insisted that she had other coats and would not be wearing it and I finally took it. It fit perfectly and seemed almost too beautiful to wear. Tiny circular designs of white calfskin, sewn together by hand, bordered the bottom, and the coloring of the matched muskrat skins and wolverine ruff were the finest I had seen.

The second morning Emily and I noticed a plane landing on the sea ice in front of the houses and a white man in polar bear pants hopped out as casually as we would leave a car. He was living and hunting with Eskimos and as one

Eskimo said, "He is more Eskimo than we are." There were a handful of white men in the Arctic who lived an adventurous, rather unique life; I half envied them.

Emily and I visited Abraham Lincoln's house. Abe had been given the name by missionaries who could not pronounce Eskimo names. He was about eighty years old and bedridden. Emily often visited him to gather legends of Kotzebue and stories of the past, as Abe had been a leader in the community. His face had a clear childlike look, his eye sockets deeply sunken beneath a sloping brow, whose gauntness revealed the bony spirituality which the fleshiness of former years had hidden. He lay in bed holding on to a rope suspended from the ceiling, his gnarled legs helplessly folded Yoga fashion under him.

Abraham remembered me from former visits, his mind was clear although his body was helpless. I recalled a tomcod fish hook that he had made for me with orange Russian trade beads on it. "I think of you whenever I look at it," I said, which pleased the old man.

A trip to Kotzebue wasn't complete without a visit to Gene Joiner, the Jade King. Archie and Gene had a running feud which delights all Kotzebue and secretly, I think, gave the two men many a chuckle when one outsmarted the other. Gene lived as if he had many lives. He once visited Hawaii on impulse: "I just wanted to get real hot after this cold and ice. I really wanted to sweat for a change." When he returned, he told me, "I bought some land near the beach; there's a lot of volcanic rock there. I plan to blast a hole and make that my sunken living room!"

Gene was born in the South of a good family. Although he was acquainted with the world, he preferred his old cabin at Kotzebue. He had a fine collection of Eskimo artifacts and used to publish the *Mukluk Telegraph* which contained news of the Arctic.

Inside his cabin was total disorder; not a clean cup in sight, all manner of objects on the bed, and the floor burned from hundreds of cigarette butts. A volume of modern poetry and a book about Plato had been tossed on a chair, and dried blue flowers that I had given him a year before were still in a jar on the window ledge.

Gene's eyes had a quizzical expression; they were alert eyes that darted piercingly through one. He wore nondescript baggy pants over a bold orange checked woolen shirt and heavy shoe pacs. He never just walked, he strode, with purpose and vitality. He was usually full of enthusiasm for his next adventurous plan, doing things with a flair and a complete disregard for convention.

If you did not care for a drink of the stronger stuff, Gene scooped out the water from a gasoline drum with a beautifully carved sheep horn ladle. A typewriter rested on a chair and blueprints for a sailing ship were spread out over the bed.

"I'm building this boat in Nome," he stated. It was a comfortable-looking boat, large, with a sail, and a place to sleep and cook; he said he planned to sail along the Arctic coast in it.

Gene piloted his plane to the top of Shungnak Mountain where he looked for jade and to the coast as a polar-bear guide. A hunter at Point Hope said: "Gene doesn't give you that big smile like some white men who hunt here, but you can depend on him if you need help."

He piloted his plane as comfortably as if he were sitting in an armchair. The previous year he had said casually: "Come on, I'll take you to Sheshalik for a ride." We walked a few feet from his house to the plane. "Hop in," he said, gesturing, slammed the door, and turned the key, and we were off.

The plane was old and appeared untrustworthy, for there was a hole in the windshield stuffed with an old rag and one wing was white and the rest black; it looked as if it had seen better years. We set out over the sea and if it had not been for his serene confidence, I would have felt shaky.

"Want to see who that is?" he asked as we flew over a small boat, dipping down until we could see the occupants' faces. We landed on the rough tundra of Sheshalik where the tents still blew in the wind. There was just time enough to say hello to everyone. It had been a poor year for beluga, nothing like the year when I was there when the catch was eighty. Only twenty beluga had been shot for the whole camp, but they had made up for the lack in seal and fish. A small bag of candy produced from my pocket made a hit with the children.

The trip back to Kotzebue seemed much shorter with the wind favoring us and we stepped out of the plane as if we had only taken a stroll. Gene had gone back to his cabin to work on his ship plans, waving off any thanks.

CHAPTER 19

Return to Tigara

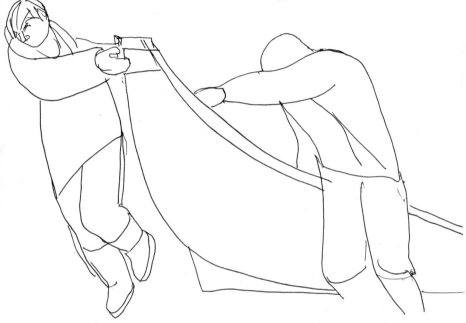

You man on the ground
I see you from above
While I fly and hover
Where is your friends
I see you from above
While I fly and hover.
            PAUL TIULANA of Nome

AFTER THREE DAYS the weather
cleared enough so that my plane could take off; but the
whole coast from Nome to Point Hope had been stormed
under with snow and fog, and flying was hazardous. Icing

on the wings added to our troubles, and I was terribly air-sick flying in a Cessna 180 on skis. The sun enabled us to see mountains which were desolate this time of year, as were the snow wastes on the sea.

In another twenty minutes it would have been impossible to land at Point Hope; the storm and fog were closing in. No one was expecting a plane in this bad weather, but at the sound of a motor, the first in weeks, the people came running out.

I tumbled out of the plane, steadying myself against the pilot's arm. It had been a rough trip and I braced myself in the wind, breathing deeply. Snow flakes beat my face and the wind tore the parka hood from my head. I had wondered for months how this first reunion would be, remembering how shy and strange I had felt at first, but nothing had prepared me for the warmth of the greeting. A woman came running up, grabbed me and hugged me tightly and we laughed and rubbed faces, our cheeks wet and our ruffs snowy. It was Hilda Weber, Billy Weber's mother; then Dinah Frankson and Ikkaheena were laughing and hugging me.

The women put my boxes and paint box on a sled, Dinah put the rope around her waist like a harness and Hilda, Ikkaheena, and I pushed from the back. I was nearly swept away by the force of the wind which blew against us. Drifted snow made it difficult to walk and we kept sinking through the soft crust. Finally weary of fighting the wind, I hung on to keep from being blown away; it was impossible to keep up with Dinah. At last we reached Asatsiak's house at the end of the village.

The entrance except for a small channel was covered with snow. Dinah, Hilda, Ikkaheena, and I entered by sliding down a short incline to the door, making sure not to step on Choosy, the dog, who was asleep in the doorway. Otoonah opened the door. She usually hid her expression with laughter, but now, her face showed shock, then her eyes grew soft and tender, and smiling widely she put her tiny arms around me.

When I came in, she took off my parka and shook the snow from it, hanging it up carefully. Then she put on the coffeepot and we all looked at one another. I was the first white woman visitor they had seen in months, and my face was paler than usual after the flu. Dinah wore a brown calico print which suited her nut-brown complexion, her smiling mouth and high cheekbones making her resemble Tigluk, her brother. Ikkaheena's parka was loose in the back; no baby filled it now and she had blossomed into a serious matron with a slow, lovely smile.

Hilda, a good-looking woman with long black hair and sparkling eyes, looked exactly the same. She just bubbled over with laughter as she looked down at her feet. Her laughter was contagious and we laughed until we were breathless. Between bouts of giggling, Hilda pointed to her footgear, white canvas army boots that she had been wearing around the house when the plane came. They were about twice as big as her tiny feet and curled over her toes in a ridiculous manner.

"My, my mukluks," gasped Hilda hysterically, "they're too big for my husband too," and she went off again, doubling over and holding her stomach.

Otoonah, who had a bad cold, served coffee and fine homemade bread; then I took out gifts from the warm lands of California that I had found in Fairbanks—an orange for each woman! The huge tropical fruit glowed, and each woman accepted it differently. Dinah ate hers right away, exclaiming, "First orange I see in long time!" The others put theirs away to savor later or perhaps to share. I saved one for Ah-gaik. I had brought eggs, potatoes, onions, and fruit, all of which were difficult to buy at this time of year in Point Hope.

The women told me of a white man living in the village who planned to hire an Eskimo crew for whale hunting. He planned to pay them by the hour and keep the whale meat for himself. If he was successful, the meat could be sold for more than a dollar a pound and at sixty tons that would be over $12,000. He had plans to take movies of whaling and show them in the States and had invented a "superior" whaling gun.

The village elders, upset about this misuse of whaling resources, had posted a sign at the Native store: "No white man allowed to hunt whale at Point Hope." It was open rebellion. There had been whispers of this at Kotzebue. The Eskimos had refused to work for the man as crew members, especially when they discovered he had no money and was living on credit at the store. His fine plans and inventions were of no use to him; one can't hunt whale alone.

Dinah, to be charitable, said slyly: "First he came all nice, new clothes; now he wear all dirty rags."

"Your heart bleeds for him," I said tartly. With this remark the last vestige of shyness dropped and we all howled.

"Weather is bad for whaling," Ikkaheena offered. "South wind closed the open lead."

Otoonah's kitchen looked the same except for the new calendars. Out of spare parts Asatsiak had rigged up a stove for my little room which connected to the kitchen stove. I put my boxes behind it but not too close, then set the sleeping bag down on the sagging cot. I was home and glad to be there at last. I had everything I needed, a stove, a basin on top of it, hooks for my clothes, and a table.

In the kitchen a blanket was suspended from the ceiling and Eugene lay behind it, asleep.

"Sick," explained Otoonah to all of us.

Asatsiak had left with Tingook to hunt duck as he did every day. Eugene tossed in bed while Otoonah's eyes and nose ran and her face perspired. I gave her one of my aspirins but later Asatsiak told me that Otoonah took pills from the doctor but never swallowed them. "The only medicine that Otoonah takes is seal oil," he said. If I had been as sick as Otoonah, I would have stayed in bed.

When his father was due home after ten hours hunting in the cold, Eugene got out of bed and paced the floor, looking out to see if he was coming.

"There he comes; soon he will be braggin' what a great hunter he is and how tired and cold he is and how his legs hurt!" As Eugene talked there crept into his voice a grudging respect for the old man which he covered quickly with cynicsm and a wish that he too could go hunting like his father.

Asatsiak arrived, his face burnt brown and healthy, glowing with good spirits and looking younger than ever. There was not a wrinkle on his face, although when he walked he moved his body from side to side, his mouth working as if to balance the effort.

Their relative positions in the house were revealing. Asatsiak had the nicest bed, with good springs and mattress, Eugene the smaller bed, and Otoonah slept under the table on a mattress which she rolled up every morning. She tucked her little sewing box and a few belongings beside it. When I gave her a cotton dress and a scarf for a gift, she quickly hid them under her mattress without looking at them. Otoonah was treated as a servant. She was older than Asatsiak and his second wife. Eugene was her stepson.

Tigluk was there in the morning when I got out of bed, looking disheveled and unwashed. I filled the basin and washed my face, brushed my teeth with everyone looking on, then had to go get my towel because I had forgotten it.

It seemed strange that this trip, everyone spoke better English than I remembered, or else they were talking freely now and did not before. The previous year I had to drag every word out of Tigluk and now we made more than equal conversation. They had lost their shyness and I mine. Tigluk talked freely of the past winter; he still had no rifle and needed one badly so he sometimes borrowed the minister's to hunt with.

I told him about Joe and the family and showed him photographs. "It's good to be back," I said.

"People are glad to have you back," he said, "because many people never come back."

"How was the egg hunting this year?" I asked.

"We got many eggs," Tigluk said. "Black and white the ducks were. When I looked up, I couldn't see the clouds, all black like mosquitoes all around, thousands of birds." Tigluk sucked in his breath as he remembered.

"When me and Keepororuk climbed for eggs, he was ahead of me on the cliffs, I climbed on a small place, so high on the cliffs, and I looked down and couldn't see far. A big rock got loose and fell on my shoulder—a big rock. I'd be gone now if my left hand had not held tight above me on the cliffs. Keepororuk helped me get down. Now my shoulder bone is split in like this." Tigluk rubbed his shoulder. "That's why I hold my shoulder up sometimes," he said and settled himself comfortably around the chair, moved his shoulder to show me.

"I was born in another village near Cape Lisburne, a place named Kalik. When I was a boy, my mother made mukluks out of beluga skin. She dried it first and it became tough, they were the best mukluks I ever had. We lived there when I was a boy, not many other people nearby. When I came to Jabbertown, I helped Asatsiak; that's how I met my wife."

"How is your family?" I inquired.

"They are well and would like to see you. We don't have a fine house but you will be welcome," he replied.

"I will come soon," I promised.

After coffee I walked him to the store, following in his huge footsteps. The morning sun was bright and deep drifts and hills cast blue shadows on the snow; our mukluks sank in about a foot with each step.

We dropped in to Andrew Frankson's store. The yearly boat had brought a pool table which he had installed, charging twenty-five cents a game, and the coffee counter held pies and homemade bread which Mrs. Frankson baked. The store did not yet have the merchandise that the cooperative native store did.

Andrew and his wife welcomed me with a cup of coffee

and told me that their daughter Nina, who fell off the walrus skin last year during the nalukatuk was fine and away at school in the States. Evidently she had not broken any bones.

Allen Rock, owner of the lodge for the polar-bear hunters and occasional reporter for the Fairbanks paper, came into the store and said hello. He gazed steadily at me, sizing me up. I must have passed for when I returned home, Joe showed me a clipping four lines long that Mr. Rock had sent in to the paper. "The artist came today from Fairbanks, Mrs. Clara Fejes. She is well known by all people. Everyone happy to see her. Mrs. Fejes plan to visit some whalers." I liked that.

There had been a wild shooting party the week before. The polar-bear hunters had given whisky to some of the younger men and one of them had gone berserk.

"One of the boys got drunk. He even hit his uncle!" one woman explained.

The polar-bear hunters introduced new problems to the village. Any man who could afford to pay the registered guide $2,000 and up might come to Point Hope by plane and hunt bear. The lodge now had one chemical toilet and beds to accommodate eight men. During bad weather the hunters amused themselves playing cards and drinking whiskey. When they offered the Eskimos a drink, they accepted, forgetting they had reason to resent the white hunter who came outfitted with the latest guns and equipment, guide and plane to hunt the same bear they hunted with a sled and dog team. As the number of bears became depleted close to the village, the situation became more difficult for the Eskimo hunter, who had to hunt farther and farther from home.

Next to the bowhead whale, the bear was the most valuable catch in terms of food and grease. The bearskin alone was worth more than two hundred dollars at the store. Great prestige was attached to the hunting of the bear and the native hunters felt the white hunter had an unfair advantage.

In addition to taking home a magnificent hide, the hunter from the States usually hired a photographer to take movies or took his own. Two planes left together in good flying weather, one spotting the bear while the other gave chase until the bear reached a place on the ice where the plane could land. Near the plane in view of the bear hid the photographer and the man with the rifle who paid for this "sport." When they had harassed, photographed, and finally shot the fine beast, they skinned him, leaving most of the meat on the ice. A few choice steaks were taken, but the food which could have provided months of meals for an Eskimo family was left for the foxes and sea gulls. The white hunter would excuse himself back in the village by saying that the plane was too loaded down with photographic equipment for them to bring back the bear meat!

Lee Holen, a guide, was an exception, for he would make another trip to bring back the meat. One year his plane was downed on the ice and he would have frozen to death if the Eskimos had not come to his rescue.

The stories the returning hunters told sickened me, as did the fact that they chose to tell them where men hunted every day for their food. The guides were for the most part quiet men who did this for a living, but the newcomers usually strutted and swaggered with their kill, photographing one another in ridiculous positions.

The bear would be mounted in the States, with its mouth pried open in a vicious growl, its tongue curled in defiance, even though it may have been shot in the back.

One hunter described his day's experience as follows: "I saw the bear but it was under the ice in the water. I didn't want to lose it, such a perfect specimen! The bear began to heave itself out of the water, bleeding from my shot. I shot him again and that darn bear sank in the water." What a waste, yet he bragged about it, deploring the loss of "his bear!"

If a hunter was hurt or lost on the ice, it was the Eskimos who spent days looking for him. Asatsiak told me the story of a relative of his who hunted polar bear: "When we walk on ice we always put stick first or we go through thin ice. If man falls in and it's not too wide, he can get out. One man, Ohnakuk, Otoonah's uncle from Kivilina, hunted on soft ice after a polar bear and two cubs. For a long distance he tracked till he shot the bear. He jumped on a little ice cake crossing a lee. The soft ice broke off and he fall in the water. Too cold. Windy. Swim back, climb up, wet all his clothes, pants. Wet feet. Pants take 'em off. Put polar-bear skin and sit down on skin, meantime, rinse off pants and socks. After awhile he put back on, then take off parka, ring out water. Okay. Stay overnight, wrapped up in polar-bear skin, keep warm."

That hunter took care of himself but many hunters have lost their lives hunting on ice. Point Hope gained in one respect by the intrusion of the polar-bear hunters; they gave employment to the women. Working all night to scrape the fat from the skin, the women earned about twenty dollars.

Asatsiak told me the preparations they had made for whale hunting. Early in March, while temperatures at Point Hope ranged below zero, Asatsiak and Otoonah had called all of the crew members and their wives to help put the ugruk skin covering on the umiak. A few days before, Otoonah had soaked five skins in a hole in the ice to make them soft and pliable. The skins had to be new and clean for the whaling season.

Tingook's wife and other expert skin sewers came to the house. Otoonah busied herself making coffee and biscuits while Asatsiak talked to the men about how the five skins were to be cut. The job of cutting fell to Asatsiak, who was particularly good at it. He cut one skin lengthwise for the bow, another one lengthwise for the stern, and three crosswise to go between them. In addition head skins were sewn at the bow and stern so that the ear, nose, and eye holes of the ugruk were visible at the ends of the boat. The men worked on the wooden frame while the women sewed the skins together with small even stitches, using sinew for thread.

The men replaced broken ribs of the wooden frame, greased it with whale blubber, and got the sealskin lines ready. The women had cut slits around the edge of the skin for the lines to pass through. Now the men stretched the pliable skin over the bow and stern, passing the lines through the slits and pulling them tight.

When the lashing was done, the men took the umiak out, placed it on a sledge, and returned it to its whalebone rack. All of the children crowded around to wish the whalers luck, for there were great expectations for the coming season.

There were about eleven umeliks, or whaling captains, this year at Point Hope. The umeliks achieved their positions through skill, intelligence, energy, and shrewdness rather than inheritance or prestige. They had to accumulate boats, hunting gear, and clothing, and since the bombs for the darting gun alone cost about twenty dollars each, a poor man could not afford them. Eugene, Asatsiak's son, might inherit his father's whaling gear but he could not be an umelik unless he undertook the responsibility of equipping and directing a crew. An umelik was under obligation to feed and outfit the crew during whaling time; it was said that generosity was his true measure.

As leaders in the community, umeliks exercised social control. Rainey related a story of one woman who persisted in having sexual relations with many men in the village until the umeliks were provoked into discipling her. One night all of the men raped her and then married her off the the last one.

Asatsiak was one of the oldest umelik's now engaging in whaling at Point Hope. Koonooyak had been ninety when he finally proclaimed to the village in a public ceremoney that his whaling days were over.

In Asatsiak's crew were his half-brother, two nephews,

and Tingook. Asatsiak was upset because his son-in-law Tigluk would not hunt in his crew in spite of the fact that he had lent him his dogs and other equipment, for Tigluk had promised to work in another crew.

Before the missionaries came to Point Hope, it had been the custom for the umeliks' wives to perform a ceremony at the first new moon. They would put on their best clothing, take their ceremonial pots filled with clear water, and stand in the entryway of their houses calling out, "Alignuk [moon god], drip a whale into this pot so we can kill a whale next season." Then the woman lifted the pot to the moon four times and, calling to Alignuk, drew a crescent moon on the frost of the skylight, holding a dipper of water up to it. According to Rainey, the Tigara people used to associate Alignuk with God. Women used to "perform . . . ritual acts so that '[they] . . . would look good to the whale,' and he would give himself up."

In the past, whales were so numerous that the crews chased only the young ones and threw ice at the older whales to drive them away. Today if the village struck four whales, the hunt was considered successful.

In the late 1800's, hunters could not make a fire while whaling, they had no sleeping bags or shelter other than ice blocks, and they ate their meat raw and drank cold water in strict discomfort. When Charlie Brower of Barrow went whaling with Attungorah, he produced a stove, made hot tea, and boiled meat. Attungorah was shocked but quickly saw the advantages, especially since the whales came anyway.

Darting guns were also looked on with suspicion when they were first introduced. The hunters hid them in the bottom of the boats, as the old people had warned them that they wouldn't kill whales. Steel knives, harpoons, and flint-headed lances were used in killing and butchering whales before darting and shoulder guns were used. The shoulder gun was never satisfactory because of the need to harpoon the whale before or after it was shot, but the darting gun had the advantage of combining these actions in one thrust. The harpoon drove deep into the whale while the trigger mechanism released the bomb that exploded deep in the whale's body. Often the bomb did not go off, an expensive miss.

In the past some villagers believed that the success of the whale hunt was due to the use of certain hunting songs, and some hunters paid money or goods to Tingook or Asatsiak in order to buy a good whaling song.

Asatsiak said: "Whales don't die; the spirit, or inyua, comes back to find a new body.

"Whales not afraid to die. Very patient. I kill many whales," he said, "and always I see whale not afraid to die. He just goes down under the water, doesn't kick like seal or ugruk.

"When umelik throws back head of whale in ocean after stripping the meat, hunter always says, 'Come back again next year,' to the whale. Whales hear good but can't see good. Patient.

"I used to give seal a drink, one in mouth, another in cut-open stomach, but don't do that any more. Get them anyhow. But whales know everything," Asatsiak concluded.

"I read in a magazine about a scientist writing a book about dolphins who talk. He says that they are very intelligent," I remarked.

"Eskimos always know that about whales," was his only comment.

When the first snowbirds flew over the village, the people knew that the whales would soon follow. When the wind and ice conditions were favorable, the hunters went out on the ocean ice with axes and shovels to make a trail for the dog teams and boats.

In the past the launching of the boats was a solemn moment charged with supernatural significance and was performed with rituals. An umelik usually sang his own special songs until they reached the open lead.

A long time ago, according to Rainey, the umelik's wife played a leading role during the launching. Crouched at the edge of the ice, facing inland. The crew paddled out a short distance with the harpooner standing in the bow turned toward the woman. The boat turned seaward again and then the woman walked homeward, never looking back.

When she was home, she placed her special pot and her husband's drum in a particular place in the entranceway. She did not work during his absence, or wash, or comb her hair, or scrub the floor; if she did, the skin of the whale would be thin. She remained tranquil and acted like a sick person so that the harpooned whale would be quiet and easy to kill. She must never use a knife, and her food must be cut for her, because she might sever the harpoon line holding the whale. In the umiak the umelik wore his wife's belt. His own charms were in the bow of the umiak along with the special left-hand mitten an old woman had knitted and used to carry her pot to the whale to give it a drink.

Nowadays the old taboos were no longer followed; it was the Christian minister who said a prayer at the opening of the whaling season. A few of the men still wore ivory charms and hid them in the umiak. Their attitude was that it couldn't do any harm.

At Barrow in the past the youngest and most powerful man was chosen as harpooner. He slept in the bow of the boat with the youngest and prettiest woman, for the soul of the whale was supposed to be attracted to being killed by a man coming straight from a woman.

When a whale was killed, it belonged to the particular clan whose boats were the first to strike it. Whether the men were present or not the meat would be shared with them. Asatsiak and the elders were the supervisors of the cutting and distribution of meat and skin and their word was law.

However, it was different in the old days and bloodshed was not uncommon. Killigivuk related this story to me.

"In those old whaling days, the umeliks Old Nannoona and Avraluk came from Barrow to whale at Point Hope. The first time they caught a whale they agreed to share it, but Avraluk wanted more share and Nannoona wanted his share. They tried to fight inside the skin boat in water. Avraluk tried to choke Nannoona but Nannoona caught Avraluk's mukluk string and pulled hard so that Avraluk's head went down in the water and he drowned.

"He left his body on the ice and Nannoona started home with his crew. Another captain went out on the ice with his crew. He was Avraluk's brother, a great fighter and umelik. The two crews happened to meet out on the ice pack. Nannoona was carrying his spear, hook, and paddle and he could not pass in the narrow space. Avraluk's brother also carried a spear. Nannoona said, 'I fell in water. I have to go home and dry my clothes.'

"The brother of the drowned man looked and looked, staring at Nannoona, and when he passed him, Nannoona speared him in the back, because he was afraid Avraluk's brother, a great fighter, would kill him when he found his brother dead."

CHAPTER 20

Visiting

THE BIG WIND

My parka is blowing,
I should have noticed;
The black cloud
Over the mountain
Is blowing hard on my face.
The big wind around Kisimelock
"The mountain all by itself"
Is blowing me away,
It's blowing my parka;
The black cloud had warned me
I should have listened.
      Composed by Asatsiak's Mother, NIKUWNANNA

ONE OF THE NICEST LETTERS
I had received during the winter was from Elmer, Ah-gaik's
fourteen-year-old son. He had written at the end, "Clara, it

is my will and hope that you can make the trip safe to Point Hope. God willing we'll see each other again."

God willing I was at Point Hope and in Otoonah's doorway stood Elmer with an indescribable expression. Those who live in cities become satiated with the crowds of people passing one another blindly, but in the isolated North the sight of a new individual was rare.

Solemnly grouped behind Elmer stood Rosa and her sister, Lizzie. "My mother can hardly wait to see you, Clara, can you come now?" Elmer said.

I was anxious to see their family so I dressed warmly and we went out together. It was storming again and the houses were unrecognizable, the familiar landmarks and paths of the previous year buried under snow. We trudged over snow mounds, at each step sinking through the hard crusts, the snow blinding us. I could hardly breathe.

The entranceway to Elmer's house was about four feet high and packed with snow, which created good insulation. We entered down carved snow steps, bending our heads until we reached the inner storm porch where dog harnesses, frozen seal and beluga meat were stored. We passed through the porch and I hesitated by the second doorway, but Elmer said warmly: "Just go in, Clara."

Alec and Ah-gaik were standing at the far end of the room holding their new baby. The house was neat and clean with bright yellow oilcloth on the table and curtains on the windows. I gave an orange to Ah-gaik and candy, gum, balloons, and other gifts of clothing to the children. Yola had sent a bunny rabbit she had made out of cotton and paper and *Heidi*, her favorite book. They invited me for dinner but since I had eaten, I just had tea.

Little Silas was fat and strong and still hostile to me. No amount of gum or balloons would change him. Perhaps I reminded him of the nurse who gave him his first shot, or maybe he was resentful because I looked different. Silas was still the "boss" of the family but no longer the baby. Pearly, the newborn, was beautiful with her triangular nose and

Ah-gaik

Silas,
Ah-gaik's son

satiny body. Silas watched jealously as Ah-gaik drew out her breast and fed the little girl. She weighed only nine pounds at six weeks, which was tiny by Point Hope standards. Her delicately flushed face reminded me of a Japanese miniature, her tiny lashes were tipped in an elegant design and the tracing of her eyebrows followed the line in perfect symmetry. Her petite mouth grasped the nipple while she drank contentedly. On her lower back were the dark bluish Mongolian markings that distinguish Eskimo babies.

I thought Ah-gaik looked tired and assumed that was because her recovery from the birth of Pearly was slow; meanwhile she remarked how tired I looked and I told her about my bout with flu. I asked about her lovely married daughter remembering how she had made *maporuks* for the whale feast and how listless she had seemed. I also remembered catching a glimpse of her and her husband one day when she looked up at him with a radiant face. They were so young and so much in love. Ah-gaik told me resignedly that her daughter was in the hospital with tuberculosis but that they were looking forward to her homecoming in six months or so.

Alec, Ah-gaik's husband, was having trouble with an old back injury but had been carving masks to supplement their income when he could not hunt.

Ah-gaik said as I left: "Come again, it's *arigah*."

"*Arigah*," I answered.

Elmer brought me by dog team to the minister's house. "I'm on the whaling crew just like a man," he said happily, as he hurried the dogs along.

Near the doorway of the minister's house at the end of the village sprawled ten dogs in various positions. Reverend Lawton, the new minister, hauled his own ice for water and was a capable dog musher. I had received a letter from his wife inviting me to stay with them and I had come to thank them and tell them that I was staying in my usual room at Killigivuks.

Young, blonde Mrs. Lawton had a baby in her arms and another handing on to her skirts. She and the scientist's wife were interested in woodcuts and I had brought a block-printing set for her to use with the children. The scientist's wife, Berit, was an accomplished artist and had tried to arouse interest in woodcuts among the hunters. A photographer was staying with the Lawtons on assignment to cover the whale hunt.

Billy Weber's father, Keepororuk, lived a few feet away from Billy and Alice near the Episcopal minister's. I went to visit him one day. Keepororuk was born at Kivalina and had lived at Noatak until he married Hilda, a Point Hope girl. He was an elder in the Episcopal church, a good hunter, and gave meat to those less fortunate than himself. He and Hilda had been chosen by the Rev. Lawton to accompany him and his family on a visit to New Hampshire the previous year. It was their first trip across the United States.

"How did you like the States?" I queried.

"Too crowded," was the reply.

Keepororuk, who kept calm in the face of a whale, was alarmed in heavy traffic. He refused to walk beside the minister through crowded thoroughfares, preferring to track behind him. He sold his parka and mukluks to admirers and sensibly bought a short-wave radio and tape recorder with the money. Hilda bought herself a bathing suit and went swimming for the first time in her life.

"It was fun but we were glad to get home," Hilda said.

The elder Webers' home was large with alcoves everywhere and an upper story that had walls of Celotex and a linoleum-covered floor.

An old woman sat on the floor by the fire skinning three eider ducks, her hands deep in their vitals. The ducks were beautiful. The male duck had a yellow beak and red, green, and iridescent blue feathers marking the face. The female had speckled brown colorations and was plain-looking in contrast.

Keepororuk had been up since three in the morning and by covering fourteen miles by team and carrying his eight-foot umiak had caught two seals and three ducks and taken a white fox out of one of his traps. The fox now hung by one leg from a rope suspended from the ceiling in the middle of the room. He squeezed the fox's neck and drained fluid out onto the floor. Then with a large pocketknife he cut the fox down and proceeded to skin the animal. First he cut the small feet carefully, slit around the nose and sharp teeth, then over the top of the eyes. He was an expert who enjoyed every movement of the blade as he pulled and cut the skin with dexterity.

I took out my sketch pad and drew him skinning the fox; also the old woman cutting up ducks on the floor. Hilda scraped a sealskin with the edge of a discarded milk can and then ran to the store with it rolled up under her arm to trade it for goods. She was wearing slacks and a red blouse and her hair was parted in the middle and tied in back like a little girl's.

Keepororuk skinned the fox down the middle and with a strong movement, leaning against the skin with all his might, revealed the fox as a poor, skinny, naked mite with its ribs sticking out. Another pull and the fox's male sex was revealed, and finally he had no skin at all. Head stretched and neck distended he held out his paws in a grotesque crucified position, a piteous object. Fox skins were now worth twenty-five dollars, but the head and body brought extra money since it happened that the visiting scientists were studying them.

Three relatives from Kivalina came indoors after tying their team, consisting of about thirty dogs, to the whalebone stakes. The men were part of Keepororuk's whaling crew and would get their share of whale meat.

Hilda usually walked with a bounce, arching her back and bending easily. Now she came running back from the store with dried vegetables and macaroni which she poured into a duck soup that had been simmering on the stove. The Kivalina men and myself were invited to sit around the table; the old woman preferred to sit by the stove. Hilda placed the pan of duck soup in the center of the table next to a batch of fresh biscuits and scalding tea. After Keepororuk said grace, I ate my first eider duck soup. The men relished the head and feet while Hilda selected a choice morsel for my plate. The duck soup had a slightly oily, fishy taste, different from soup made from grain-fed ducks.

I had a difficult time finding Tigluk's house which was only a mound of snow and ice with the chimney protruding. One could stand and look down into the house through the skylight. The entranceway was carved through ice and dropped downward to a small door the height of a short midget. Apparently Tigluk, who was over six feet, had to bend double to enter his house.

The inside of the door was made of an old wooden

*Anahkaloktuk
and baby*

crate; on it was a cross shaped from adhesive tape, and over
the cross hung a calendar and a written prayer. About three
feet from the door stood the iron stove and on top was a pot
of boiling water, over which hung four child's mukluks to
dry. For added insulation Tigluk had nailed dismantled cor-
rugated cardboard cartons on the walls. Clothes partially
covered an enema bag hanging from a nail and a crude
cupboard held plates, pots, flour, canned milk, and the gas
lantern. There was no electricity here, but the skylight allowed plenty of light.

   Anahkaloktuk called to her children playing outside,
"*Don't* walk up there," meaning on the skylight. Since the
roof was the only dry spot, the children were drawn to it
rather than to the snow. There was a danger of crashing in

through the skylight, as one of the panes was out, and a child could land in a pot of boiling water.

Standing in the middle of the room I could stretch out my arms and touch the bed with one hand, the stove with the other. The whole area was about ten by twelve feet. Under and over the cots that lined the wall were clothes and fur coverings. A discarded mattress had a handy purpose; when Anahkaloktuk wanted to cook, she added kerosene to a bit of mattress stuffing and pronto, there was a roaring fire in the stove.

Tigluk had been carving a whalebone mask and he swept aside the leavings with a short broom and set out a chair for me. More children wanted to enter but five besides three of his had already squeezed in and were observing us quietly.

"I didn't want to invite you to my poor house," said Anahkaloktuk.

"Don't say that," I answered. "Someday you will have a fine house."

"Yes," answered Tigluk. "Maybe I could build a new one."

Behind the stove was a pailful of caribou bones; on top was the head, freshly skinned out with the eyes intact, staring at us. It was difficult not to stare back. The fur of the caribou legs had been stretched flat and nailed to the wall behind my chair; it would dry and provide hide for mukluk tops of the warmest type.

Anahkaloktuk nursed her youngest, a healthy strong baby. The whole family looked well fed; Tigluk was a good provider.

Rather than go all the way back to Killigivuk's for lunch, I often carried such snacks as dried apricots, which I now passed around. Anahkaloktuk who was a relaxed, hospitable hostess, served coffee, while Tigluk began to work his whalebone mask again. The children sat on the cots in their red, blue, and multicolor parkas. Their straight black hair, long bangs, and rosy cheeks were so appealing that I

Three children in Igluts' house

asked Tigluk if I could paint them. He gave permission and leaning the sketchbook on my knee, I drew the children sitting on the cot with the stove and the clothesline of mukluks as background.

Anahkaloktuk amused little Elizabeth when she began to fuss by pulling out a Sears catalogue from under the bed. "See the little girl. See Elizabeth," she said, showing her photographs of little girls in bathing suits.

Little Elizabeth was silent, then cried, "Look she has no pants!"

I had not realized how educational a catalogue could be. It classified material things for people who had never seen a bathing suit, lawn mower, or modern stove. The bathing suit and lawn mower will probably never be needed at Point Hope, but some day the modern stoves might be in use.

So much of our modern world was unknown, yet beginning to be known. By the next generation the great transition will have begun. Perhaps some of the younger people of Point Hope will have children who will choose another way of life, yet they will have inherited the Eskimo culture.

The entrance to Ahksivvokrook's house had three ice steps and three pups nursing at the bottom. I carefully stepped over them and moved aside a polar bear hide inside the door. A small cramped room was the dwelling place of his family of nine. Along the back and side walls ran a hip-high wooden board over which was thrown the family's disheveled bedding. Most of the children slept on the floor beneath the bed board, wrapped in skins. On top of a little box near the stove was an assortment of broken cups, a can of milk, and sugar. The only "adornments" in the hut were two seal stretchers on the celing and a gas lantern, both basic utilities. A dog harness hung on the wall and a washtub with a scrub board leaned in one corner.

Nathlook sat with her blouse open to the waist. She had

just finished nursing the baby, who looked ill and pale although her cheeks dropped from the weight of fat. Nathlook was a strange woman, different from the other women in the village, shrewd, dirty, tough, and wild looking. When she laughed she had the zaniest sense of humor, revealing her missing bottom teeth. Her hair was greasy, unkempt, and hung over her face.

Somewhere in her ancestry she had acquired the profile of a Slav with Mongolian cheekbones. Her eyes were perfectly proportioned, her nose the right length, and had she been bathed and gowned, her hair arranged, and some front teeth repaired, she would have been a beauty in any country.

As she was, she was an easy mark for TB germs and had transferred them to her sons. Because her husband was not a good hunter but lazy, the family suffered from malnutrition. She and her husband prided themselves on being "Eskimo" in capital letters, which meant to them being completely free of the responsibility of work. They were noted for their indolence and performed only the most basic acts necessary to stay alive.

Earlier Nathlook and her older daughter had been skinning a polar bear on the floor and the blood, hair, and grease had dried into the darkened wood. The gentle, sloe-eyed daughter was as beautiful as her mother must have been. She picked up a short battered broom and pretended to sweep the littered floor. She threw seal blubber, duck feathers, and odd bits of garbage into the stove. Then, without washing her hands, she prepared to make bannock. In a basin used alternately for preparing food and washing dishes she mixed the flour with water and bear hairs.

I had brought with me my shiny metal oil box with its many tubes of paint and brushes. The family stared at my box and finally Ahksivvokrook said: "You must be very rich!" I hadn't realized that the box and its contents were costly looking. Every object in this house could have been packed on a dog sled. It made me feel humble.

"This baby had fever last night," Nathlook said, "but she is better now. I rubbed her with whale oil and covered her good."

Koahk looked better, too, not so peaked as when I had seen him. He had been to the Anchorage hospital for several months for a TB checkup and had been fed well to counteract his malnutrition. His shoulder blades still protruded pitifully and his head between his hunched shoulders had the look of a bird of prey; he held his face down and his hair was a dark wing over one eye.

After my last trip I sent him a good winter coat and brand-new fur-lined boots; but no matter what he wore, it was soon reduced to shreds. If a button came off, no one sewed it on; and if the cloth tore, it remained so for the lifetime of the garment.

His oldest brother wore new mukluks that had been furnished him as a member of a whaling crew. The mukluks had a band of white bleached sealskin across the tops with cross ties of white. He helped himself to some hot water from the teakettle and colored it with canned milk and sugar—all he had eaten except the lunch supplied at school. The schoolteacher had told me that the children lost weight in the summertime when the free lunches were not supplied, but that may also be because of the extra summer activities.

"I made twenty dollars cleaning bearskin. First time we make so much money," said Nathlook. "We made three hundred dollars skinning bears and spend it all on food."

"She works all the time, too much work," said her husband. The groceries seemed to be all gone.

Nathlook picked up a mask and showed me her crude carving, then her son took it and began to chip it in a haphazard fashion. They needed the money and the whalebone mask would bring credit.

The whole family had the funniest sense of humor, sharing jokes and laughing at anything. Every time I said anything, they tried to find the humor of it.

All the homes I had visited were different; most were clean and orderly, some overcrowded, others poor, yet in two respects all were alike. The first was their cordiality and warmth toward me, their guest, expressed in part by their generous sharing of what they had; and the other was their concern for favorable whaling conditions. The whole village was united in one effort to this end.

"Cara, Cara," call the children and converge on me from all directions.

"How come you're not in bed? It's late and tomorrow is school!"

"Our mother is cleaning polar bear. Do you want to see it?"

"Sure," I replied and pulling my hands the girls lead me to their house.

It was the sod house of one of the best hunters in the village. Under the glare of a single electric bulb, five women sat on the floor skinning a huge white polar-bear pelt with their ulus. Two tubs held the scraps of bear fat while another contained the red meat, and upon this one was enthroned the ghastly skull with shreds of pink-red flesh sticking to its bones and holding in its sockets the glassy, bulging eyes of the unprotesting beast.

The hunter sat on a box supervising the operation while the children and I watched the proceedings. Each of the women held one section of the bear and chatted as they handled the skin and carefully scraped off the loose fat. The bear was huge; his rubbery nose flopped around in loose folds, and there were holes where his eyes and ears used to be.

Two of the women stopped to casually light cigarettes as they greeted me and the hunter turned over the skin to the fur side to show me the bear's head. A baby crawling on the floor poked his fingers up the nostrils of the bear.

The children were still up when I left at one at night. Two of the oldest ones offered to walk me home to the end of the village and I was grateful; although I carried a stick at night, I was afraid of loose dogs. It was bluish dark, a few dim lights shone from the few windows and the moon was obscured behind clouds. We sank into snowdrifts, it was hard walking, but we kept good company, the children and I.

CHAPTER 21

Ice World

O Allingnuk, Dweller of the Moon—
Allingnuk, great and generous giver of whales,
I, Nikuwanna, whose wife I am of Killigivuk,
A young and hopeful new whaler of Tigara,
Implore thee for they life-giving gift. . . .

                    HOWARD ROCK

APRIL SIXTEENTH dawned clear;
it was the kind of day when whales, migrating along the
coast, might come close to Point Hope. The north wind
blew with an icy concentration and every hunter woke that
morning glad in his heart for the good wind.

I hopped out of my sleeping bag, washed, and ate a
quick breakfast of mush and coffee. Eugene was asleep and
Asatsiak had left earlier for the whaling camp. Otoonah,

in answer to all my queries, had one answer. Pointing to herself, she said: "You come . . . me."

Quickly assembling what gear I thought I might need for a prolonged stay on the ice, I threw sealskin pants, long underwear, a change of mukluks, caribou socks, wool socks, two down sleeping bags, and painting supplies into a duffel bag to be picked up later. I wore quite a combination of clothes—red underwear, slacks, blue sweater, red windbreaker, mukluks, and parka and carried sketch pad and fur mittens. I brought two pairs of sunglasses but neglected one important item—sun lotion.

I followed Otoonah as she walked to the south side of the spit. She preferred to walk the eight miles to the whaling camp for she believed that whales could hear dogs bark. She prided herself on observing the old customs and was the only one who still made the special pair of mittens and the little bone pot with which to "carry water to give the whale a drink."

Land and sea were covered alike by ice and snow, but we knew we were on sea ice because we could see the Killigivuk house and remember how far the land extended when there was no snow. The air was of indescribable purity, and each breath filtered through frost crystals sifted to a rare fineness.

Choosy, Otoonah's white husky pup, followed us on the narrow trail. Otoonah led the way, walking faster than I, even though she was an old lady. At one point she turned around and retraced her steps, realizing she had taken the wrong trail.

This was my first experience on sea ice and at first it all looked alike to me. Near the shore were huge masses of blue pressure ice piled in ten-foot ridges, or higher, which formed a strange white ice world. It was an eerie feeling to know that we were walking out on the Chukchi Sea bordering the Arctic Ocean. To Eskimos sea ice is natural, an extension of solid ice on which they felt completely at home, since it is the source of all their food—seal, polar bear, walrus, whale, and fish—but to me it seemed strange, barren, and fearsome.

Blue chunks in strange shapes towered on both sides as we walked. My eyes were glued to Otoonah and the single trail. We saw no life in this ice world but an occasional flock of ducks overhead. I wondered if we might come upon a polar bear that had followed the open water looking for seals, and I imagined the bear would be a fatty yellow color distinguishable from the blue-white ice. Otoonah had walked on ahead and was out of sight. Picking my way carefully in the white expanse, I experienced moments of panic as I viewed the seascape in all directions and saw only the ice stretching endlessly in all directions. I knew that ridges and floes extended all the way to Siberia.

"Otoonah," I screamed as a furry yellow shape appeared from behind the jutting ice. My fears had been realized and I stood poised, defenseless, unsure of which way to run.

The furry form had shrunk in size when I opened my eyes and Choosy's friendly tail wagged before me. Far ahead a little blue-clad figure swung easily along in a rocking fashion. Otoonah stopped to take off her parka and sling it across her back while I quickened my steps to catch up, giving Choosy a disgusted look.

Several miles out we came upon Asatsiak and Tingook resting upon an ice block. Asatsiak carried his rifle across his back, horizontally balanced in the crook of his elbows; and Tingook carried his under his arm, for his small three-legged stool was strapped to his back. The stool is handy to sit on while waiting for seal on the ice. The farther we walked, the worse seemed the condition of the ice. Wide open cracks hampered us; if we had stepped off the trail, we would have sunk down up to our knees in ice water. As we approached a large open water hole, I asked Asatsiak, "How do we get across this hole?"

"Just follow my footsteps," was his advice as we slushed through the soft ice. "I took Rainey on seal hunt one time.

Tell him, follow me. Don't go off the trail, just follow me. He went off and fell in the water. I fish him out, save him." Asatsiak laughed at the memory. "He learn."

We had covered about six miles when the sun forced me to take off my heavy fur parka. Asatsiak tied the parka in two places with the string of my fur mitts, and I put my arms through the string and carried the parka like a knapsack.

Ahead lay an ice world of fantastic shapes, a universe of silence. The atmosphere created a peace not found in the woods. An Eskimo once told me he felt strange when he traveled through the forest where there was no ice. "I hate to spend the night among trees," he said. "They whisper and groan; it's a language I can't understand."

Sea ice spread before us endlessly to the horizon, meeting the pale sky, yet it had a variety of shapes and forms and I was beginning to even distinguish color. Its opaqueness had a variety of whiteness and variations that I would learn to read in the days ahead.

The ice muted sounds by absorbing them, yet any sound seemed clear as a bell. A sea gull swooped down and made an isolated curve above us in an eloquent gesture. I felt myself melting, blind to everything but hot sun and cold ice. This strange never-never world demanded everything of me, all feeling, all action, and left no room for other thoughts.

A spot far ahead turned out to be a black figure on a tall pressure ridge, the ice being about ten times taller than the man who clung to it. Coming closer we could see it was Ahksivvokrook's eldest sun scanning the distance to see how the wind was opening the ice.

Ahksivvokrook, Nathlook, their oldest son, and Koahk were scattered gypsy fashion on the ice. Their paraphernalia was spread all over the ice while they stopped to make tea. Their eight dogs were stretched out resting, tongues hanging out, while assorted boxes and gallon cans lay strewn about. Nathlook started the Coleman stove and set the kettle to boil. We had arrived just in time.

Packed cleverly on their rough sled was all the equipment needed for a journey on ice. In the umiak, which rested on a sledge with wooden runners, were caribou skins, darting guns, seal pokes, a three-legged stool, an ax, ropes, and raw beluga. In a homemade wooden box were flour, coffee, tea, lard, and some sugar. From this box Nathlook drew a loaf of bread and proceeded to cut thick slices with her ulu. Her baby's head rested on her naked brown shoulder; the little face lolled contentedly, its black hair moist from the heat of the mother's body. The strap that held the baby rested on the upper part of Nathlook's breasts, which seemed painful but may have made for better balance. Nathlook's stringy hair hung over her eyes as she presided over the stove, squatting on the ice puffing a cigarette.

When Otoonah walked into view, she was greeted with hoots of laughter by Nathlook and her family. I couldn't understand why until Nathlook pointed to her. "She look like Point Hope Lady, not Eskimo."

It was the pair of fashionable slanted sunglasses I had lent her; they dominated her face and clung precariously to the tip of her button nose. Under her regular sweater and skirt she was wearing the new dress I had given her, and the combination of slanted sunglasses and modern dress out on the ice was too much for the present party. They needed to laugh and laugh they did, rolling on the ice hysterically as Otoonah grinned delightedly like a child at the joke.

Nathlook poured us tea and served large slices of bread, after which the men went off by dog team to investigate the ice conditions. Her son came down from the high ridge to report that the nearest Eskimo camp was about a mile away.

"How can you tell?" I asked.

"I can tell by the barking of their dogs," he said, and with one graceful motion he pulled his parka over his head and ran about for the sheer pleasure of it. He frolicked and leaped over ice crevices in a sort of "ice ballet," seemingly unaware of us. Then, just as quickly he tired and, since there was nothing else to do, climbed into the umiak, curled up on a bed of caribou skins, an inflated seal poke under his head as a pillow, and was soon snoring in the sun.

Nathlook, Otoonah, and I settled ourselves for a long wait. I took the short three-legged stool out of the umiak and placed it in the snow. I tumbled off several times until I finally mastered the art by placing the legs firmly on the snow at the same time.

Nathlook's baby cried with hunger so she swung it around from back to front and let it nurse contentedly. After a few minutes she hastily plucked the infant from her breast and pulled off the cloth diaper, holding the little one between her legs over the ice.

"I do this since she's one month old." explained Nathlook. "In olden days we use dried soft moss for diaper, put in caribou fawnskin. Soft for baby." It was easy to see the necessity for early training when one carried a baby constantly on the back. When the baby again began to fret, Nathlook put her back in the warm nest of her back. Walking back and forth on the ice in a jigging, rocking fashion Nathlook began to sing an Eskimo lullaby. It was a soothing tune, unlike any lullaby I had ever heard.

The sun had left and in spite of heavy wool socks and caribou mukluks, my feet were cold, so I got up and stomped alongside of Nathlook.

Flocks of eider ducks were returning north, a welcome sign. The dogs were returning, bringing the men. "No whale, no lead, no use. We go back," Asatsiak reported.

Ahksivvokrook was silent; he wasn't too happy to have me along. He packed the sled with boxes in a certain order while Koahk fished out pieces of raw beluga muktuk for himself and his brother. He sliced off a hunk of meat on the sea ice, then gripped the muktuk in his teeth while he cut off a piece with his knife, letting the juice squirt over his chin.

Then we began the long haul home, forming a procession—first Nathlook with the sleeping baby on her back pulled the eight dogs to lead them on the trail, then came her husband, who stood on the runners of the sled, and next the older son guiding the sledge with the umiak on it.

Tingook and Asatsiak, the two old cronies, had decided to stay and salvage the rest of the day hunting eider ducks, so they settled themselves on the ice to wait, amusing each other with stories.

Choosy and Mako, another pup, were tied to a small sled which Koahk managed; neither dog had been trained and they tried to run in different directions. Otoonah and I helped to hold the back of the umiak steady on the sledge. Every once in a while when the dogs' going was smooth and fast, she swung her arms and body up onto the stern of the umiak and coasted like a child, swinging and bending her legs in the air. She hung on, grinning and enjoying the ride, until it got too rough; then she ran behind the umiak to hold on so that it would not tip over.

Nathlook kept running ahead of the team burdened by her baby; it seemed hard to understand why her husband didn't take her place and let her ride the sled. Women were never pampered even when pregnant, but even so her strength and endurance were incredible. I was puffing from exhaustion just holding on to the boat, and fell behind, forced to accept a ride with Koahk on the little sled pulled by pups. We took turns riding the sled but he managed the dogs better; when I took them, they tried to run off in the wrong direction.

After a few miles Ahksivvokrook pulled to a halt on the sea ice and readjusted the pack on his sled, studiously avoiding me. He was the master in charge of the expedition and it was his sled; I was an outsider and he had no particular fondness for white people. Most of the white men had paid him for dog team trips but Asatsiak had insisted I be treated like one of them.

Ahksivvokrook unloaded the umiak, the sleds, and the whaling supplies, and covered all with a tarp, leaving them in a safe place on his big sled the only transportation left.

I was at his mercy out on the ice. With nonchalance I

glanced off in another direction, waiting for him to make up his mind. If he didn't ask me to ride the sled home, I would walk back; after all, we had walked in that morning and I could follow the trail marks. Nathlook was the last to climb into the sled and sit down.

"Want a ride, Clara?" It was Ahksivvokrook. There was no use leaving me stranded on the ice if I didn't care. Without hesitation I jumped on the sled in front of Nathlook and rode all the way to Asatsiak's house.

I was burnt red from the sun and my eyes and leg muscles were tired. The oldest son came into the house for some coffee. On the ice he had acted coldly, tough as his father, his eyes a slit as he surveyed my useless presence there. He had a standard of his own, when I needed him, he could afford to be hard; but when he wanted my food, he could afford to be nice.

I remembered an incident on the ice. Nathlook had put a cigarette in her mouth and asked him for a match. As in a movie, she bent her head coquettishly and with a flirtatious look up through her lowered eyelashes had said, "Got a match, Bud?"

Then he had turned straight as a perfect gentleman, bowed and scraped the ice, "Here it is, madam."

Nathlook bowed to him in return and said, "Thank you," with elaborate courtesy.

At that they both laughed satirically, showing me a white man's world as seen through an Eskimo's eyes.

Ahksivvokrook's family felt hostile to me and they were contemptuous of Asatsiak's friendliness to me. When Asatsiak came home that evening with two ducks, his first words were, "I thought I saw your footsteps in the snow coming home," thus trying tactfully to find out if Ahksivvokrook had asked me to ride in the sled or if he had made me walk home.

"I rode home in the sled, Ahpah," I answered but Asatsiak shook his head in disbelief.

I slept that night with visions of ice floes and polar

bears, tossing restlessly, my face burning hot and my muscles aching.

The north wind blew and howled; the prayed-for whaling wind. It hit my face with Arctic force as I walked over to Alec Frankson's; he had promised to take me out to the whaling camp. Ah-gaik, her dress flapping in the wind, came running from their dome-shaped house to help us tie the dogs. One husky got loose and all three of us chased him around the house until Alec caught the wily culprit.

Finally Alec called the gruff signal and the dogs were off. We were soon gliding over the land ice and skimming out on sea ice, with Alec singing snatches of happy tunes and talking to the dogs.

The day smelled of promise, a crystalline day. The ice looked shiny from the sun and the trail had taken on sharp ridges worn by the many dogs. Eight miles out we heard the barking and howling of other dogs and soon we pulled up in front of a tent in the whaling camp.

For over a month every able-bodied hunter in the village had chopped and cleared the trail to make it wide enough for the loaded sledges. Now everyone was putting up a tent and getting the camp ready for a prolonged stay. The scene was a confusion of Eskimos, dogs, and tents. Some of the men were cutting chunks of ice to use as weights to which to tie the tent guy ropes, while others were staking out the dogs. I stood by bewildered, wondering what use my sketch pad and camera were to the rest of the community. I was dressed as an Eskimo, but my white face and gait made me feel strange and apart. There was no work for me to do to help set up camp and I was feeling useless when a heavy parka-clad figure came running up to me.

"I've been waiting to meet you," the woman said. "I'm Judith Allen, daughter of Quavuk of Noatak." I was drawn into her arms and the "apartness" vanished. Quavuk's daughter had her mother's warmth and spirit. The year before, her mother had taken the fur parka off her back to put on mine so I would not be cold and had shared her meager catch of fish with me.

Judith smiled at me warmly. "My mother told me about you, Clara, how you helped the women cut beluga at Sheshalik."

"How come you're at Point Hope?" I asked.

"This is our first time here. We promised the Noatakers we'd bring them back some muktuk. We came by dog team; it took a week because we stopped over at Kivalina."

"What happened?" I asked.

"We had lots of trouble this winter. Our little girl baby got sick one day, took fever and choked; we could do nothing for her. No doctor. When she got high fever, I brought her to the schoolteacher. It was at night, but there was no help but aspirin. She died. I cried and cried. Clarence planned this trip to help us forget our troubles. We brought our two-year-old girl with us on the sled. "That's my Clarence there unhitching the dogs." She pointed to an amiable man leaping nimbly among the dogs. "We never went whaling before. Our dogs are hungry but they won't eat seal meat, they are used to fish."

Clarence was having a hard time handling the dogs and Judith ran to help him, calling, "Come and visit our tent later."

Eskimo women in multicolored parkas were busy about their tents. In the midst of the activity I spotted Ahksivvokrook. He was calmly sleeping in his umiak, his head resting on a seal poke.

The largest tent was Donald Oktolik's. The stove was set up and the smoke of seal blubber came out of the pipe invitingly. Oktolik's wife, a strong, nicely made woman with a gentle voice, was stirring batter for bannock. Inside the tent to the right was a dog sled covered with caribou skins; to the left was a stove with about three inches of melted ice water around it; and in the back of the tent was an ice block elevation strewn with polar bear skins.

Mrs. Oktolik motioned me to come in and put down my gear on the dog sled. "Lots of room for you to sleep here." She pointed to the polar-bear skin bed. "The men will be out on the ice." I thanked her for the invitation and told her I would be back.

I followed Alec about half a mile from the tents out to the open lead. The ice was rough with big cracks showing greenish water below and as we came closer to the open water, the cracks became larger. I lifted my fur parka to jump across the wide gaps in the ice, and Alec warned, "Be careful, that ledge is sharp enough to crack a man's leg."

The open water, or lead, grew wider from the force of the north wind. Rotten bluish ice drifted away from the ice pack, widening the gap gradually until there was an opening of about half a mile wide.

Meanwhile back in the tents the women were cooking, water was boiling for tea, and seal meat was being prepared for the evening meal. Seal blubber, stored in tubs outside the tents was used for fuel as there was no wood.

The dogs growled and fought until a boy tumbled out of a tent to separate them. Dogs were not allowed too close to the open lead; in the past it had been taboo to bring them at all on a whaling expedition. Alec said: "We used to catch more whales before we brought the dogs." It was thought that the dogs' barking frightened off the whales.

Most of the women in the tents were the umeliks' wives and daughters, but there were a few unmarried woman who helped with the cooking and chores.

Out at the open lead some whale hunters were perched on high ridges looking through binoculars across the water for signs of whale blowing; other men carried and pushed umiaks, straining to bring the boats to open water. They were dressed for whaling in immaculate white drill parkas which they wore over their fur garments, and the umeliks were distinguished by a stripe of white fur at the tops of their mukluks. Each crew set its umiak down, poised near the water at a good vantage point, with the bow projecting over the water in order that they might push off instantly; the harpoon and guns were set pointing toward the open lead. Only then did the hunters sit down on the sledge to wait. They sat on caribou skins placing poles with long hooks behind the sledge.

Donald Oktolik's crew had the spot nearest the open trail leading back to the tents. His crew seemed to be perched on a precarious chunk of ice, yellow and rotten behind them and not connected very well. As I stepped onto it, I felt it could take off into open water with a strong wind behind it, but Oktolik, an experienced umelik, had chosen his spot, testing and knowing the thickness of the ice.

He had chosen his crew from Point Hope and Kotzebue, and it included his brother John who ran the native store and three relatives from Kotzebue. The young Kotzebue hunters stared hypnotically at the water, refusing to look at me; they weren't too happy about having a strange white woman around. The umelik, didn't mind my presence, so I sat down quietly on the sledge.

I took off my fur parka since it was warm and under it shone my bright red windbreaker. When Oktolik saw the red windbreaker, he immediately made a strong stipulation: "Take it off." I hid the offending jacket without a word. The Kotzebue men looked at Oktolik as if to say, "She just got here and look what she did. She'll cost us the whale yet!" I tried to shrivel into the sledge, sitting on a small corner.

As time wore on I sat silently, unmoving. Some of the men lit pipes, others lay back on the skins for a short nap. The wind pushed the lead wider and wider as we sat for hours facing the sun's reflection on the ice and water.

It is favorable for whaling when the lead is not too wide, for the whale must pass close to the ice to make it easier for the men to approach it. Strong north winds can break up the ice, rendering it unsafe and forcing the crews to go ashore even when there is plenty of open water.

All of the hunters, each umelik and his crew of from

Daniel Lisbourne

five to ten men, were by now stationed around the open
lead. Some of the crews paddled by in their skin boats looking for a better vantage point on the ice. The water reflected
their bent white figures and pensive dark faces, as they
glided by in their umiaks, a scene reminiscent of a Japanese watercolor. It was dreamlike, the stillness broken only
by the dipping of the paddles.

The Allens and their crew paddled by and Judith
waved. Ahksivvokrook walked by on the ice with his sons
carrying behind him their umiak. Asatsiak was nowhere to
be seen but Otoonah came into view perched on a cake of
ice. She didn't recognize me as I was now wearing one of
the hunter's extra white drill parkas, my hair hidden in the
hood, hoping to make my presence unobtrusive. If only I
were invisible! The sun was so strong that my eyes were
glazed, my cheeks burning. Staring constantly into the
water for signs of whale had a strong hypnotic effect.

Sitting there for hours I had memorized Oktolik's
umiak, a symmetrical work of art fashioned from sealskin
and wood. The wooden frame was about forty years old and
still sturdy, although it had never seen paint or varnish. The
driftwood oars had been sanded smooth and they rested in
the sinew thongs. The skins enveloping the frame were soft
and white, the stitches holding the skins together invisible.
The boat was watertight, and the lashings would give, not
break under rough ice. Rifles, shells, darting gun, gloves,
inflated seal pokes, three-legged stools, fathoms of rope, and
long gaffs were placed in the umiak in an orderly fashion so
that the men would know exactly where to reach for what
was needed.

Oktolik passed me his binoculars to let me view four
belugas cavorting in and out of the water, young whales
diving in plain sight of the hunters. Two shots and one
beluga was dead; the others quickly disappeared.

The beluga was pulled out of the water onto the ice
and dragged off to the tents on a trail that had turned from
white to shiny yellow from continued use. The ugruk soles

of the people had polished each chunk of ice and a trail of beluga and seal blood was now beginning to stain the ice red. It looked as though the hunters would supply the women with meat for the evening meals.

Several of the young boys had stayed out of school to help the crews; they kept the blubber fires going, made trips into the village to pick up additional clothing or supplies, and occasionally prepared food or tea.

Donald Oktolik's son, who was fourteen, bailed out the melted ice water under the stove. His job was to keep the tubs filled with ice for drinking and cooking. If the crew was shorthanded, he could sit with them when the whale was sighted and by observing them, learn how to hunt whale.

"When I first sat in the back of the umiak with the crew," he said, "I rowed fine until we saw the whale and then I started to row backwards as hard as I could. I tried to get away from the whale. My father laughed at me afterwards."

Another chore for the boys was to feed the dogs and to separate those that fought. One lone dog of the Noatak team had the temerity to break loose and eat the fresh beluga one of the woman had set out. The woman screamed and everyone ran out of the tents to watch the loose dog running in circles, then all bedlam broke loose when the rest of the team escaped and came after the beluga meat pulling the sled. A young girl grabbed the sled handles as they went by but she couldn't control the dogs even though everyone shouted advice. She hung on to the sled and the dogs barely missed the tents. Oktolik's boy kicked the dogs away from the meat and I tried to help by picking the meat up but it kept slithering away. The huskies made off with some beluga and a crowbill duck that was to have been made into soup that evening; finally Clarence came and stopped the dogs.

The woman whose meat it was gave the dogs a sour look as she picked up the meat and salvaged the rest of the ducks, dropping them down again on the ice close to the tent flaps. Outside the tent lay caribou skins, wet pants, mukluks, anything that didn't fit in the tent was dropped outside of it.

Judith and Clarence's tent rested on a wide section of ice that was cracked down the middle.

"That's not safe, is it?" I commented, visualizing the ice parting in the middle of the night and setting the occupants adrift. Judith confided that their camp had been purposely built over the crack since it was easier for throwing away garbage and for urinating. "It's handy!" she remarked.

However, old hunters such as Asatsiak took a dim view of the large cracks in the ice. "It's not safe," he said. "If the wind changes, ice go out." He gestured to show how the ice chunks could separate along the wide cracks if the wind got stronger.

The hunters could jump into their boats but how could the women and dogs be saved in such an eventuality? They could not run back to shore fast enough as the route might become separated from the main ice. There were several feet of water above the ice in places and it did look dangerous even to my inexperienced eyes. There were about seventy-five people on the ice and about that many dogs. The men had been hunting at the open leads for a month now and not one large whale had yet been caught. How long would they have to wait and how long would the ice stand up as the weather turned warm in the month of May?

CHAPTER 22

Waiting for Whales

Greater grew my fear
When the fresh-water ice split in the cold,
And the frost-crack thunderously grew
Up over the heavens.

THE ICE CRACKS widened each day. If these precarious ice conditions worried the hunters, they did not show it. They knew it was getting late

in the season but they knew they must have a whale in order
to exist, for their children were hungry in the village. They
were determined to stand resolute for as long as necessary,
never moving far from their stations while they waited, and
waited and waited, scanning the open lead.

Each took a turn standing on the high ridge of ice with
binoculars, a one-man sentinel, lonely against the gray sky.
The rest of the crew took turns sleeping on the sledge.
Oktolik the umelik stood watch pacing in a circle, never
taking his eyes from the sea. I tried to sleep for a while
curled up on the caribou skins but did not want to miss
anything.

The Kotzebue hunters were growing amiable toward
me, my silence convincing them of my obedience; humility
was earning me the privilege to participate. The men joked
and talked only in whispers.

"Wake me if you see a whale," I whispered to the
Kotzebue hunter.

He said he would, but in the established manner. Eskimos never make a sound when a whale is sighted; they
just grab hold of a sleeping person's arm or leg and shove
him awake. He told me that the Point Barrow whalers never
take a woman with them because the ice is so dangerous;
they prefer to set up their own tents and do their own
cooking.

"Have any of the Point Hope women ever hunted
whale?"

"Only one that I know of," he said. "Dinah Frankson. A
long time ago I heard stories about a famous woman whaler,
but I don't remember them."

At night it became darker and colder as the sun lowered. It
did not set out of sight and would not disappear during the
whole month of May. All day the hunters had soaked up
its warmth, lovingly turning their faces to it, while I had
tried to protect my pink skin, knowing the penalty I would
pay. Their dark faces and eyes had a natural resistance to
sun which mine did not; and their faces had burned a deep

brown-black while mine had grown steadily redder. Their cheekbones seemed to project more sharply and their deep-set eyes had sunk deeper into the frosted fur rimming their faces.

The hunters changed into warmer clothing—seal, caribou, or polar bear pants and extra socks under their mukluks. For the most part they sat patiently and silently on the sledge, their faces set and stern, their eyes and ears sharp for only one thing: whales! They strained to see or hear a black shape leap from the water, a flash of flukes, a sign of spouting, any sign.

My legs were cramping and stiffening so I got up and walked back to the tents, guilty over not helping more with the cooking, but I did not want to miss seeing the whales. In the tent I put on my sealskin pants and added caribou-skin socks.

When I sat with the men again, the lead had opened to about six miles in length. The evening was still except for the call of the sea gulls, but as the sun hid behind the reddened ridges a flock of guillemots suddenly appeared.

It was about two A.M. when I went back to the tents, but Oktolik's son was already asleep, curled up on a caribou skin near the fire. He had come in and dropped in his tracks, falling asleep immediately with no covering over him, his ragged jacket inadequate in the cold night. Black curly hair hung over his forehead and he slept with the same good-natured expression that he had worn all day as he carried out his many duties.

His mother slept soundly on polar-bear skins on the raised block of ice. I threw my extra sleeping bag over her peaceful form and lay down fully dressed in my other one on the dog sled, ready to leave at a moment's notice. In spite of long underwear, sealskin pants, and a muskrat parka under the down sleeping bag, I shivered, finally covering myself with a caribou skin and sleeping fitfully. According to Stefansson I should have taken all my clothes off and then crept into the sleeping bag.

The boy awoke several hours later with his jacket

Waiting for Whales

sleeve soaking wet, having lain in the ice water near the stove all night. When I reminded him to dry his jacket before going out, he just shrugged.

"Boys!" I muttered and tried to go back to sleep.

But sleep was impossible, although it was about four-thirty in the morning. Five youngsters who had played hooky from school were outside the tent having the time of their lives. They had no idea I was awake.

One boy presided on a caribou skin with five others sprawled around him. Pulling out a deck of cards he dealt them to each boy with a flourish; then placing a pair of large glasses on the tip of his short nose, he jerked his collar up and pulled his hair down over his eyes. The boys giggled in expectation.

"Now, youall, youall boys," he began. I recognized the Southern accent of one of the schoolteachers. He went on in the best Alice in Wonderland nonsense tradition, mimicking the teacher while the other boys rolled on the ice in fits of laughter.

Next came a parody on rock 'n' roll sung in a quavering falsetto while the listeners frolicked and tumbled, whooping it up while Oktolik's wife slept. True Eskimos could sleep or stay awake all night but I threw the covers over my head to drown out the racket.

The youngest Kotzebue hunter came in to change his wet mukluks at about five thirty in the morning, having slept all night at the open lead. He stirred up the fire by adding blubber and filled the kettle with ice water. Groggy and bleary eyed, I watched him take a handful of tea leaves, throw them into the pot, and stir and stir as the tea boiled until I thought it would never be done. Finally he offered me a cupful and it did live up to its reputation as the strongest, darkest brew I had ever swallowed. It got me up and I combed my hair (breaking a taboo); it was a mess. A dash of ice water on my face served for the morning wash.

We carried the teakettle, sugar, and cups to the men who had slept the night with a pillow of ice under their heads. When we appeared they told us, "No whales yet."

The silent watch continued. Every man's eye focused on the water and in the distance we could see water spouting and the noise of it came softly. At first I couldn't hear it, then the hunters pointed to their ears, meaning, "Listen." A sound like "pooouf" came to my ears.

The men tensed in prayerful attitudes. The whale had sounded and gone, the crew nearest to it on the other side of the lead had taken off but we saw it come back. No luck.

The previous night three crews had taken off after a whale and the whale had also escaped. One of the crews had a strange experience; the whale had come right up under the ice near them and while they ran to the umiak prepared to strike, the whale had sounded below. When the whale came up again, it aimed right for the boat. Instead of overturning it, however, the whale's back supported it and the hunters, balanced and ready, remained on the massive back until the whale went under again and out of sight. They could not strike in that position but remained unharmed while the whale escaped. The boat smashed and grated against the ice but the skin was slippery and did not break as wood would have done.

"The whale knew we were waiting there for him," one of the men said. "He tried to smash the boat against the ice. We were lucky."

No one could remember anyone's being killed by a whale in their lifetime but one forty-year-old man recalled that his grandfather had been killed by a whale. The whale lifted his skin boat into the air and tossed it; five crew members had drowned.

The hunters stretched out again with their feet hanging over the sledge; they never showed impatience, or talked about "luck," but always showed extraordinary patience at waiting—the skill of a lifetime. Ice glided softly out to sea, breaking off with a "sppplishhhh."

Ducks flew in formation overhead and the call of sea gulls and crowbills broke the stillness when an occasional shot hit its mark. The waiting was not dramatic or tense, but natural, the natural waiting of the land and its people, as natural as the small darkness of birds that appeared on the horizon and grew in magnitude and then disappeared again.

Oktolik's wife and her young son brought the evening meal along with a printed calico bag filled with plates, cups, and spoons. A three-foot wooden board was the table and our supper was boiled beluga muktuk soup with macaroni. For an extra treat our cook had made doughnuts fried in seal oil. The small, round, cut-out centers floated in the soup. Our crew was well fed, finishing each meal with strong black coffee served in thick mugs. The night before, we had boiled seal meat with rice, and Mrs. Oktolik had picked out the choice fin for me. The duck soup was delicious; everyone relished it, leaving only a pile of clean bones.

Once a wounded black and white crowbill came drifting down in the water; someone had been unable to retrieve him, so Oktolik fished him out with a hook on the end of a string. The poor crowbill was half dead and bled on the ice, his bill shaking with his convulsions while a mile away his mate called piteously. Old Kovanna, one of the Kotzebue hunters, told me his mother used to make him good warm socks from crowbill feathers.

Most of the time I sat quietly, but I couldn't resist a giggle when it came time to get up from the low sledge in my tight sealskin pants, for it took some effort. The giggle sounded and broke the stillness. Hours of continuing silence with only a whisper now and then were hard on a woman. Whales have small riduculous ears for their huge size, but they hear everything. I wanted the whale to come badly, if only to show that I was not—and my mind wouldn't let me think the word—a jinx.

I asked the youngest Kotzebue hunter a question: "How come, out of all the men that hunt, Daniel Lisbourne always gets a whale?"

"Because whales like certain men," he answered seri-

Daniel waiting for whaler

ously. Daniel was a good hunter, reliable and strong, and a leader in the community.

Some time after we finished the evening meal, the minister drove out by dog team to see how the whalers were doing. He had come to spend the night and had brought his own bearskin rug to sleep in. If only his presence helped the men to strike a whale, I prayed.

The sledge was full now with the minister on it. "No room for a woman," Oktolik said, pointing to the tents. "You sleep in the tent," he ordered, and that was that.

I walked back about fifteen feet and stood on a large piece of ice, reluctant to leave. An occasional umiak glided over the water, the men paddling in unison. The red sun sank near the horizon between ice ridges, giving the illusion of squareness as it went down between two icebergs. The redness was vivid and I wanted to absorb it, living as I had for so long with the whites and grays of the stark landscape. The gray-white cliffs carved in intricate forms turned pink as the sun turned the hummocks bright with light.

It was an unforgettable sight and I didn't want to leave, so I lay on the wooden board we had used for a table and tried to sleep with my head on a snowbank.

South wind and fog found the hunters resting in the damp air—still waiting. The open lead had threaded and widened as far as the eye could see. It reflected none of the blue sky overhead, perhaps because above it hovered the fog, that smoky barometer registering open water.

Kovanna, the Kotzebue hunter, cut large squares of ice and put them behind the sledge with two upright gaffs at either end supporting a canvas windbreaker. The men slept on that icy ledge wrapped in furs while Oktolik kept a walking watch in the early morning. Hoarfrost had covered the men's fur ruffs and eyebrows while they slept.

The south wind caused the ice to move closer, lessening imperceptibly the width of the lead. Several spouting whales had been sighted but disappeared before the men could get after them. The water was quiet, the run of whales had come and gone, and they had missed them.

We heard a straggler whale spout and then the massive hulk of black flesh writhed in the water, his flukes slashed out, and his head rose up threatening and gigantic. The umiaks took off, the men padding fast after the black shape, but the small ears were alert and the whale disappeared down into the darkness, giving us a glimpse of tantalizing tons of food.

I gripped the wooden sledge tensely on shore as the men paddled back. The other crews had also seen the whale and the explosion had gone off but missed. The men waited for another chance but none came.

No more whales ran through the lead—the wind was against the whalers. It played havoc with the rotten ice, forcing new cracks. The south wind was closing the lead and the hunters looked up at the fog and the leaden skies and shook their heads in disappointment. One by one, independently, the crews decided to take the umiaks and return to land ice. They packed the furs and other supplies in the umiaks, put the umiaks on their wooden sledge runners and pushed it all back over the cracks and soft ice to where the women waited. They too had read the warning signs and were packing everything, including the tents, onto the dog sleds. Oktolik's wife and I gathered up the stove, clothing, even the pot of boiled muktuk, and put it on the sled.

The dogs began to bark, eager to begin the trek home, and one after another the people left the treacherous ice. The Allens offered me a ride since the Oktoliks had a heavier load. The ice looked as though a good stiff wind would push it out to sea with all of us standing on it!

The Noatak team of one-and-a-half-year-old huskies were large and strong with black and white markings. Judith and I climbed on the sled and before Clarence could give the signal, the dogs were off. He had just time to grab the sled handle, for the dogs, unused to sea ice conditions, ran wildly ahead, knocking down the lines of the neighboring tent and collapsing it. As we rounded the curve, an Eskimo woman stood with her arms over her head ready to catch the weight of the tent poles falling around her. Another woman opened her mouth in disbelief as we sped out of sight down the narrow ice ridged trail.

Judith and I sat down with a thump on the sled, I on some sleeping bags and Judith on boxes behind me. We were violently thrown from side to side and leaped in the air with each thrust. Crash! I thought my neck would break in mid-air; we felt in danger of our lives. Coming in with Alec had been child's play compared to the reckless speed at which we now traveled.

Carelessly the dogs crashed around the curves between huge ice cakes with the sled half turned on edge. We leaned with all our weight on the opposite side to right the sled. It was hard to see how Clarence remained with us; he had lost control of the dogs completely.

Judith kept mumbling, "They are ruining the sled, they are ruining the sled!"

This diverted our minds temporarily from our own danger. The sled, a beautiful piece of craftsmanship, crumbled as the front bow smashed in and the sides scarred and broke as it jarred against the sharp ice edges. The Point Hope sleds were crude and functional and now I know why.

The dogs took us right through open water over huge cakes of ice and bounced us down over larger ones. When we hit level ice again, I leaned back against Judith and breathed more easily. Every once in a while she peered over my ruff at my face.

Clarence was hanging on with a grim grip and when we came upon another team, without halting to let it pass our dogs ran full speed ahead. Both teams bottlenecked between two huge wedges of pressure ice, the only trail. The Noatak dogs had no sense of sportsmanship at all; they were hopelessly wolfish and solved the problem by simply running over the other huskies. Our sled runners, with three passengers and about half a ton of boxes, went right over three of the dogs' bodies and heads. I winced, imagining bones crushing and turned expecting to see bloody dogs dying, their bones broken beyond recognition. It was amazing but they hardly yelped as they pushed on behind us.

Clarence had no time to turn around and apologize to the driver or even see the damage, as our dogs took a wrong turn onto rotten ice. We thought we would sink but speed made up for direction as we flew over the water and made it to land ice.

When we were safe on land and Clarence had finally stopped the dogs, we got out gingerly to feel our bones. Later Judith related to everyone, "I thought we'd be killed and I looked at her and she never minded!" What else could I do!

The short-wave broadcast that night brought news of an Eskimo couple in Kivalina who had perished out on the sea ice. The ice had broken away and they had drowned.

CHAPTER 23 *Wind, Snow, Rain, and Sleet*

My face is turned from the dark of night
My gaze toward the dawn,
Toward the whitening dawn.

OTOONAH WITH WATERY EYES
and a towel wrapped around her hair stuck her head in my
door. "Coffee?"

"Is everyone up?"

She answered with a shake of her head.

"Did the wind change?"

"*Nahka*," she replied in Eskimo.

I looked out the window but could see nothing, no horizon, no meeting of sky and land, just a "whiteout," so I crawled into the sleeping bag to snooze some more. I woke an hour later, washed, and creamed my face, which was getting rough from the wind.

No whaling that day. The wind howled and twisted in a gray-white snowstorm. We heard the Kotzebue weather forecast over the short-wave set: "Wind, rain, snow, and sleet!" Of course no planes could land. Asatsiak had gone duck hunting despite the weather.

The men's faces looked gaunt; they had been hunting all night for seal. Our neighbors had dragged home two seals, one for the dogs and one for themselves.

While I was eating my mush and coffee, Rosa came over to visit. She told me she had stayed up late the night before playing "Big Clara" with the other kids.

" 'Big Clara' !" I asked naïvely, "What game is that?"

"Oh you know, we play we are you. I be Big Clara, and the other children follow me around." With coaxing, Rosa proceeded to show me how she walked like me, her little mukluk'd feet taking big steps pointed outward as she carried a sketch pad and pretended that the other children were marching behind her!

Otoonah patched my furs; I had torn the parka during the race back to the village. She had been scraping muskrat skins for Asatsiak's parka, using a handmade stone scraper sharpened to an edge. I watched her sew the skins together with sinew with tiny stitches, exactly alike.

Ahksivvokrook and Asatsiak were discussing the new Assembly of God church. "It's fun; it's lively. The minister plays the guitar and sings good, but you can't smoke or play cards in that church."

Ahksivvokrook picked his teeth with a sliver of wood. "Can't chase around any more, says the minster."

I looked at him and said, "I doubt if that would stop you," and he grinned slyly.

The Assembly of God minister's son was not living with his parents but with an Eskimo family in a sod house "because he smoked." I had met the tall pale boy in the store and he had offered to carry my groceries.

I roamed the village all day while it snowed miserably. The children followed me. "Don't you have to go home and eat?" I asked.

One of the girls indignantly told me, "Eskimos don't eat like that."

Koahk interrupted her. "Eskimos only eat when they're hungry!"

Only Koahk accompanied me the length of the village, as it was dark and I was afraid of the dogs.

At Killigivuk's I shared some canned spinach and boiled muktuk with Koahk; then I flopped into bed and fell asleep. When I awoke, Koahk was still there, sitting in the kitchen. I gave him some peanuts and as he went out the door he called: "Remember, Clara, I was your first friend here."

Otoonah made bread in her large bowl that she kept under my cot, so I offered to bake a pie with dried apples that I had bought at the store. I thought Asatsiak and Eugene would enjoy it and Otoonah had never tasted apple pie. Mixing the flour, lard, and water, I simmered the apples at the back of the stove while Otoonah kneaded bread. Since I had no rolling pin, I patted the dough with my hands; a milk can would have been fine but I did not think of that until it was too late. I put the pie and apple filling in a bread pan and then cut strips for the top. The "pie" baked in the oven along with her bread. Otoonah tasted it cautiously, none of the Killigivuks enjoyed it as much as I did.

Otoonah and I could not converse with each other, but I had a deep compassion for her. The night before she had coughed all night as she lay on the floor, her chest badly congested. I had given her a jar of mentholatum to rub on her chest but she took it suspiciously; I doubted she would use it.

Otoonah used seal oil as a cure-all for most illnesses. I remembered the red flannel, the mustard plaster, the goose grease, and camphorated oil of my youth. We once had a neighbor who made poultices of flannel combined with thin slices of salt pork and onions sprinkled with black pepper.

Asatsiak was not home when I came in at night but was out playing pinochle with his cronies. His son was sitting up and smiled strangely when I asked, "Where is Asatsiak?"

Otoonah was asleep on her mat under the table and without the old man at home I felt strange.

Gene now replied, "Asatsiak is in your bed."

I quickly walked past him to my room, shut the door, and stood behind it. I kept my parka on, too uncomfortable to stay, but it was too late and dark to go anywhere. Where could I go?

Asatsiak finally came home and then I unrolled the sleeping bag and lay down fearfully without saying a word. With Asatsiak there I felt less unwelcome. Gene had gone to bed and pretended to be asleep; and if Otoonah had heard anything, she did not say.

I got up early the next day and left the house without breakfast. Asatsiak had gone out early again to go duck hunting. Otoonah followed me out to the door, for she knew immediately that I was leaving; our eyes met and without a word she understood.

The Assembly of God minister greeted me as I walked toward the village. He remembered me from the year before and when I told him of my predicament he said warmly: "We have a spare bedroom now that my son is gone. Why don't you come and stay with us?"

I did not need to be invited twice since space was at a premium and every house full, so I carried my gear over. They had built a new house which was a large room sectioned off in back into two bedrooms and an indoor bath.

My room was magnificent by village standards as the double bed had a box spring and comfortable mattress and stood about four feet high! Underneath the bed was a year's supply of canned stuffs, everything from nuts and dried onions to cake mix. They had come well supplied and I could not help noting the comparison with Eskimo homes, which held very little canned food but usually only staples like flour, sugar, tea, and coffee. Canned butter, jam, or even canned milk for the children was a luxury.

The comfortable house with many windows was heated by a large oil stove. A modern gas cookstove, modern kitchen sink, cupboards, and an indoor chemical toilet made it attractive. I thanked them for the loan of the bed and hoped not to inconvenience them, explaining that I would be out on the ice watching the whalers and would be gone most of the day.

I spent part of the day out of doors sitting on an empty oil drum in the center of the village, sketching the men as they sauntered by with their hands in their pockets. I sketched Ah-gaik's house with the children playing in the snow, the staked dogs, and the snow-covered roof.

The children held their positions and I could draw them quickly, using the felt pen boldly, then watercolors sparingly. My hands were freezing without gloves so I went into the store to warm up, sketching there for a while, perched on a case of milk. The store was full of people passing the time and the men clustered around the hot stove, hands in pockets, talking casually in Eskimo, about whaling no doubt.

Tingook was in the store and as he placed his few groceries in a bag and slung it over his shoulder, I asked him if he could come to pose for me. I had wanted to paint him from the first time I had watched him dance and seen his fine face. It was as if I knew how the painting would look and the feeling had crystallized within me. He promised to come the next afternoon to the minister's house.

When Tingook came, I seated him in the late afternoon

light streaming in the window with his head lifted as if in the dance. It was a pleasure to paint his fine, spirited, wrinkled face as it was beautiful, his goodness shining like a prayer unspoken. I painted him while he told me in broken English that he was an orphan boy from Kobuk village who came to Point Hope when he was fourteen.

"What does Tingook mean?" I asked.

"It mean seal liver," he replied.

He told me little things about his life. "I see first white man when I am eight. Those days we make nets of willow branches tied together to catch fish in the Kobuk River. Size of net," he measured with his hands, "was so big! When I come to Point Hope they make nets of stripped baleen. . . . Me and Asatsiak shipped with *Karluk* whaling boat in 1900. We travel to Banks Island. I met Stefansson; he spoke good Eskimo. Sang Eskimo songs with the people."

Tingook's head nodded and he fell asleep. The wrinkles, the sparse faint gray whiskers, the white hair bushing out from his short sloping forehead, the half-closed joyous eyes, and the mouth as if to sing, all painted themselves; the brush seemed to know everything. A song, an Eskimo song, seemed to burst from his heart, his head seemed about to move in dance, to the drums of his youth. Old Tingook was the beloved man of Point Hope, even though some of the people still called him after forty years "That Kobuk Man."

Since I had deliberately invited Tingook to pose for me and he had left his own chores I paid him for his time, made lunch for us both, then washed the brushes in turpentine while Tingook went to the store to spend his earnings.

A hunter was returning empty-handed from the ice, his face brown from the sun. He was a handsome young Eskimo from another village, whose two wives had died and left him three children. His first wife had died of pneumonia and the other of a freak accident. His brother had fired a shot that went right through the house, through the walls into the bed where she lay asleep. He was now contemplating marriage again with a Point Hope girl who had borne him a child. He confessed that he was afraid to take another chance after the two tragedies.

I noticed a few of the hunters had red lips; they had found that a good prevention against chapping and blistering: lipstick!

The Kotzebue dentist, Dr. Lathrop, was at Point Hope for a week, working in the building behind the church; he gave the children Novocain injections and filled their teeth. The Eskimos received free dental and medical care from the federal government. The dentist said that their once perfect teeth were getting worse each year because of their consumption of candy and sugar. He asked me if I had met Macheena, the old hunter who was supposed to be about one hundred years old. "You should really draw him," he urged.

Donald Oktolik's wife accompanied me to Macheena's house, where he lay on a bed in a small back room. The place was crowded with eight people of three generations; behind one curtain a young hunter lay asleep.

Since Macheena understood very little English, Mrs. Oktolik explained the object of the visit. Macheena had been a superb hunter until he became ill and bedridden. Propping himself up on one elbow, his shrunken shoulders barely supporting him, he looked at me with great interest. A shock of gray hair hung over his withered lined face and sunken eyes, and his mouth twisted to one side slackly. Surprisingly his cheeks were smooth. Behind him on the wall was a large cross. I sketched the old hunter in that pose with the cross in the background. I slipped some money under his pillow and went into the other room.

The family invited me to a snack of tea, doughnuts, and store cheese. Their daughter, just returned from Mt. Edgecumbe School, put on a parka for the first time that year, strapped a baby to her back, and walked out in the snow with her new red shoes.

Pt. Hope at break-up time

I had many new impressions to digest, wandering, roaming the village with my sketch pad, alive to everything. I was "Big Clara" to the children as they followed in my tracks through the snow. The wind and sleet had lashed the village and the whalers had to confine their activities to hunting seal, since there was still no open lead for whales.

A restlessness was apparent in the village, an unspoken struggle, the continual search for food.

Back in my room I watched the teen-agers coming home late from the beach after midnight. It was getting bright, the fog had lifted, and a pink cast enveloped the sky. The whole village lay bathed in its light, the little houses, nestled in the snow, with the silhouettes of whalebones projecting against the sky. Perhaps our luck was changing; perhaps a new day would bring the change of wind!

The dogs' howling woke me; they had chewed through their harnesses and broken away from their chains to get at some caribou meat hanging near the house. They had half-chewed through a caribou leg before the minister came and tied them up again.

The spacious room of the Assembly of God church-home was a fine place to paint, and all visitors were cordially welcomed. Koahk's mother and father came to see me and Anahkaloktuk and her baby. It was their first visit and we had coffee.

Ahksivvokrook picked up my camera asking, "How much is this?"

"I paid thirty dollars for it secondhand." It was an old Ikoflex.

"That would be three dog team rides out to the ice," he hinted.

"I'll never ride with you." I replied.

Undaunted he threw back his head and laughed. Anahkaloktuk sat placidly, while I did a drawing of her holding out her arms to her baby.

I had been drawing a lot and my work was crystallizing, flowing easily and expressively. Gone was any hesitation; I was unconscious of drawing, it had become second nature.

Everyone waited for a change in the weather, scanning the clouds constantly. Should it warm up too fast, the ice would melt and break too early. What if the whales were late this year? The villagers' food supply was running low and the evening soup had little meat in it unless one of the hunters had shot a duck.

Asatsiak and Tingook had been up at five every morning to hunt ducks in all weather but without success. The families were sharing every bit of meat, stretching it out. If one hunter was lucky, he shared his catch; another day he came home empty-handed and was given meat.

A bad rumor circulating in the village turned out to be true. The young U. S. Fish and Wildlife man who had arrived in the village told the people it was illegal to hunt ducks out of season! The Eskimos had always hunted ducks in the spring; it was their way of life. Larders were lowest in the spring before the whales came and the ducks provided a change in their diet from seal meat. It was shocking news. "What are our children going to eat now?" The women asked: "We have no money."

The weather continued with strong winds that made whaling impossible; the men watched for a change of wind.

One afternoon some little girls came into the house and noticed a caribou joint with some shreds of raw meat on it sitting on the cupboard. The children got very excited over the bone and offered to get a rock to crack it; then taking the bone outside they broke it open and fought over the raw marrow, their favorite food. The children lived with their grandparents, having been given away by their mother who had no husband. The minister's wife cooked the rest of the caribou scraps with the leftover gravy and gave it to the little ones, who acted as if they had not had a meal all day, which perhaps they had not. These good people fed a few children each day. I also shared my food with the children, usually carrying dried apricots or dried apples in my pockets. A little boy came to the door crying that something was wrong at home but would not say what. He was given milk and a sandwich by the minister's wife.

Restlessness and hunger drove the hunters farther and farther from the village to hunt, and they came back tired, many without game, and with empty stomachs.

A boy walked into the minister's home and stood there uncertainly. It was the first time he had come and we wondered what errand had brought him. His hair reached his shoulders, giving him a peculiarly feminine look, and his wide-set eyes stared out of his bony ridged face, one eye moving far out like an Indian Yoga's. Finally he whispered to the minister's wife that he would like her to cut his hair. She had cut some of the other children's hair and he had heard about it.

She answered: "I will if you'll wash out the grease."

He ran home and said he would be back. I had noticed the boy earlier; he was one of Koahk's brothers. The minister told me the boy had been away in the hospital with TB and confined to bed for a long time. When he returned, he had lain in his father's house in a lice-ridden corner in the darkness, perhaps remembering the whiteness of the hospital, the nurses, and the three meals a day. He was better now but terribly thin, although he managed the dog team, was able to get driftwood and water and hunt a bit.

Only the day before I had passed Nathlook's hut and noticed them clustered around the dog team. I saw Koahk throwing something and as I walked closer observed a large bearded seal lying on the snow, its head bloody but still breathing.

Nathlook explained proudly: "Tula got his first ugruk." Usually he looked abject, pitiful, but now he looked proud, lifting his head.

Tula told me what happened. "I went out hunting with the dogs for driftwood and came across this large ugruk on the ice. I lifted a piece of wood and beat it on the head, smashing the brain; then I put it on the sled and raced home." It was a huge bearded seal. I could not see how he could have lifted it alone.

Koahk threw another rock at the seal and I scolded him, watching the animal breathing weakly and feeling pity for the beast in its pain. One of the polar-bear hunters came over and said: "Why don't you put it out of its misery?" But Ahksivvokrook was not going to waste a shell and just shrugged. A younger brother picked up a large rock and aimed it at the exposed bloody skull of the beast.

The polar-bear hunter in desperation drew out his knife to stab the seal in the neck to kill it, but his hand could not do the job. He stopped in mid-air and said lamely: "I guess I'd spoil the skin."

When I walked away, the family was still contemplating the ugruk proudly. I did not want to be there for the bitter end.

Tula came the next evening for his haircut.

The minister's wife placed a towel around his thin shoulders and began to cut his hair. Some children had followed me into the house for an art lesson. I diverted their attention so that Tula would have some privacy as the long, still greasy black hair fell in thick clusters all over the clean floor. He had come in long-haired and was soon transformed into a modern boy with short-cropped hair.

I heard his "barber" say: "Your hair is still too stiff; let me get it wet," and putting his head into a basin of hot water she proceeded to scrub it, knowing that with the scarcity of snow water he had not done a good job. She washed his ears and neck too for good measure, scrubbing hard, then dried his hair with the towel, parted it and slicked it back neatly as a trained barber would have done. She gave him a mirror so that he could see the results.

When the job was done, Tula sat down in a chair in a corner of the room and proceeded to read a comic book while the children and I kept busy drawing on white paper at a table. The room was full of that pleasant hum and busy scratching of pens and crayons. I happened to look up for a minute and saw the sixteen-year-old Tula, not reading at all, but staring at the book while tears coursed down his cheeks. Perhaps he was remembering something out of his past; except for me, no one noticed.

CHAPTER 24 *Give Us This Day*

Aja'—ja'—japape!
Hard times, dearth times
Plague us every one,
Stomachs are shrunken,
Dishes are empty.
Aja'—ja'—japape!
Aja'—ja'—japape!

IT WAS SUNDAY, a clear bright day but windy; the people were going to the Episcopal church, pouring out of every entranceway with the same destination. Hunters loped across the village in clean parkas, hands in pockets, children and wife following.

Ah-gaik and I walked to church in the blinding sunlight, suddenly Ah-gaik ran to the house for something she had forgotten. "My box," she explained breathlessly.

It was a little box all the people carried to church that day. "I put a penny in it every time Alec caught a seal. I give thanks," she said. I closed my eyes tightly. "Thanks, Lord, a penny for a seal, exchange my pennies for a whale. Lord, an offering, our humble offering this day. A whale, a whale."

We found our places in church among the hunters and their families who were harmonizing in clear powerful tones, Dinah, behind us, singing loudly as always.

White-robed Eskimos on the platform surrounded Reverend Lawton, who also wore white, his beaded mukluks sticking out beneath the long pleated robe.

The lovely color of wood benches, polished over the years by loving hands, glowed in the candlelight. The sermon was about "the whale and the reverence for it as food and fuel" and how the hunters' hearts ached and prayed for that whale. The church was packed full—I had never seen it so full. The people needed that whale badly; they felt it proved that they lacked courage and faith not to have caught one. Something was wrong! Two years before, twelve whales had been caught and the year before four, and now it was May first and no whale.

Disease, poverty, and starvation had plagued Tigara in the past. The new prohibition on shooting ducks made it harder than ever. The children were stuffed full of tea and pilot bread, that flat cardboard-like cracker which fills the stomach without nourishment.

The minister pleaded with God for the whale; the people bent their heads low as one, kneeling on the green floor; even the children were quiet. These people had a power and strength as they prayed together; I could feel their presence and it moved me. They had to get that whale; I prayed with them silently, tears pouring down my face. How I yearned for their sakes for that plentiful muktuk, that great mound of pure food, whose every bit of tongue and heart was eaten, even the very bone used. That beneficent whale.

"Oh whale, come to us," I prayed. "Dear whale, offer yourself as sacrifice, give food to our babies and sustenance and strength to our bodies so that the hunters may not be weary and lose courage, so that their spirit shall not feel defeat and their hearts not be leaden.

"Oh windless day, bright with blinding light, bring fulfillment—tomorrow. Bring the north wind; perform a miracle for us. We are a prideful people, living in hardship and poverty, but give us this fulfillment; fill our pots and our caches, our stoves, our bellies, and our hearts. Bring us the great whale."

I had felt like a compass with a shifting and useless needle, wandering, wandering from home to home, and from home to ice, waiting for the wind to change. I had wandered and sketched and been ready to go at a moments notice across the village, past the snow and dried earth, past the wet grasses, poking up over the mounds of snow over the icy ridges.

The people regarded me as from the "outside world," talking in wonder of places where there are stores in which you buy what you like, a dream world like their Sears Roebuck catalogue. The women did not know from one day to the next what would be in their cook pots; they think of only one day at a time. The insight struck me sharply and I wiped wet cheeks on my fur hood.

Reverend Lawton spoke about a "harvest of whales," his face a blur. I looked up and saw the eyes of a hunter, who usually wore a brutalized and bitter expression and I saw his face transformed, shining with an inner light, purified of doubt, and I was glad.

Out on the tundra dried grasses, ocher-colored, poked up in the snow; spring must be coming, but where, oh where, were the whales?

I saw an old man sunning himself for the first time all year on the roof of his sod house. He wore a bright blue hand-knit stocking cap and he was carving whalebone. A young hunter sped by swiftly with his dog team on the way to Jabbertown to hunt.

The sunlight blinded my eyes and the vast white snowy expanse in front of me gave me a sense of isolation and barrenness that turning back to the village could not dispel.

What will the destiny be, I thought, a full harvest or an empty one this year? Will this be the rare year of no whales of which no villager will speak, the year of starvation that is quickly forgotten, although one old man said it had happened twice in his lifetime?

Ka-you-tuk, Ah-gaik had called me today; after her dead grandmother. "Kayoutuk, you are just like a sister to me."

Walking along the snowy shore I stopped to avoid a water hole and saw the sky and clouds reflected in it. "Bring the whales," I prayed. "Let me not see them, just let the whales come soon."

I walked out to the village at eleven-thirty in the morning, but everyone seemed to be asleep, not a soul was out, and the weather was grayish and windy; not even a dog was howling. After searching I found an old rusty can and sat on it to paint with the wind blowing my fur ruff and cutting my face. My hands were frozen when I finished the watercolor. Rosa and Lizzie, her sister, had spotted me and came running, so I added them to the painting and went with them into Ah-gaik's house to warm up.

I did not knock on the door as I noticed no one else ever did, they just walked in—when I asked about it I was told, "One never knocks when entering a house; it would seem that he was boasting his importance."

The oldest boy was still sleeping on the cot and their uncle from Kotzebue who had come for the whaling was asleep in the middle of the floor in his sleeping bag. Ah-gaik had just finished nursing Pearly and was starting the fire to make hot coffee.

The hunters had been out early to the open lead and Ah-gaik reported that the Frankson crew had harpooned a whale but it had escaped. The men had seen twenty other whales but they were too far away to strike. The hunters came home early in the morning, for the wind shifted and closed up the open lead. "No use for whale today," Alec said, discouraged.

The conditions might have been bad for whaling but they were good for duck hunting. Alec brought home a bag of four and his son five eider ducks. Asatsiak, after trying all week, hit the jackpot, killing fifteen ducks. Almost every home had the aroma of duck soup swirling out of their chimneys today—a welcome change.

Ah-gaik cut up the ducks on the floor for soup while I played with Pearly. The eider ducks had beautiful striped heads and she skillfully slit the skin down the middle, separated the skin from the meat with her ulu, cut every part of the duck into pieces, and threw everything, including head and feet, into a big pot to boil with a handful of rice, but adding no salt.

I sketched her as she cut up the duck, then sketched Silas as he stared stony-eyed at me, his mouth full of bubble gum—that suspicious character.

Elmer came in from a long stay out on the ice at the open lead where the whaling crew had missed their whale. His lips were puffy from the wind, raw from the sun, and his face was very red. "Ma," he said, "I haven't eaten all day; I'm hungry." His mother set down biscuits and hot tea and he fell to it. He had been out on the ice all night, curling up on the caribou fur from time to time to snatch some sleep.

Ah-gaik invited me to a duck soup dinner when it was done, serving fresh store bread and a special treat, red Jello with canned fruit in it. When I told Ah-gaik that I had eaten boiled beluga at Otoonah's, Alec asked, "You like it, Clara?"

I said, "I swear," such was the disbelief in his voice.

Ah-gaik had set the table with white dishes, and the soup was delicious. We finished with hot tea, then Rosa and Lizzie did the dishes.

Ah-gaik's father, Chester Seevek, came to visit. Many years before, he had been in charge of the government reindeer herds. He was a strong active man over seventy, and Wien Airlines hired him every summer to be host to the tourists at Kotzebue and demonstrate the Eskimo dances. He was a widely traveled Eskimo, for Wien's had sent him to Hollywood, Japan, and Hawaii for publicity purposes. His second wife, Helen, was a comfortable fine woman who accompanied him everywhere; they had appeared in Edna Ferber's movie *Ice Palace*.

Chester used to greet the tourists with "Welcome to Kotzebue," but after his trip to Hawaii he welcomed passengers as they get off the plane with "Aloha," smiling broadly in his elaborate fur parka.

Chester and his wife had a house at Point Hope where they rested up from the tourist season. Now sitting on Ah-gaik's cot he informed me, "A long time ago over three thousand people lived at Point Hope, further out. . . . The white whalers came and brought disease and now—few people left.

"Eskimos reduced to three hundred and twenty-six after three schooners in 1600's came to visit Point Hope. They brought measles and other sickness. People died. Finally U. S. government brought medicine. White men brought in first tobacco, dishes, copper, and traded whiskey."

Chester was right, epidemics had wiped out large numbers of Eskimos, for they had no immunity to disease. Tuberculosis was still the greatest public health problem in Alaska. It was estimated to occur at six times the average rate for the nation because the native population suffers from lack of immunity, crowded housing, and borderline nutrition.

Chester gestured with his hands. "The world is divided in three parts, sky, earth, and sea. We believe in God. In the early days Eskimos eat only animals, nothing from under the earth; we were like animals, no disease, only pure and kind to each other."

I visited Ah-gaik and Alec often, enjoying the neat cheerful house with its bright yellow oilcloth and curtains, often sketching there. Otoonah was visiting one day and spoke to me in Eskimo, which Ah-gaik translated.

"I'm coming to see you soon," I replied. She complained to Ah-gaik in Eskimo that she had no money and was eating my groceries; I told her to go ahead and eat them, giving her money to buy more. I had seen Asatsiak at church and he asked it I was angry with him, and I said, "No, of course not."

Otoonah was invited to a meal by the Assembly of God minister's wife and she enjoyed being served for a change. When the children came in for their art lesson, I turned the tables and had them draw me while I did a drawing of one of the girls and gave it to the minister in exchange for his hospitality.

Sometimes it was difficult to communicate with the people for in addition to not knowing their language I had to remember many simple things such as never to put a question in the negative. If I asked a boy, "You don't have a sister, do you?" he answered, "Yes," meaning, "No, I don't have a sister."

It was also difficult to get information from anyone. The men answered in monosyllables. Some of them did not understand me at all and gave me bleak looks. One of the Eskimos told me the reason he could not understand English was that "It sound like mouth is full when they talk."

Early one morning I was invited by Alec to accompany him on a trip to a nearby lake to get water for drinking. The day was gray-white with snow falling in big cold patches and a south wind blowing. I had wrenched my knee somehow and it hurt, and after a sleepless night I hesitated to go seven miles in the wind and snow, being tempted to sit instead by the cozy fire with Ah-gaik; but torn as I was between comfort and the trip, I chose the latter. Dinah, who was good at doctoring, had rubbed my knee muscles the day before but I still hobbled around.

After coffee Alec went out to harness the dogs. His team had ten dogs, including father, mother, and four of a year-old litter. The mother with strange spotted marks on her face had chewed her harness and ran alongside the team for the whole trip.

With a fast team it was a two-hour job to get ice from the lake, but Alec's team was slow and as it turned out we were gone over eight hours.

On the sled was an ax for chopping ice and a shotgun just in case. As we started off in the gray cold, Alec casually mentioned that he sometimes brought home over a thousand pounds of ice on his sled. "It will be a heavy load." I envisioned myself running behind or in front of the team like an Eskimo woman, or perhaps, hopefully, sitting on top of a half ton of ice.

The trail was slushy to start and then firmed up as the black spots that were houses disappeared in the distance. I rode the sled, feeling pampered, and we passed the grave-yard with the grave markers and fence of upright whale-bones.

Huge pressure ice ridges three times the height of a man were an eerie sea blue. The whiteness of ice and snow met the whiteness of sky in a barely perceptible line, touch-ing one dark lonely spot, a hunter returning with a seal, pulling it by a rope.

A flock of crowbills crisscrossed a flock of eider ducks. The shapes were easily recognizable; the eider ducks were heavier and rounder, their wing spread was different, and their wings made a rushing, whirring sound overhead. We could see them in the distance, the black tracing line disap-pearing as they turned and maneuvered.

We passed Ahksivvokrook dreaming on his sled, pulled by his dogs, lazy man's style. The dogs knew the trail and needed no urging.

We traveled slowly, savoring the day. "When my son takes the dogs, they go fast; he scare them," Alec said and with that picked up a stick and banged on the wooden sled;

immediately the dogs trotted faster. "Older people not in such a hurry."

A dark, blackish blue streak appeared across the gray haze of the sky, and Alec said, "Now the hills are open all around. Hope the south wind get tired," by which he meant he wished the north whaling wind would come.

Little pieces of driftwood and whalebone structures jutted out of the ground. Alec pointed. "That's Keeporuk's cache and that's Frankson's." We came to a corral surrounded by a whalebone fence that had been used for reindeer herding in the early days.

The dogs stopped while we loaded the sled with a good supply of driftwood. I spotted a three-foot beluga backbone, intact, bleached white in a beautiful design, and set it in the sled along with the driftwood. There were other whalebones too large to move and walrus skulls from which the ivory had been removed; one had ivory teeth and Alec tried to pry the mouth open but could not budge it. Bits of duck feathers lay scattered on the tundra, whose whiteness was beginning to show some faint green stains, although more snow still showed than earth this time of year.

At Jabbertown, where the eighteenth-century whalers came to hunt, to procure the precious baleen for the corset manufacturers of the East, we found a nine-foot-high strip of baleen and I put that on the sled. It had a feathered edge along its hard black smoothness. When fresh, baleen has a horrible smell which one white man described as "whale's halitosis"!

Murres came over in huge waves going north to Cape Lisburne to nest. At last we reached the huge lagoon seven miles from the village where everyone got their drinking water.

The lagoon had large water areas over the ice, which froze to a depth of five feet in winter but was only about three feet deep now. When Alec chopped out a chunk, I could see that the ice was rotten and splintered, too soft to cut out and useless to bring home on the sled.

To travel over the water spots on the ice seemed dangerous and I was glad when we left the center of the lagoon and the dogs led us once again to shore.

I remembered vividly a story about the lagoon that a white man who had lived two winters at Point Hope told me. He was an experienced hunter and used to ice and Arctic conditions. One night during winter, when the drinking water in his host's bucket was almost gone, he offered to get more. His Eskimo friend said, "Don't go; the wind is bad tonight," but he insisted upon doing his share and left. He had hitched up the team and driven almost four miles when the wind became so fierce that it was impossible to distinguish direction. However, he kept going until he reached the lagoon. Once on the lake the dogs kept slipping and sliding on the glasslike surface; their lines became twisted, and they finally refused to venture further. With the wind howling around him he unhitched the dogs and staked them out, and struggling to push the sled over the icy surface he began to chop out great chunks of ice.

Just as he was leaving, he saw another dog team approach from the other end of the lagoon, driven by a small boy barely able to see over the handle of the sled. The boy went to the same spot with his team, lifted a pickax almost as big as himself, and proceeded to chop and load the ice; then expertly tying up the load, he quickly jumped on the sled runners and mushed home before my astonished friend.

The hunters learned to be adept on the ice even when it was rotten. Billy Weber had shot a seal about three hundred yards away on rotten, water-covered ice. He was on foot, but he ran quickly over the ice, balancing himself with his hooked pole, and was able to throw his line over the seal and make it back to shore, dragging the seal behind him. He appeared to fly over the ice without touching it, maintaining his balance like a ballet dancer.

I was brought back from my reverie by a rifle shot. The dogs had begun to bark, spotting fat squirrels poking out of their holes, and Alec had shot one that ran back into its deep nest. With a pointed stick, Alec tried to pry it out; then putting his hand way in he dragged out by the tail a plump squirrel with reddish fur. Alec showed me the places where the animal had gnawed on little willow roots and grasses.

Alec aimed at a white spot on the snow several yards off and shot a white ptarmigan, a small bird good to eat; then with another blast he shot its mate.

He showed me the place where his ancestors wearing ivory breast plates had fought Noatak Eskimos with knives and spears. Once, he said, the Noatakers had crept up, surprised the Tigara men, and had driven stakes in the ground in such a way that the enemy would impale themselves.

The legend of the war had been told me by an old man. "One time in morning Point Hope people found right at Point, little fish, tomcod, drifting ashore. Many people go to Point to get some fish. Only two families lived in house and that man was a good fighter. His wife carried boy in back. She walked east along coast, she walk little way, see many people on beach crawling, crawling, to Point Hope village.

"She quiet, baby quiet, walking little way towards people, turn slowly, gently, making baby sleep, try, to get husband. Then husband called: 'Men, people, they come to fight us.' Other man call over Point. When he called, that man fight bow and arrow. Fight. Before fighting Point Hope people one mile away from village is make ivory and bone sticking up on ground and beach. When people fight, ivory and bone backward sticking in feet. They fell over stick in back, killed all people, not save one. When one enemy came and smell salt water, all dead."

The sun was a pearl mist in the gray-blue sky, reflecting a mysterious light; its ultraviolet rays burned my face but I was unaware of it.

When flocks of eider ducks crowded the sky, Alec aimed, raised his rifle just as they flew overhead, and shot a beautiful male, a white and black duck with yellow bill, ringed neck, and green-blue markings, then the fatter female with her plain brown feathers; I think the latter was a Pacific duck.

We had obtained no ice but the sled was full of drift-wood and old bones and the pouch on the back contained ducks, squirrels, and ptarmigan. When we turned to go home, I sat on top of the driftwood load until Alec let me drive the team; then he sat on the sled. We went slowly, enjoying each new scene and change of ice pattern. I lost control of the dogs, fell flat on my face in the snow, and had to run to catch up.

Two Kivalina teams, racing to reach the village, slowed down to say hello. They had come to buy flour for their village since their store had no more.

My face was red from the wind, my hood pulled back from the wind's presure. We passed a hunter waiting patiently behind a blind of blue ice cakes; he had shot only two ducks and a seal in several hours and stood shifting his feet from the cold.

The sparse landscape reminded me of whales, the whalebones projecting in lieu of trees, a lonesome land, desolate, where once many people hunted. We reached the village at nighttime, my wrenched knee forgotten; I remembered only Ah-gaik's happy face as she ran out to see what we had brought.

CHAPTER 25 *Wandering*

I call forth the song
I draw a deep breath
My breast breathes heavily
As I call forth the song.

Across the sky
A song I call forth
As I draw a deep breath
Aya aye.

ONE OF THE HUNTERS was sitting on top of his sod igloo carving a mask, blocking out the main forms with a homemade adze. I talked to him for a long time earnestly about carving figures in the round using all sides of the whalebone instead of masks which use only one side. When I was finished, I asked him if he was interested and he looked up at me and said honestly, "No." Basically the men were proud hunters, carving only when they needed groceries and had no skins to exchange for food. I bought the mask he was carving because it resembled Attungorah, the other carver, with its high cheekbones and projecting nose; oddly enough the tongue was sticking out! I had previously seen Indian and other primitive paintings depicting this expression.

The wind changed and one of the boys offered me a ride out to the open lead, but we did not get far because halfway there we met the hunters coming back. The change of wind brought lower temperatures and frost. The south wind was closing the lead again and they would have to start from the beginning when the north wind returned.

The women worried about the duck situation. "If my husband can't hunt now for ducks, we'll starve," they said. "The ducks are fat and good now, but later in September, when the wardens want us to hunt them, they are stringy and tough." Besides in September the men are out hunting caribou which is plentiful then.

I felt sympathetic but helpless—what could I say! Point Barrow had an Eskimo representative in Juneau; I knew the decree would be fought. When I returned to Fairbanks I would fight to change the prohibition.

I started out to visit the Killigivuks and Attungorah, but I walked into the wrong sod house by mistake. After bumping my head through three tunnels, I came upon an old man whittling on a wooden oar. He looked like a gremlin, smiling as he worked; I had only to ask him and my wish would be granted. In the middle of his underground room he had set up a tent to keep out the leaks, and he sat snug and comfortable with the light pouring in from one bright naked electric bulb. I apologized for the mistake, backing out and bumping my head; the spot was sore.

His outer storm porches were made completely of whalebone and except for the leaks, he had a very interesting, unusual, large house.

At Asatsiak's house I found him and Otoonah sitting in the little room where I had slept. The cot was gone, the sun was pouring in, and Otoonah sat sewing muskrat skins together while Asatsiak carved a piece of ivory. Gene was still in bed in the other room.

I asked Asatsiak, "What do you think about the whaling situation?" I thought that as one of the elders in the village he could tell me what was happening.

"Something is wrong in the village because the whale won't come near it. He stays out so far and won't come near. The whale can hear," he said, "and feel. That sign the council they put up about white man not hunt whale—no good. Hate. That's why whale won't come.

"No one follows the old customs at all any more— maybe just me and Daniel Lisbourne still pour water on the whale and use the mittens made by an old woman," he said. "Young don't believe. Young change it."

So we chatted until I got up to go to Attungorah's house; Asatsiak said he would meet me there later. As I walked away, Otoonah came running out of the house to wave at me again.

Attungorah's sod house was almost buried in snow. He remembered me from former visits and I asked how his masks were coming along. His wife was home. I had seen her limping behind her husband, using a homemade wooden crutch to climb the ice. Her face sweet and shy and I would have given much to know her, but we could not speak each other's language. When Asatsiak came, she served us coffee and maporuks and the men spoke in Eskimo of days gone by when masks were made of driftwood to cover the face and were used for dances. Meaningful masks, "not like nowadays." Asatsiak explained to me.

Frequently a man who had experienced a vision would carve a mask representing what he had seen. Some of the masks were normal or slightly distorted human faces, some of them representing the caribou people or whale people and thus combining the spirit of man and beast.

Asatsiak had masks that he used only for the ritual masked dance held annually on New Year's Eve. I had seen him wear his special headband of a loon's skin and tail feathers which had significance to his family.

Before I went home, I sketched Attungorah's sod house, gray and earth colored, with dark wheat-colored grasses covering the doorway and growing out of the sod hung over the entrance. Whalebones surrounded the house and from the top of the house was strung an electric wire connected to a nearby telephone pole.

It was a sunny day with a north wind blowing; perhaps the wind would blow the lead open. A few hunters took their teams out to investigate the open water.

The Allens were leaving for Noatak, for the snow was melting fast and they were afraid that if they stayed longer they would not be able to get home with their team. They were living at the midwife's house and Judith was washing clothes.

The midwife was a large capable woman who had many children, most of them gone from the village. Her photo album contained pictures of her family and grand-children, and she showed me her baby book recording every baby she had delivered at Tigara. The book opened from back to front and all the names, dates, and weights were written down; most of the babies weighed in at ten and twelve pounds!

"Sometimes such a big baby tears the mother," the mid-wife said.

"What do you do then?" I inquired.

"We leave her torn until the doctor comes two months later."

Donald Oktolik's wife and Dinah Frankson were also midwives. They all received twenty-five or fifty cents for a delivery, or sometimes nothing. They had a "baby box," or satchel, containing bandages, scissors, and other necessities. The women for the most part had their babies easily, sometimes squatting and sometimes lying down.

The midwife went on with her work of pleating skin soles with pliers while her daughter scraped fur off the skin with a sharp rock. I offered to help Judith get some snow water for rinsing clothes and took the bucket outdoors.

When I came back the women were laughing. It seemed I had done everything wrong, taking the snow from the top where it seemed clean but was dirty instead of going farther away from the house and digging deeper; then I tamped down the bucketful with the shovel and they thought I would damage their new pail. At even so simple an effort I had failed!

Cyrus Norton, son-in-law of the midwife, had one of the finest teams in the village, fourteen dogs in top condition. I teased him about being more interested in them than anything else. He spent hours caring for them, stirring their food over an outdoor fire. Cyrus, a Noatak boy, had married an intelligent Point Hope woman who had been educated by a mission school in the States. She had a serene expression and complete faith in God. Both of them assisted at the Assembly of God church and held meetings and Bible readings in their comfortable but small wooden house.

Cyrus and his wife, Viola, who was seven months pregnant, had just returned from Kivalina by dog team, bringing Cyrus's relatives to help in the whale hunt. During part of the trip Viola had carried her two-year-old baby in her parka to shelter her from the wind, but around Cape Lisburne she put the baby in a sleeping bag. The ice was dangerous and the wind made sled travel treacherous, and the bag would tend to protect the baby if the sled rolled over. They made the trip down in twelve hours, stopping to make tent for the baby only once when she cried.

Viola kept the floor and house spotless and there were curtains at the windows. She had lost her first baby at birth, the second birth had been difficult, and now she was approaching her third. (A few months later she gave birth simply by walking down to the beach alone one day; then she walked back carrying her baby.)

Viola did not know how to make mukluks or how to prepare sealskin; she wore shoes and rubber boots. We had a good cup of coffee and over their powerful short-wave set I heard the fantastic news: a man had flown in space in America!

How remote the rest of the world seemed here. As far as the village was concerned, it was almost itself another "space world," an ice world cut off from the rest of civilization.

I went to David and Dinah's house one evening and was invited to join a game of pinochle. David and I were partners and Tingook and Dinah—the rest were "advisors." Everyone who dropped in to the post office remained to watch. David was a clever, shrewd player; compared to him I was a rank beginner. It took me a while to learn the interesting motions—small liberties with the rule book—used to inform your partner after you meld. If you had a jack, it was legal to walk your fingers over the table; for a ten you waved your hand horizontally over your head.

Tingook did not speak much English, but it was surprising how revelatory of character a card game could be. I felt I knew everyone better and they me when the game was over. Dinah was the most fun, a reckless, hilarious player who laughed good-naturedly when she lost.

I was still eating and sleeping at the Assembly of God minister's house; the weather continued to storm and no one was whaling. The minister's son was heading for Nome and they prayed constantly for him, especially in the morning, adding a long prayer for me. I felt rather sinful to merit such a long prayer.

The Church of the Assembly of God was trying to establish itself at the village and broadcast a religious sermon each evening in hopes of converting the Eskimos. I was ignorant of my hosts' beliefs and found out later that they disapproved of card playing, smoking, dancing, and lipstick. Apparently the concern for me reflected in their prayers was due to my card playing and dancing! But I didn't know any of that at the time.

I was told that my sleeping at their home had caused an Eskimo woman to remark, "Even though she stay with them, I still like her." Whether I had intended it or not, I was embroiled in the middle of a controversy.

When the Episcopal minister's wife came for coffee, the two women avoided mention of the churches, talking instead about clothes, food, and women's things; about how Eskimo mothers blow on a baby's head to get it to urinate, or about the habit of women of exposing their breasts.

Ah-gaik dropped in and I showed her the modern gas stove and oven, for I didn't think she had ever seen one except in a catalogue. When we had cake with whipped cream and chopped walnuts, she exclaimed, "I never tasted such cake, *arigah*—first time, *arigah!*" When I walked Ah-gaik home through the slushy snows, she told me that there was to be an Eskimo dance at Brownie Hall.

Upon my return, the minister's house was filled with about ten children washing clothes. In return for their help they were all invited to dinner—a feast of a dinner—caribou meat, mashed potatoes, gravy, peas. I contributed a loaf of bread from Frankson's store while the children set the table.

After dinner I thanked my hosts for the delicious meal and got ready to go to the dance. It occurred to me much later that the whole reason for having the children to dinner was to discourage them from attending the dance! I could not believe that anyone would wish to stop the dancing which meant so much to the Eskimos.

The photographer staying with the Lawtons was impatient for the whales to come since he had an exclusive assignment to "cover" the hunt. "I have to pay for everything and my money is running out. I have to pay for use of a dog team wherever I go," he complained.

One of the boys told me what the trouble was. The photographer had stood up in the umiak when he was out with the whaling crew and begun to take photographs without permission. The men thought he could have jeopardized their chances of striking a whale. The photographer had set his will against the Eskimos and vice versa, and from then on no one would help him without pay. When he sat on the ice ridge by himself, no one even offered him a cup of coffee.

There were three schoolteachers this year and one of them, a young bachelor, asked me to give his class an art lesson. The children's paintings depicted an ice world, ice shapes being as familiar to them as trees are to our children; the animals and skin boats and people were also sketched. Daniel Lisbourne's daughter drew an aerial view of a charming kitchen with linoleum on the floor.

The photographer came into the art class wearing a baggy wolf parka with the hood up, his bearded face red and his nose peeling from sunburn. He pretended to frighten the children, hunching one shoulder, distorting his face, and saying hoarsely, "I am a bear and I like to eat little children," and then sat down next to Rosa and began to tease her: "I especially like little children with green dresses!"

He meant only to tease the children—he had many children himself—but these were Eskimo children and some of them were afraid of "the white man."

After a while Rosa came up to me bringing her drawing, her face white and strained. I felt her head to see if she was feverish, for her eyes stared glassily into mine; she mumbled something and then her composure broke and tears poured down her cheeks. I guessed that she was frightened of the man with the red face who said he liked to eat little girls. I took her into the outer room and tried to console her, reassuring her that he meant no harm, but she sobbed in my arms. Afterwards the photographer apologized, feeling bad about the whole thing.

Later at the request of the teacher the children undertook to entertain me with an Eskimo dance. Four boys sat on the floor and beat books with their rulers to keep time. Some of the boys began to make the motions of the dance but the girls needed to be coaxed. The older boys were reluctant to perform and satirized the dance; instead of the words they sang "ABC" self-consciously.

When the dance began at the parish hall it had a few strikes working against its success for the people had been told that dancing was a sin. First the school had shown the children new ways to eat, providing them with white man's lunches every day; then they were urged not to speak Eskimo at home; and now the last vestige of their culture was being undermined.

The dance was different from the one I had attended the previous year. Tingook led off again with the opening dance; he was not as strong as he used to be, but what he lacked in strength he made up in spirit. Asatsiak and the elders drummed and sang as before, but the crowd was small. Many teen-agers were down at the lodge, dancing to rock 'n' roll from the juke-box.

Something was lacking. When the dentist's wife danced, she was applauded warmly; then Dinah asked Mrs. Lawton to dance with her but somehow Dinah reversed the order of the dance and the switch confused her partner. A twenty-two-year-old visiting scientist danced, imitating the Eskimo cry of joy, but it sounded satirical even if not so intended. Only the Episcopal minister in his kind serious way seemed to put things right, for by his dancing he again affirmed the cultural importance of Eskimo dances.

When I came back late to the minister's house, the door was locked; I knew then that it would be my last night there. According to my "hosts," I had erred badly in attending the Eskimo dances.

The next day was gray, rainy, wet, foggy, and damp and I did not know where I was going to spend the night. My wrenched knee ached and I felt like a pauper carrying my gear out, Ah-gaik had a houseful, they were already sleeping on the floor there, and the lodge was full of men. Every house was overcrowded on account of all the visiting relatives. I walked over to Cyrus and Viola's house which was close by and explained the situation. With Cyrus's relatives staying there they were crowded too but he welcomed me warmly: "There is plenty of room, come in and stay with us."

We had a dinner of caribou soup and afterwards Cyrus blew up an air mattress and said, "Follow me." I climbed up a ladder to the attic floor where there was plenty of room and privacy.

I hung my wet mukluks and inner soles on a line over the stove and washed in the basin. Cyrus had brought home some *akootuk* his mother-in-law had given him and we had some.

Cyrus's assurance of "plenty of room" was more than a token gesture. He had gone far out of his way to help a stranger in the village. That night in his attic I slept comfortably and well, warmed by their generosity.

In the morning when I came down, my considerate host had run out to the store to buy special groceries for my breakfast: expensive white man's cereal and canned meat.

Nathlook came to visit the next day with her family. The dentist had pulled a number of her teeth and she smiled to show me the wide spaces. The baby was ill with a fever of 104 degrees and had been given a shot of penicillin by the nurse but here she was, out in the cold, protected from the high winds by her mother's parka. Poor baby had a runny nose and looked pale and pasty. She had been fed some rotten caribou meat that had been left too long and had spoiled. Some of the other children had wheezing chest colds; their feet were wet all the time from playing in mud puddles.

The weather had been growing warmer and the snow was melting fast. Spring was creeping up; it was May! The melting snow revealed dog feces everywhere, the stench terrible as I walked through the village. It was difficult to avoid stepping on it and tracking it through the houses. Toilet refuse was thrown out into fuel oil drums and disposed of by each family—some put the drums on sleds and dumped them into the sea.

Snow piles remained on the cooler sides of the houses and the women used them for washing clothes, hanging them out of doors in the sun for the first time that year.

"Given away just like a pup!" a woman told me, still smarting after twenty years. Her mother had too many little children and could not afford to feed another girl. To this day this woman could not bring herself to call her own mother "Mother."

Many children were given away, some harboring feelings of rejection while others took it for granted. One little girl whose mother had given away her sister said, "She is my sister but she lives with the —— family."

Mrs. Lawton, or Jackie, as everyone called her, invited me to stay at their home as the photographer was spending his last two days at the schoolteacher's. Reverend Lawton and his wife were hard-working and dedicated young people. Their two little red-headed sons were pictures of health and the youngest, a plump baby with golden eyelashes, fell asleep in my arms at our first meeting. There were puppies and toys underfoot and little Eskimo boys playing everywhere. We had a wonderful Sunday dinner, including cabbage cooked with caraway seeds. After dinner I demonstrated watercolors for Jackie and the girls of her Bible class.

The minister had changed from a shy young man to a

mature confident spiritual advisor; he traveled up and down the Arctic coast with a dog team, like an Eskimo, gaining and giving much. Both he and his wife would be sorely missed when their term was finished.

My bed that night was between two brown bearskins on the couch. Someone from the States had sent these warm coverings to the minister. First I laughed, then I shuddered, then I crept between them thinking, "Now I have tried everything!"

My bed at Killigivuk's had been a cot, hammock style; my bed in Oktolik's tent had been a dog sled on the ice covered with caribou skins; at the Assembly of God minister's house I had lain in a four-foot-high "real" bed; at Cyrus's on an air mattress in an attic; and now I was bedded down between two brown bearskins! Needless to say I was warm—too warm!

The next morning Tingook's son came to the minister's house to see the painting of his father. "I want to buy the painting; I'd like to have it," he said.

The painting was unfinished, only the head blocked in. The belligerent way in which he asked for the painting made me feel he wanted it for reasons he wasn't telling me and at which I could only guess. He was angry. He didn't say he liked the painting and I was puzzled. Could it be that he felt I might take his father's spirit away when I left Point Hope with the painting? The old people had joked that if one took their photograph with a camera, it took the spirit away. Did Tingook's son believe this? I hoped not.

He was one of the best ivory carvers in the village and I had bought one of his bears at the store. I reasoned with him, "You are an artist yourself. It is just a rough piece of ivory in your hands before you make a bear out of it."

He was amazed to see what I had accomplished in a few hours.

"But it has taken me years to learn how to paint. I'll send you a colored photo of the finished painting," I promised.

I don't know if I convinced him that it would not hurt his father in any way, rather that it was an honor to him. He seemed to feel that it belonged to him; that I should not take it away. I gave him one of the two sketches I had made of Tingook and appealed to his knowledge of art until his threatening look subsided. I didn't know if I should feel flattered or not. Perhaps he wanted to find out what I would charge for the painting. Perhaps he could not understand that it was only a canvas until I put my impressions on it. I think I finally made my point when I asked him, "Would you sell your plain ivory for the same price as the finished bear?"

After Tingook's son left, one of the ten-year-old boys

came to see me and I invited him upstairs. The boy said with awe, "This is the first time I go up stairs!" Only later did I wonder whether he meant he had not ever been in a two-story house or that he had never climbed a flight of stairs.

Otoonah came walking across the tundra, arms swinging, face hidden in a huge fur ruff, her old figure straight and proud. Her white pup followed. As she caught up to me, she showed me what she had purchased with the money I had given her for groceries. Giggling like a schoolgirl, she held out her hand to reveal a silver wedding ring.

Since I expected to leave Point Hope soon, we walked together to Ahksivvokrook's house. I wanted to see how their baby was faring before I departed. Nathlook was just getting up from nursing the infant, who seemed to be better, and Ahksivvokrook was sitting near by, sleepy-eyed and tousle-haired. The children were at school, the fire in the stove was burning, and the coffee was ready.

Donald Oktolik's wife came running over with a small parcel wrapped in white paper. When I opened it, out fell a tiny whorled shell! "I took it out of a duck's stomach this morning," she exclaimed. I thought it lovely and we both wondered where that duck had eaten such a shell. Then she handed me a sack filled with Eskimo artifacts she had dug up from the old ruins. "This is for you, Clara."

In the bag was an ancient wooden wristband with little designs around it. Otoonah fitted it on her wrist to show how it was worn a long time ago. Some jade arrowheads were next and then a wooden board which Nathlook promptly took. Jumping off the high bed board, she ran to get her ulu and a bit of sealskin, proceeding to use the old wooden slab as a cutting board.

"Real old, real old time," she stated. It was only a small piece of old wood, about seven inches long, but it had had a purpose in this world.

Otoonah handed me a tiny ivory bird; the ivory was

very old, pitted and scarred. Later when I showed it to Louis Giddings, the anthropologist, he said it looked like a piece from a game the Eskimos used to play.

Not to be outdone, Ahksivvokrook reached under his bed and dragged out three objects: part of a walrus tusk made into a snow scraper, another with holes drilled into it to form part of a harpoon, and the last a huge ivory labret which had been worn in the skin below the mouth in ancient days. He handed them to me.

I registered surprise and thanked him, remembering how he had almost left me out on the ice. He said sheepishly, "You the nicest white woman I ever see."

He had allowed an animal to be stoned to death, he and his family suffered, yet they knew it not. They lived in sickness and deprivation, one of the poorest families in the whole village, yet in spite of everything I could not help liking them. They lived so nonchalantly; to them suffering seemed nothing; they laughed about everything.

We heard a motor roaring and a plane landed out of the fog. I had to run and gather my things. The Kotzebue radio had reported foggy weather with poor visibility and I had not expected the plane that day. The photographer had left without seeing the whale he had come to photograph and now I was leaving so as to be home on Mother's Day as I had promised.

In the plane were ten 50-pound sacks of seal and ugruk skins going "outside" to be tanned. I had three cartons full of mukluks, sealskin pants, other clothing, whale discs, a beluga backbone, and starfish, as well as an oil box, wet canvases, four notebooks full of drawings, and watercolors. But I felt that my work was unfinished because I had not seen the whale.

I would not see the whale on the ice, the people delving into the animal's choice delicacies, drunk with the tender flavorsome meat and the happiness that wells from a full stomach for oneself and one's children and from caches full of meat—tons of it—for the whole village. No, I wouldn't see it, but I could imagine it.

The pilot was the same one I had flown with in the fog and rain several years before. Before I got in the plane, the wind changed; it was a north wind at last. Then I knew that the people of Point Hope would get their whale before the ice was gone, but I had to leave.

We flew north over ice floes and snow mountains, around the cliffs of Cape Lisburne, over the stretch of barren coast, and then landed at the military installation. The lieutenant waiting at the airport was surprised to see a woman pop out of the plane, especially a white woman in an Eskimo parka.

The weather was good this trip and we flew above the clouds, taking a short cut through the mountains instead of following the coastline. I had a short wait at Kotzebue airport, where I changed planes.

I felt contemptuous of trees when I first flew over them coming into Fairbanks; open ice and snow spaces seemed to have much more meaning—nothing could be hidden.

CHAPTER 26

Fulfillment

Know you the smell
Of pots on the boil?
And lumps of blubber
Slapped down by the side bench?
Joyfully
Greet we those
Who brought us plenty!

I WAS HAPPY to be home
with my loved ones again but the inanity of the radio adver-
tising was intolerable. Olaus and Mardy Murie came to the

house to see my paintings one afternoon. Olaus, an artist as well as writer of the wilderness, had a great love and understanding within him of all things. He discerned immediately how I was feeling and said, "I feel the same way after a trip." The vast wilderness spaces become part of one; freedom is precious.

I seemed caught between two ways of life, resentful of the limitations on my independence and the repetitive demands of housework. Sometimes I hated inanimate mechanical objects, feeling a slave to them. Monster-like they sat in my kitchen, shiny white, waiting to be fed and cleaned, devouring soap and water. I admitted that the bathtub was a great invention, but in my mood I felt like holing up in a tent, for possessions demanded obeisance.

From Tigara came a flood of letters, among them this one: "I heard when you leave from Point Hope. Sample God preacher to quarrel you, locks the door, you not to come in to sleep. Why not you tell me. I am very very sorry full."

Then a long letter from Killigivuk:

Dear Papnikluatak,

I'm going to tell you about Daniel Lisbourne caught a whale. Yes. They caught 13 May morning. They called all crews. Everybody rush start run and dogs team. When they cut whale can't make it. 100 yards pull the whale on the rough ice. Broke ice. When the wind started windy from the northeast.

Allen Rock caught whale when the broken open water close by point. No winds started open the water. Fine weather sunshine. He caught it. Cut whale close on beach. Everybody enjoy. Jawbone long about seventeen feet. Twelve feet baleen. Everybody very happy. Enjoy.

Your ahpah,
J. A. Killigivuk

Daniel Lisbourne had caught the first whale on the thirteenth of May—the day after I left!

In my mind's eye I had pictured the event a hundred times: Daniel harpooning the whale, throwing his sealskin floats overboard, then perhaps singing the special song to alert the other crews; the umiaks in which the men poised to strike the whale, waiting for the floats to rise.

Then the hunters fixing their lances and harpoons into the bleeding whale's vitals; the crews swarming around the *arvik*, reaching for his heart with long lances until he spouted blood!

Then Daniel driving a smaller harpoon into the whale's lower lip, fixing a towline to it and towing the carcass to ice. The months of work and prayers climaxing in success. I could hear the joyful cry going up from all the men's throats, the cry I had heard during the nalukatuk dance and again when the umelik was thrown up from the nalukatuk skin and he "danced in the air"—the cry of the triumphant male hunter! The great arvik brought in at last.

A boy would be sent to the village to tell everyone that the whale was there, and he would run as fast as he could with the dog team, yelling, "Arvik, arvik!" The minister would ring the church bells, everyone would stop what they were doing and rush out with their cutting knives to the ice to help with the butchering and feasting.

The feasting, of course, would begin right then. Women would set up their stoves and put pots of muktuk on to boil, and the men would begin the ritual division of the whale. Right at the shore's edge they would eat what had taken them so long to hunt.

When one of the schoolteachers came to Fairbanks, she told me that Allen Rock, the lodge owner, had killed the second whale of the season, a record whale, one of the biggest ever taken at Point Hope, measuring about fifty-nine feet.

Allen Rock wrote, "I caught my first whale, as captain of the crew, on May 24th. The longest of the baleen measured ten and one-half feet and each jawbone measured nineteen feet."

The schoolteacher said the whale was immense, that they had to cut it in the water because the ice kept breaking under its weight and they could hardly drag it in. The heart itself was so big that they had to cut it in nine parts in order to haul it ashore! The whale represented about fifty-nine tons of food!

Allen got his whale in a most unusual way. About seventy-five Eskimos were encamped on the ice—same as when I was there—when the heat of the sun loosened the ice to such an extent that a large floe broke off from the main section of ice containing the women's tents. The hunters were beginning to drift. Quickly one man gave the danger signal to alert everyone—three gunshots. Those who could escaped with their teams over the thin thread that held the ice close; the rest loaded their belongings—dogs, sleds, tents, stoves, everything—into the umiaks and paddled to shore.

One hunter had gone farther out to hunt beluga but they managed to warn him. Jackie Lawton, the minister's wife, had fallen into the ice water but was rescued. The chaos, the rush to sound ice, was accomplished with everyone safe. Not a life was lost.

They were resting on shore and helping the stragglers when Allen Rock saw a whale come close. He took careful aim at what appeared to be a small whale. It turned out to be a mother, a monster of a whale, and angry! Had he known the baby was near the mother he would not have shot at it for mother whales are dangerous and become violent when attacked. The mother, trying to protect the baby, had been swimming back and forth, sheltering it with her body.

Allen hit the mother in the spine near the kidneys and the bomb exploded well, which fortunately slowed her down. She thrashed around lifting out of the water, leaving a bloody stream behind her. "Some of those swipes came to about six inches of my face, almost tipping our boat over," Allen said.

The umiak of the second crew that came to Allen's aid was lifted out of the water to about four feet and almost broken in half by the force of the whale's body.

The bloody, wounded arvik was roped and brought

safely close to shore ice, but they could not hoist it up with block and tackle and heavy ropes so they left most of it in the water, flensing the huge mammal in the water from their umiaks with flint blades set in ten-foot shafts. The water soon turned red from the mother whale's blood and the baby, who had also been shot, disappeared, never to be seen again.

In the past, dividing up the meat had sometimes been followed by bloody fights; but these days the older men like Asatsiak made the actual divisions on the skin of the whale before the butchering was done, and each cut was pre-scribed by ritual followed meticulously.

The top of the head was eaten on the spot by all the people. The umelik got the heart as well as tail and flippers to give away at the feast. The first umelik to strike the whale received all of the carcass behind the navel except for the strip behind the stomach. If it was his first whale, as in the case of Allen Rock, two crews divided up the tail and the umelik kept only one side of the lip and two lengthwise strips along the belly. The fore part of the body ahead of the navel was divided equally between the crews of the second and third boats; the lower side of head around the tongue was divided between the fourth and fifth boats. Usually the rest of the lip went to the sixth and seventh boats.

Each umelik placed his meat in separate piles on the ice and apportioned it among his crew mambers; the task of hauling the meat back the several miles to the village was left to the women and boys. Until dog teams were used, the women hauled the meat in sledges. The butchering of the whale took a week, the men and women working day and night, stopping only to eat fresh whale meat every few hours and to sleep when they were too tired to continue.

I could understand the Tigara people's faith in their ancestor's knowledge of how to kill the whale, for wasn't it the most important element in their survival? Did they not feed on his sweet flesh and burn his vital oils?

I was happy for the Tigara people but I knew personal disappointment in not having witnessed the finale of the whale hunt. To think that I had missed it by one day and had experienced everything except the most important part. Now the more superstitious among the Eskimos would say, "I told you so; it was that white woman on the ice that prevented the whale from coming. You see, the minute she left, the whale came!" And who among them would refute it?

I searched for the meaning, groping for understanding. And I was inconsolable. Why had it not been given to me to see the whale? Why was it given to me instead to see the hunger and not the fulfillment? I could not find the answer.

Another blow fell. Word reached me from the village that little Rosa Frankson had died. Someone later told me that she had been stoned to death for her choice of churches. The boys pelted her with rocks, he said, and when she became ill she was flown to the Kotzebue Hospital where she died. He believed that she had died a martyr's death.

It was shocking news, and I wrote to find out more. The villagers were silent about the whole thing. The Lawtons were gone from the village when it happened but did check at the hospital and found that she died of rheumatic fever.

Evidently Rosa had had a severe sore throat, diarrhea, abdominal pains, and a high fever. The family gave its consent for an autopsy. It seems that some of the boys had really hurt her, so that hung in the air as a dubious implication.

The state police were called in. The state trooper reported to the village council that Rosa had not been murdered and that there was no evidence that she had been beaten. There were also no eyewitnesses to any beating. The doctor found no bruises and the autopsy revealed a rheumatic heart condition complicated by a blood disease.

The conflict between the churches continued and a few Episcopalians had themselves rebaptized in the other church. Dear Rosa, whose beautiful face had shone out among the others, would not be seen at Point Hope again.

Amid all the confusion and rumors, I did not know

what to believe. Maybe Rosa's death had been due to a combination of all the alleged causes—malnutrition, rheumatic fever, rock throwing. I remembered hearing about the fights that occured at Kotzebue when the Catholic church first came there.

Point Hope was split into two camps. Ah-gaik in her grief began to attend the new church regularly while her husband and sons stayed at the Episcopal church, forcing a cleavage within the family.

I looked at my portrait of Rosa again; it was wistful, her eyes large and clear and full of longing. I couldn't forget her. I did a large painting of Rosa lying with her mother kneeling in front of her holding her hand and the other women and men behind her. One man had his hand raised in blessing. It was inspired by Giotto's "Death of St. Francis" but had Eskimos instead of Italian monks as subjects, and it comforted me a little.

I drew a child lying in a woman's arms, and the woman mourning was Ah-gaik and all mothers facing the loss of a loved one. A series of whale paintings followed, the whale as a fiery furnace, the whale as a harvest, the ice and the hunters waiting for whales.

The University of Alaska Museum bought the largest painting. I finished Tingook's portrait, changing the background about ten times, and I mailed a photograph of it to his son as I had promised, along with some tobacco and little things for Tingook.

Tingook, I learned later, had accompanied his wife, who was dying, to the Kotzebue Hospital. He had stayed with her all day and when night fell, had brought his rolled-up caribou skin and spread it on the floor next to her bed. He had lain beside her, comforting her till the end.

Further news from Tigara: Nathlook was in the hospital with tuberculosis. I remembered how she had run in front of the dog team, outracing the dogs.

I also remembered the time Ahksivvokrook went hunting on the ice without food, umiak, or dog team, taking only

Nathlook and baby

a rifle. He was stranded on drifting ice and did not come home that night. Nathlook ran to the older women, worried, and they told her what to do. "First put his mukluks on the shelf over the hot stove; that help to keep his feet warm. Then put inside caribou skin. Every day change the caribou skin and be sure to keep them warm. Then keep yourself warm, wear parka in house, don't get cold. Don't move around too much. Just walk on your knees and don't go any place. If you do, Ahksivvokrook will hurt legs!

"If mukluks fall off shelf, that mean Ahksivvokrook jump off ice pack. Be sure you string line of sealskin from one corner of room to other and pull very tight. When line is loose it mean he's asleep on ice; when it is pulled tight it mean he walking; when line does not move, it mean he dead."

Nathlook did not follow the advice exactly. She went visiting, and sure enough when Ahksivvokrook came home he was limping and his legs hurt.

There was good news too, however, along with the bad. The U.S. Bureau of Indian Affairs was building an addition to the schoolhouse, hiring local men to do the work. Tigluk was one of the carpenters, and he had made enough money to buy lumber to build his long-awaited house. He and his family now lived in a new plywood house like John Oktolik and others.

Killigivuk had been invited to Anchorage to demonstrate the Eskimo dances to the tourists. He had no doubt been chosen because few Eskimos knew all the words and motions and music as he did. He had visited his sick daughter in Sitka and on the way home had stayed with us. He brought us a treasured gift, a pair of caribou mittens Otoonah had made for the New Year's Eve dance and the whaling ceremonies. The mittens were unusual; they had no fingers and were edged with wolverine fur. We were very happy to see Asatsiak, who looked marvelous but was using a cane now to get around.

"*Quayanna,* the mittens are beautiful. How are the dances coming?" I asked.

"I have five young boys about eleven years old and I teach them the words and to drum. They follow me," he answered firmly. Due to men like him the dance would not die out at Point Hope. It was Killigivuk and the Point Hope dancers who were chosen from Alaska to dance for President Johnson's Inauguration in Washington, D. C.

The federal prohibition against shooting ducks out of season was fought by Alaskans from all walks of life. State Senator Eben Hopson, Eskimo representative from Barrow, led the fight in the Juneau legislature and our Senators in Congress, Bob Bartlett and Ernest Gruening, along with Representative Ralph Rivers, demanded an investigation.

One of the most dramatic protests against the decree was made at Barrow. There every hunter went out and deliberately shot one duck, bringing it in and asking to be arrested. "We're not going to give up our natural hunting rights," they proclaimed.

After many months the Eskimos won their case, so once again they hunted ducks in the spring as their great grandfathers had always done before them in order to survive in the Arctic.

PART V

The River

CHAPTER 27 *Kotzebue*

And the great, dear paddlers
Were leaving out there—
Great grief came over me
While I was picking berries on the fell.

> Rendered from the Eskimo
> by WILLIAM THALBITZER

THE WINTER OF 1963 was rough;
temperatures fell to fifty below zero in Fairbanks and I had
"cabin fever" (a term we use to describe a restless, cooped-

up feeling). In March the temperatures were cold but at least the dark days were over. In April the sun warmed the river ice and breakup was close. When I went outdoors to chop the remaining snow and ice away from the front of our house, I could feel winter tensions snap and disappear. The earth was appearing where the snow had melted and we could walk again on terra firma. Strength poured into me from the tree roots; flocks of geese honked overhead; I could have wept for joy. It seemed as if I had hibernated like a bear all winter, dead and feeling no pain. "The flowers appear on the earth, the time of the singing of birds is come," probably means more in the North than any other place. Spring was here, yet I yearned for the Arctic, the freedom of Eskimo life, which was stripped of everything but the essentials.

It had been five years since I had visited Sheshalik. I was eager to see my Eskimo friends, for we had corresponded and their letters urged me to come to Noatak.

I wanted to paint Eskimos again in their own environment. Working on the tundra with an icy wind blasting my face or in a tent was more satisfying than painting under artifical studio lights. When I was among them, my brush seemed to pick up the Eskimos' vitality and translate it to paper. Studio paintings were a must only afterwards, but I never made a small sketch to be translated into a larger painting, I felt each drawing or painting to be a complete statement, and the studio painting at home were something different, something from the subconscious, a predigested statement about Eskimos.

The river trip was exciting to contemplate. I loved the unknown, and a river opening up at every bend in the wilderness had the aura of adventure. The Noatak was little traveled except by Eskimos and an occasional barge loaded with supplies. Most white people flew to Noatak. The river, navigable for only a short time in the summer, was said to be hazardous; it was frozen over most of the year.

The Jensens, two wonderful schoolteachers from Kot-

zebue, offered me the key to their home as they would be
gone until school started in the fall. I decided to go to Kotzebue and travel with my old Sheshalik friends by river boat
up the Noatak River.

When I arrived in Kotzebue at the beginning of August, the first person I met was Quavuk. We went immediately to the postmistress's tent. Ethel was no longer the
postmistress, for she had resigned to go camping with her
husband. Noyuk was in the tent, eight months pregnant
with her seventh child. How warm was their greeting; immediately food was set on the stove. I had forgotten how
grand was the gesture of an Eskimo woman bending over a
stove.

The women were preparing to go to the Friends Church
so I accompanied them in the rain. The church was crowded
with wet Eskimos, colorful in their parkas and fur ruffs. It
was the quarterly meeting time and Kivalina, Kotzebue,
Buckland, Noorvik, Ambler, Selawik, and Noatak villagers
were represented. The program was in Eskimo without an
intrepreter. It was the "Blessing of the Infants" ceremony.
The Eskimo missionaries stood in front of the congregation
and held the newborn infants. It was then that I saw Leela
for the first time. She had not changed much, but Gordon
was grayer. After the blessing three women knelt at the
altar, and cried a confession. The whole assemblage knelt
and prayed fervently with them.

Puyuk walked down the aisle and I reached out to
grasp her hand. What a look of surpise on her face! After
church Puyuk and I walked through the mud to where I
was staying, our faces red from the wind and our clothes
wet from the rain. It was building up to a storm as severe as
one in winter and it was only August!

The Jensen house, one of identical schoolteachers'
homes, was government built and luxurious for the Arctic;
it had running water, a washer and dryer, three bedrooms,
a modern bathroom, kitchen, and living room. A pantry was
filled with canned stuffs and groceries to last the winter.

The Jensens' grocery order came only once a year on the annual boat from the States. Grocery prices in Kotzebue were a full 25 per cent higher than those in Fairbanks, while Fairbanks prices were about 25 per cent higher than those in the States. It hurt me to think that the Eskimos paid the highest prices when they were among the lowest income groups in Alaska, but freight costs were high.

The Noatak people's tents were a few miles away from the center of Kotzebue near two tall beacons. The people had come from Sheshalik to fish and pick berries until it was time to return to Noatak, usually at the beginning of school.

After hot coffee Puyuk walked out into the storm. How her eyes lit up at my invitation to stay, tempted as she was by unknown luxury. She decided firmly, however, "No, I can't stay; they look for me all night long."

The next day I walked out to the Noatagmiut tents. En route I met an older Eskimo woman, a nurse at the hospital. I asked her about Rosa and she said she didn't remember anything about a beating, that the child had died of rheumatic fever. "But," she said, "it's not uncommon for children to be beaten who change to another church. Kotzebue children do not go to church as they used to, but when the Catholic Church first came up here there was a lot of fierce fighting against anyone who left the Friends Church."

When I reached the tents, it seemed as if I were back at Sheshalik; there was the same arrangement of tents, the same racks in front, but instead of beluga and seal meat there were rows of trout and salmon.

Leela and Gordon's tent was clean, orderly, and peaceful. "Here is my place to sit on the box near the stove," said Leela, brushing back the hair that had fallen over her cheek and setting her bulk down carefully. "I just cook, put wood, keep place warm."

She spoke better English than I remembered. "I had to learn English," she said. "My boy was in the hospital and when he came home, I couldn't understand him."

Her biscuits were light and better than I had remembered too. We had fresh trout and coffee with them. While we ate, Leela told me about her childhood. "I was brought up by my grandmother who was blind. She followed me by holding on to my parka. My own parents didn't know me hardly. When I was twelve, my grandmother left me to live with an uncle and then I took care of myself. Okukchuk is my sister but from different fathers."

Gordon told me that there were many bears along the river this year. "One man counted forty bears inland."

"Bears have been coming close to Fairbanks all summer," I returned. "Homesteaders have been shooting them. No one knows the reason why there are so many this year. How was the hunting at Sheshalik this year?"

"Bad hunting. The water is rough and the boats couldn't go out. Altogether we got one beluga and one ugruk. When you were here, it was different; we got more than eighty."

"Things are different now; the men have gone to work for the cannery with their boats, netting fish. The women are busy picking berries," said Leela as she refilled my coffee cup.

After eating, Leela went outdoors to feed the huskies. I tried to paint the sea and distant mountains with boats and dogs in the foreground, but my hands got cold so I went into Okukchuk's tent next door to warm up.

Okukchuk had spoken so much of her husband that I was eager to meet him. He was a quiet unassuming man of about sixty, with a prominent nose and strong chin. Okukchuk had sewn his white rabbit-skin parka with a border of beads. Originally from Kobuk, Jack had worked in the gold mines at Fairbanks and the fisheries in southeastern Alaska. I asked him when he was leaving for Noatak.

"I don't know but we'll be glad to take you with us when we go," he answered while Okukchuk beamed. She hadn't changed at all, although the flood at Kotzebue the previous year had wiped out their tent and possessions.

"I hope we don't have a flood this year," she said. "The weather doesn't look good; too much rain and storm."

When I walked back to the Jensens' house, the wind

was so strong that it nearly pulled the petals off the daisies by the roadside.

That evening I went to watch the Kotzebue dancers led by Chester Seevek, Ah-gaik's father. The dancers were full of vitality, the little ones imitating their elders. The best dance was a Diomede Island bench dance in which three women sat on a bench and did rowing motions as in an umiak, turning and swaying. One of the women was Abe Lincoln's wife, the other the wife of Sakarna, a relative of Asatsiak's, and the third unknown to me.

Sakarna was short and full of pep. He had the body of a young man but his old eyes had cataracts. It was difficult for me to understand his English as his sentences always ended with a question. He spoke with an animated expression and it was only afterwards that I realized I couldn't understand his pantomime. He probably had the same difficulty understanding me; however, he sold me a set of teeth, probably from a wolf, strung on old seal gut. (These white people will buy anything!) I planned to combine them with some old Russian trade beads in a necklace.

Sakarna told me about the meaning of one of his motion dances, dancing around the room to illustrate. "First time Eskimo know coffee. He cook whole can with little water. Strong. Thick coffee. He drink. I dance." He made circular motions with his hands to show a man opening a can of coffee and then drinking it with disgust.

Sakarna's house was well insulated with cardboard; there was cardboard on the floor, on the walls, and covering the table. It was cardboard from broken-up grocery cartons.

Sakarna's wife, a heavy-set, strong woman with black hair severely tied in the back, brought out an old seal oil lamp, two old combs, and labrets for me to examine. She called the labrets *kutooks*. One was of a strange white polished stone about two and one-half inches long. I paid her the price she asked for the labret and the combs but left the lamp, as it was broken.

Their thirty-year-old son was reading on the bed, his

black eyes sunk in his sallow face. He didn't hunt but liked to play pool at night and sleep all day. A naked bulb hanging over his head flooded everything with a dim yellowish light. Assorted clothes hung on hooks around the wall, casting lumpish shadows.

Their lively, adopted grandson was getting ready to leave for Chemawa, a high school for natives in Oregon, on his first trip to the "outside world". A boy friend gave him a hair cut after which he went into the other room behind the curtain and took a bath in a tin tub, chatting excitedly all the while.

When he came out in his new shirt and pants, his hair brushed back, I helped him roll up his shirt sleeves. It was a brand new shirt bought at Kotzebue but by mistake one sleeve had been sewn in backwards.

The friend, who had been "outside" to school already, told me he liked to draw and asked me to show him how to paint with watercolors, so I painted Sakarna's head. His wife laughed at the result; to her it must have looked strange, although it was a good resemblance.

The boy gruffly said, "Old women always laugh at art." Evidently he had not been encouraged to paint. He walked me home, as it was well after midnight, and I tried to inspire him to work at it.

"I'd like to stay here for a year and paint," I said.

"You would soon do nothing, just drift," he replied.

Interesting. The atmosphere at Kotzebue certainly was a lazy one; most teen-agers stayed up half the night and slept until noon. There seemed to be a lack of incentive and little employment except hunting. Welfare checks had lulled many adults away from taking the responsibility of planning for their own futures.

Kotzebue was a village bubbling like yeast. Dissatisfied with the old ways it faced transition, struggling to find the answers. Few fresh ideas came to the Arctic, for isolated people were shut off from the mainstream of life and ideas became ingrown as did their marriage relationships. Young people coming home from schools and using modern equipment were not content to remain on a hunting economy.

The outlying villages offered few jobs but there were rumors of a copper ore find at Kobuk, oil strikes on the north Arctic slope and the young were hopeful.

Because of my comings and goings in the Noatak tents, the Noorvik and other village women had been asking, "Who is that *nalogme* [white woman] who comes here?"

"She's the one who helped us cut beluga at Sheshalik," answered Gordon. They look at me again, this time with warmth instead of suspicion.

I sketched the waterfront houses, the fish racks, and the hills, drizzly gray in the rain. Everyone in the village seemed to be eating salmon for lunch, including the tourists at Wien's Hotel. The fishermen went out daily, bringing in boat loads of fish which the floating cannery in the middle of the sound took to process. Okukchuk and some other Noatak women left for Sheshalik by boat in the rain to pick berries; a twelve-year-old boy ran the motor for them.

The children ran up and down the beach, their hair flying in the wind, pushing a stick nailed to a coffee can lid which revolved like a wheel. Maybe I should have gone with Okukchuk, I thought, for the atmosphere around Kotzebue was stifling. The village slept, dreamed, and sometimes erupted into wildness. Some of the men played pool at Ferguson's all night. There was lots of drinking and a feeling of restlessness in the air. The wind and rough sea intensified the sense of an impending storm.

When the storm finally burst that night, it sounded like a human wail. The wind lashed the schoolteachers' house, causing some loose appurtenance in the house to answer back with a loud squeal. Windows rattled and a pot fell off the oil stove. The Alaskan flag on top of the schoolhouse snapped in the wind as if it were going to be torn in shreds, and the huge "lakes" in front of the house were wild with waves.

Everyone must have spent a sleepless night, expecting a repetition of the previous year's flood, for the wind buffeted the tents hour after hour. The wind gave no peace, and summer seemed to be disappearing in rain and storm.

After a week-long storm the sun came out, luminous along the beach where the boats bobbed on the water. Once in a while a motorboat whirred by with an Eskimo woman sitting in it, her ruff blowing in the wind, her baby humped on her back, and her husband standing stoically at the tiller.

White sea gulls squatted on the sea, clustering, bobbing, dipping their wings, some with their heads under water as they dined on fish scraps near the cannery. One of the fishermen commented at the weather change, "The water is smooth today."

I walked away from the weatherbeaten Kotzebue houses to the northeast beach where the Noatagmiut tents were flapping in the wind. Lichens flamed silver and orange, pale olive and scarlet, among the gray rocks, and white balls of Arctic cotton flowered among the caribou moss. Myriads of red cranberry globes, black crowberry, Arctic daisy, and ankle-high willows covered the flat terrain. The earth was very black, peatlike and wet from rain.

I saw groups of women picking berries and greens at all hours of the day. They picked sourdock, wild rhubarb, wild spinach, and willow leaves. They gathered cowslip, or marsh marigold as they called it, cooking the leaves and letting the brew ferment.

In front of Leela's tent the women were cleaning berries, pouring them in the wind from one bucket to another. I had brought some soap and other stuff and hidden it in a corner of Leela's tent and I could hear her saying, "Oh, soap-a!" The day before, she had tenderly discovered a wee "mouse-a" and his nest near her stove. Smart mouse.

She was boiling reindeer soup with rice for a change of diet and Gordon said happily, "I'm a caribou meat man; fish is okay, but meat is for me!"

Okukchuk had just returned from Sheshalik where they had waited out the storm. "We had plenty of fish to eat, plenty of berries." The young boy had shot several ducks, and their only mishap had been a torn fish net.

In the evening the sky was dark blue with a band of pink rising behind the ranges. The houses were gray shadows with square patches of yellow light—windows silhouetted in front of the sea.

I felt like standing in the darkness to paint the mysterious night sea. I remembered Abe Lincoln's telling me that the original Eskimo name of Kotzebue was *Kikiktogruk* until Captain Otto von Kotzebue named it after himself. There was also a legend that in the water there was a strange creature with long human hair called a *newyukpolik*.

In olden days boat sails were made of walrus or ugruk intestine. It must have been a sight to see these carried across the water up the Noatak River by the wind.

I invited Leela and Gordon for lunch one day.

"I can't understand how the Kotzebue people can live all winter without wood to heat their homes like we do at Noatak," said Gordon, shaking his head. "Fuel oil is so expensive, but I guess they can't help it. No trees."

Leela looked radiant in a violet calico. I noticed a copper bracelet she was wearing. "It made my arm feel better; before I wore it, I had bad rheumatism," she explained. "Gordon made it from an old copper tube."

Gordon told me about Manuneluk, a legendary Eskimo of Kobuk. "He married a Noatak woman and once he stayed at Sheshalik. Manuneluk never believed the old-time angatkoks. He was always looking for rules to break. In those days at Sheshalik when they ate beluga they never ate berries and roots or leaves at the same time. Manuneluk went and picked some wild rhubarb leaves and cooked them and went down to the edge of the water where they were cutting beluga and asked for a little piece to eat with the leaves. He ate it and never got sick. Before that time, even if little kids broke off leaves while the people were hunting beluga, all the people got sick; but after Manuneluk did that, nobody ever got sick any more.

"Other angatkoks tried to kill Manuneluk but they didn't have the power. Manuneluk foretell the airplane, he said it would come out of the sky. He said boats would go against stream fast some day, he foretell motors. He foretell Ambler would have many people some day. There never used to be a village there, now they have many people. He was prophesy all these things," said Gordon, his eyebrows raised like Puyuk's.

"Manuneluk didn't think girls should go away from village to have baby, so he went up to one girl and asked for a drink from her bucket. That girl didn't want to give him a drink. The other village people said she had to stay by herself, but Manuneluk drank her water. He said to the people when a woman is going to make a baby she should not have to go away from village.

"The last words Manuneluk say, 'All the people—I don't know what they going to do, all the people.'"

Gordon said proudly, "He was our prophet."

"People were better than now a long time ago," said Leela. "They help one another like brothers and sisters. They were good people even before we had Christ." Leela believed, "We are born again; when we die, we come back into another life."

Leela and Gordon left in the afternoon thanking me for the lunch. That evening I visited the Kotzebue Catholic priest, Father Pat Spoletini, a remarkable, warm, cultured man, originally from Rome. He had home-baked bread and tomatoes that had been sent by air which he generously offered me. It was the first tomato I had tasted in a month. Afterwards I sketched him sitting by the stove drinking tea.

Father Pat lived behind the church with many books and a collection of records that included Gregorian chants and Tebaldi. He tried to bring a little art and music into the

lives of the Eskimos but it was a difficult task; the youngsters were not interested in Bach or Rembrandt.

A volunteer carpenter from Minnesota was helping
Father Pat add a recreation room onto the church. "The kids
have no place to be alone to think, or study; their houses are
so crowded. I thought a room where they could come to
read and be quiet would help them."

"Have you ever poured cement before?" I asked.

"No, but I'm learning. Some of the Catholic boys from
the radar site are helping me in their spare time."

He showed me slides of Florence, Italy, and of Diomede Island where there was a Catholic Mission. Altogether
it had been a memorable day, spent in good conversation; a
day full of happenings and drawings.

I discovered Tingook's daughter living in one of the new
plywood houses, a box without insulation. She had married
a Diomede ivory carver named Charlie, who made a living
selling carvings to the tourists. Just the day before, Father
Pat had performed the marriage ceremony for Charlie's
cousin, an ivory carver named Kayoutuk too, and a lovely
young Eskimo girl.

When I first came to their door, Charlie looked up from
his work with a closed, unfriendly look. But when his wife
told him that I was "Clara, who knows Tingook," his face
opened to a warm welcome.

"I didn't know you at first," he apologized.

He sat with his legs crossed. A large cloth, spread to
catch the ivory dust, contained a vise, gouges, files, and
other small tools. He quickly cut a chunk of walrus tusk and
carved a seal out of it. After he polished, sawed, and filed it,
he drew in the nose and claws with a steel pen and black
ink. In the other room he kept a converted sewing machine
which he used as a lathe to make beads. If the sewing machine needed repairing he used bullet casings for bobbins
and carved ivory gears to replace the metal parts. Charlie's
ivory bow drill had a sealskin strap which he wound around

a stick; then he stuck one end of the stick into the bow held between his teeth and the other end where he wanted to drill the hole. It was an ancient Eskimo drill, simple but workable.

One of the white men told me he had offered Charlie an electric drill but he refused it. He was used to the ritual of the bow drill, a ritual learned in boyhood from his father, while the electric drill was foreign and required electricity which wasn't always available.

This story reminded me of José de Creeft, my sculpture teacher in New York City, who preferred to make a nail rather than interrupt his train of thought to go out into the street, walk a few blocks to a hardware store, and explain to the clerk what he needed.

Charlie scoffed at the idea of using a mask to protect him from the ivory dust, although his father had been hospitalized with TB and his wife also suffered from it. The baleen especially had an acrid smell when it was filed and made me sneeze and cough. The door was open but it was too cold to leave it open for ventilation in winter.

Ikkaheena, who now lived in Kotzebue, came to visit Charlie and his wife, having seen me go in. Charlie's wife made coffee while I sketched their son, also named Tingook. He sang a Japanese song that he had learned from the short-wave radio.

Ikkaheena told us that someone had hit Horace, her husband, over the head with a heavy board that had a rusty nail in it. "He had twelve stitches and his head is all bandaged." She was as beautiful as ever; the new baby sleeping in her hood was fat and his cheek sweaty from the heat of her back.

Later we walked to her house in the rain. They lived in a small hut containing one room about eight feet wide with a small stove, two cots, a table, and wooden crates for storing clothing. A glass jar holding artificial flowers brightened one corner.

Horace, who had returned from the army, sat on the

cot, his head swathed in bandages. Without resentment he
said, "They wanted me to bring charges, but the man who
hit me was drunk. He didn't mean it."

"My little girl named the doll that you sent her after
you, Kayoutuk," said Ikkaheena as she washed diapers
while I played with the baby. "Kotzebue is sure different,"
she said. "You even have to buy meat from your own relatives. In Point Hope they give it to you. But one thing is
cheaper here—oil. At Point Hope it cost us fifty dollars a
month."

Their future looked uncertain, but Horace had applied
to the Department of Rehabilitation of the Federal Bureau
of Indian Affairs to learn a trade, maybe in Chicago. Quite a
few of the younger men were applying to move to the
States. The families were given housing and sustenance
while the men learned a suitable trade. Strange to city ways
and lonely for village life, a large percentage would return,
but they would return with new skills and knowledge they
could put to use.

Quavuk, Noyuk, Charlie, and five others left for Noatak in a
boat loaded with three large oil drums. Noyuk, huge with
child, sat in the middle of the crowded boat and since the
trip would be against the current and would take about
fifteen hours, I asked her how she would sleep. Comically
she nodded her head to show me.

"You'll be scared, I think, when you make the trip," she
said. "The river has rapids."

After they left, I walked back to Okukchuk's tent. Her
son-in-law had returned from the cannery in southeastern
Alaska; perhaps they would be leaving for Noatak soon.

I sketched the interior of the tent, including the wonderful details like the teapot, lamp, and pots. The men spoke
in Eskimo and every other senence contained the word
Evinrude-a.

Jack said they would be leaving for Noatak soon and it
made me happy. I sang all the way back, thinking about the

coming river trip. I felt like leaping and frolicking over the fields, or at least whinnying like a horse, if I could.

The cranberries were so thick along the trail home that I could not help stepping on them, remembering Gordon's wonderful description of their abundance: "Crunch, crunchhh crrrunchhhh!" I loved the way he talked and saw things.

"Some of the children are ashamed to eat dried ugruk. I'm part white but I like Eskimo food best. I love it, can't get enough of it," a fifteen-year-old Kotzebue girl told me. I had been teaching her how to paint. "One day at our camp upriver I shot a porcupine and ate it. Grandma boiled it and it tasted good, especially the fat on it. We put nothing else with it. I like bear meat too."

She gave me an early Eskimo baby bottle made of dried animal intestines. It was used if the baby was adopted or for some reason the mother could not nurse. It was tubular, with holes at one end for the baby to suck, the other end tied with sinew.

Margaret Hunter had a little shop in Kotzebue where she sold ivory jewelry, Eskimo mukluks, and artifacts to the tourists. She was a grand woman with a generous heart who had lived among Eskimos for years, traveling by dog team and skin boat and trading at various villages. She slept behind the counter on a cot and I often stopped by to chat or sketch, sitting by the window and drawing people as they walked by or traded in the store.

Margaret was a fascinating conversationalist and sewed furs as well as an Eskimo woman could. She gave me a pair of ivory earrings and a whale's tooth and sold some of my watercolors for me without taking anything in return.

One morning I sat in her store sketching an Eskimo girl with a baby on her back as a young Eskimo watched. His pregnant wife sat quietly near him. One of their five children was in the hospital with TB. I asked him if he carved.

"Nope," was his answer. After about three hours of sitting in silence he finally got up and went to the counter, plunking down a bag of artifacts containing an ulu and some broken pieces of odds and ends from the old diggings. He argued with Margaret about the price until they settled it, then went out disgruntled with his wife behind him.

One of the white men living in Kotzebue dropped in to talk to Margaret and told us about his life. He had run away from home and stowed away on a boat at twelve, enlisted in the army at sixteen, and came to Alaska at nineteen.

He spent his first winter isolated in a cabin on a mountain. When I asked what he did on the mountain, he answered, "Sunk a few holes." He did not find any gold so he came farther north seeking adventure and remained among the Eskimos.

He hunted like an Eskimo and visited many of the surrounding villages. Once a minister called on him to discuss why he was taking a fifteen-year-old Eskimo girl away from her home in one of the villages.

He replied bluntly, "I have to; she wants to get away from her father before she gets pregnant."

"Some of the girls are given away like playthings," he said. "When a white man is accepted by Eskimos, the wife is told by the husband to ask the stranger if he wants to sleep with her."

I asked if he had to give something in return.

"Not at all," he answered. One time before he knew the customs he asked a homely woman in hopes of getting out of it, "Won't your husband mind?"

The woman had replied, "No, he told me to ask you."

In the past the parents chose their son's marriage partner. It had also been the custom to exchange wives on a mutual basis.

Rainey thought the old custom of wife exchange was mostly a practical arrangement used to bring unrelated Eskimo families together for mutual protection. Moreover, when one man exchanged wives with another, he might be expected to borrow his boat or hunting gear. The immediate families of men who exchanged wives were considered to be blood relatives and the children could expect support.

There were quite a few mixed marriages between white men and Eskimo girls. White men often represented another way of life with greater economic advantages. But many Eskimo girls had babies out of wedlock and the government paid the child support.

CHAPTER 28

The Noatak River

Ah, I tremble, I tremble lest the storm and the seas
Send me down to the clammy ooze in the depths of the waters....

THE MOUNTAINS WERE COMPLETELY hidden by fog, and the sea was rough and choppy, unsafe for an open wooden boat. At Okukchuk's invitation I decided to move my duffel bag and paints to Okukchuk's tent so as to be ready to leave at any moment if the waters became calmer. As I walked across the tundra it was still raining, a dreary morning. The tents were quiet when I arrived, the dogs docile for they knew me.

All week long the men had been scanning the sea in hopes of leaving. Jack stood at the water's edge, hands in pockets. Inside the tent Okukchuk was preparing coffee. Suddenly Jack and one of the men rushed in and began to pack, putting pots into a wooden box and carrying them to the beach. Another boy arrived to take a load and then Okukchuk ripped off the bedding. No one said a word. They had waited for the right moment and this was it. We were going at last!

I pitched in to help and soon our three boats were loaded and ready. The long wooden boat we would ride in had 28 h.p. and carried four drums of gas and a year's supply of flour and sugar in fifty-pound sacks that had been covered with tarp so as not to get wet. Stowed in the three boats were all manner of foodstuffs, barrels of seal meat packed in oil, ugruk, rolled-up sealskins, dried fish tied together, seal pokes full of berries, the team of huskies, the utensils, stoves, baskets, pots, basins, bedding, sourdough pot, fishing nets, rifles, poles, and Blazo cans. Two young men from Noatak were in one boat; Jack was in another with the dogs; and his son-in-law was to steer our boat, the third and longest one with the heaviest load.

Okukchuk and I climbed in, squeezing into a small space near the flour sacks. I waved good-bye to Gordon, who happened to be standing on the beach, and we took off quickly. It was five years since I had traveled to Sheshalik and it had been in the same boat with the same helmsman and the same Okukchuk, but now we were all going in another direction. I remembered how rough the sea had been then; it looked much worse now. The men decided to head for a point in the opposite direction from the mouth of the Noatak but safer and within sight of land. Okukchuk looked frightened. The boat seemed frail and heavily laden; altogether it carried more than two tons. Soon we could see no land. Rain had accumulated in the boat; surely we were too heavy for the small motor and the rough sea.

We made it within a mile or so of the point, then swung out into the confluence of three rivers, the Noatak, the Kobuk, and the Selawik, which all drained into Kobuk Lake. (The Eskimos call it Kobuk Lake but it is listed as Hotham Inlet on all maps.)

On open sea without sight of land the whitecaps formed higher, smashing against the boat sides. The water was brackish, turbulent, seemingly stronger than our craft. I prayed for a safe journey and for the first time wondered why I had undertaken it. Our boatman, a swarthy taciturn man, kept his eyes straight ahead while the other two, smaller boats, struggled far behind us.

Okukchuk's fear was contagious. In trying to distract us both I suggested that we sing, but her choice really frightened me. "The Lord is my Shepherd," she sang. Loudly. That is the song I want them to sing over my grave, I thought, not now.

I kept quiet, too fearful to join her.

When we entered the mouth of the Noatak, it was a choked angry mass of churning water. The boat struggled against the current, slowly warding off the raging water. Finally we entered the calmer river waters and the boat with the young men caught up to us. Okukchuk asked them to transfer her bedding, a quilt with goose feathers, and we fixed up a seat of flour sacks and threw the bedding over our feet. Ah, the comfort of it; we had been so cramped.

"Do you want coffee?" Okukchuk asked. I thought she meant to pull over to shore and build a fire but before I knew what was happening, she had lit a primus stove near the gas drums, primed it, and put river water in the pot! Contrary to my expectations the oil drums did not blow up. When the water boiled, she poured it over the coffee grounds and let it settle. How good that coffee tasted in that moving boat!

Short scrubby willows appeared now, growing on flat terrain with other low brush; but as we went deeper, the trees became taller and the willows stronger and higher. Mountains sheltered the plants here and the wind was not as severe as on the coast.

The surrounding country gradually rose and finally assumed the outlines of rugged mountains with rocky cliffs. The banks became lower and marshy, all traces of timber lost in places. The river had a marked current, so swift that our progress was slow. Tangled masses of fallen timber along the shore and dense growth of bushes along the banks gave the scene a forbidding wild look. The heavy, protracted rains of the past few weeks had brought about the high waters and strong current and every mile plunged us deeper into the solitude of the region.

Dark green spruces, yellow alder, and willows clung to the earth and we saw an occasional hare. We passed an old cabin where an Eskimo couple lived. "Sauer's place," remarked Okukchuk. "Around 1920 when the price of fox fur was high, old man Eckhardt used to have a fox farm back in there."

We entered higher and more rolling country; in places the river widened to twice its ordinary breadth. The scene was one of utter desolation in every direction, with small lakes dotting the tundra. I did not see a vestige of life, yet this was where Gordon had spotted the bears on the trip down. We could see the berry patches from the boat.

"In the old days there were two groups of people," Okukchuk related, shifting her position on the flour sacks, "the Naupatarmiut who lived in the parts around here—that means the 'People of the timber or wood'—and the Noatagmiut who were river people following the game inland. Our people travel into the Brooks Range, sometimes into Canada, following caribou. Especially in the year 1902 when there were no caribou. They just disappeared.

"In those days they used seal or caribou kayaks or larger boats made of ugruk skins called *umayaks*. A man and wife pulled the umayak with sails by a rope from shore up this river against the current, all the way home. In those days we just ate meat and oil, hardly ever tea, coffee, or flour."

Okukchuk began to cut up reindeer meat with her ulu and put some into a pot of river water to make soup, adding two handfuls of rice and some salt. I must have dozen off for when I awoke, the delicious smell of soup floated past my nose. She ladled a bowlful for me and one for the helmsman, and also gave me a chunk of pilot bread. Bowls were handed over to Jack and the other men as their boats passed. The huskies never made a sound; they were either frightened or used to the trip and knew they were going home.

The boats plodded steadily ahead and when I opened my eyes again to change my cramped position, it had begun to rain and Okukchuk had covered me with the tarp. The air was still and it was quiet except for the throbbing of the motor. The water and sky were silvery gray, no dividing line visible. Dark massed trees in shadow were misty with fog and rain.

We passed a canyon, a mysterious rock shape that I could barely make out in the dark, and Okukchuk pointed to an eagle's nest, "The baby eagles had their beaks open when we came down the river," she said.

The river narrowed at the canyon and we had trouble passing. Another tributary led to the right and it was rough. The opposite bank was about three hundred yards away. It was in this spot of churning water, I learned later, that several of the Noatak people claimed to have seen a sea monster large as a whale, black and fearful.

As it grew darker, our boatman stopped and lit a match, then waited until he saw the answering flicker up the river. The three boats stayed together as much as possible and when it got pitch black, I became uneasy. I could not understand how the boatmen could possibly find their way, as nothing was discernible, neither water nor sky nor either bank, unless they had some supersensory perception of the river. They must have known the river from boyhood.

We were carried along on a river unknown to me, struggling against the surging high waters. When we hit a wild stretch I huddled closer to Okukchuk's bulky figure.

Again the light flickered in the murky darkness and we waited until we could hear the motors of the other boats coming closer.

Once a shear pin from the motor shaft broke and the men pulled up to shore to fix it by flashlight. We women climbed up the bank to get our feet on land. Dark shapes loomed like bears so we did not linger long on shore but clambered down the slippery banks into the boat.

No matter how uncomfortable, cold, cramped, wet, or miserable I was, I would rather suffered more torment than utter a single complaint. Every bone in my body ached; but I reminded myself that although a plane would have been much quicker, I wanted the feel of the boat trip, to know the river, to know its people better. Okukchuk, as if reading my thoughts, said, "Wait till the women hear you have come by boat with us; they won't believe it." I felt a weary pride at having been accepted.

As Jack's boat went by, the muzzled faces of the huskies looked out at us patiently. One dog hovered near his mate, protecting her from the rain, licking her wet coat, for now it was really pouring and we had to take complete shelter under the tarp. All this scenery, I mourned, gone under cover of night darkness.

I slept fitfully until three in the morning, a misty morning, foggy. The river appeared broad with low brush; the tallest sights were the spruces dotting the landscape. Low reflections of the brush willows made patterns in the water. The river was unruffled, still as silver glass in the morning light.

Our helmsman had the immobility of a man asleep with his eyes open. He had found the proper channels, guiding our boat past the shallow water and the deadfalls of trees that threatened us, unerringly coming through the dark river.

Rushing high waters had caused great undercuts in the

banks and many roots were exposed. Okukchuk said she did not recognize the land, so greatly had the river changed it in a few months.

We pulled up to the banks. Not one of the men said a word. I respected their silence until I could bear it no longer. "What are we stopping for?" I whispered to Okukchuk.

"They don't want to get to the rough part in the dark; they are waiting for more light."

We had more coffee and pilot bread and I tried to be jovial but the men were stern, tiredly supping their coffee. They spoke in Eskimo about the motors—I could hear the word *Evinrude-a* again. The other two boats had 18 h.p. and they kept up with us only because we carried such a heavy load.

As morning came, Okukchuk poked me from my reverie, "Look, this is where we make fish camp."

The men were fighting a swift whirlpool current; eddies of water broke the surface of the river, yet one boat followed another carefully. Our heavy boat rocked and we were sprayed with water but we plowed ahead.

A hare watched us from the banks and birds appeared; flocks of ducks came and one of the men shot at them, but no duck fell. The landscape now looked like one of those trite water and duck paintings, with only the sunset missing. It was a glum morning, wet and cheerless, until Okukchuk made coffee again, supplying a welcome break. Our pilot grinned as I handed him his cup; I must have made a sad appearance, tousled, bundled, and wet.

"Now the river banks look familiar," said Okukchuk. "There is where I hook trouts through the ice." She pointed to a spot near the banks. "Fall is the best time of year, soon as the river freezes in late October."

When the helmsman handed me his cup for more coffee, I ventured one question, "Are we getting close to Noatak now?"

"Not far now," he answered and no more. He might

have meant ten minutes or three hours. It turned out he meant something in between; there were only two hours to go but they seemed like ten. We had covered over ninety miles since the previous day, moving slowly, resisting the current. The sun began to show faintly, wrapping the tops of the willows in golden color. The banks were lined with reddish brush, vivid against the dark green-washed spruces. Mountains, misted over, were faintly visible in the early morning light.

A few sea gulls circled overhead as we discerned the village at last, perched on top of high, black, muddy banks. Weather-beaten wooden houses were set in haphazard rows.

The old log cabins leaning with age, set without plan, were scattered like seeds. About fifty houses faced the river. Dog sleds perched on top of a house or leaned along side. There were fish racks and poles for hanging caribou, bear, and other skins. Near the racks were wooden scarecrows clothed in women's parkas to scare off ravens.

Distant hills gray and elephantine in appearance rose beyond the river, some of them dotted with snow. Okukchuk made a wonderful motion with the side of her palm toward a mountain. "That is where we hunt fox and that is where we camp for caribou."

Every hill was familiar to her and Jack. They had traveled the trails together by dog team, up and down the hills to Kotzebue, Kivalina, Point Hope, and north into the Brooks Range.

CHAPTER 29

Village Life

I love to go walking far and away,
And my soles are worn through
As I pluck the buds of willow,
That are furry like the great wolf's beard. . . .

JACK'S HOUSE was to the left
of the village; it was newer than the rest, built of plywood
and boasting green paint, with a small storm porch as entranceway to the kitchen. The house had two rooms,
wooden cupboards, table, chairs, and a great double bed

and dresser. His was the only dwelling that had an electric light plant and he shared it with his in-laws. The church and school had their own light plants.

Jack threw a pallet down on their bedroom floor for me to rest on. I had been mostly awake for over twenty-nine hours and fell asleep promptly while the men attended to feeding the dogs and unloading the boats.

When I awakened, Okukchuk was trying to keep the children quiet. Daisy, her niece, who had occupied a tent next to mine at Sheshalik, was now a young girl of fourteen, wearing teen-agers' tight pants and blue shirt. Kanayak, her father, was the new Noatak postmaster.

Daisy and her little cousin accompanied me around the village. The ground was muddy and high rubber boots were a necessity. There were no wooden walks, just deep black organic-looking mud ruts leading from house to house. Had I been a housewife here, the mud would have been the bane of my existence. Dried grasses were strewn in front of doorways and wooden planks laid to scrape the mud.

I had chosen the worst time of year to visit. September's rainy season had turned the village into a black morass of mud, almost as bad as at spring breakup. A cleaner, more satisfying time to visit would have been one month later, in October, when the houses were covered by white snow and the earth frozen solid.

Meat houses, storage shacks, fish racks, the wood chopping rack, and the inevitable brace of dogs chained to stakes were evident near every home. A huge ram's skull hung over one doorway. Boats were moored at the water's edge and drying racks lined the banks, making it easy to strip and hang the fish as soon as the boats came in. The wind carried the odor of drying fish that had been rained on and begun to rot. Puddles of stagnant water also had a foul smell.

The children accompanied me as I went from house to house, stopping to say hello and shake hands and introducing myself if I did not know the person. One woman was chopping wood, another feeding dogs, another hanging fish to dry. The aroma of coffee from the entrances told me that the Noatakers were getting up early.

The Bureau of Indian affairs was building a new schoolhouse and schoolteacher's home; when finished they would be the most modern buildings in Noatak. A gravel road led from the small airstrip to the school, where supplies for the coming winter were delivered.

The school was set in the center of town, a meeting place for the younger set who joshed one another as they passed. I stopped to greet the schoolteachers, the Harkeys, and went on my way. If a man and wife taught, it was possible for their combined salaries to total $17,000 a year, depending on their qualifications. They had modern conveniences and were the richest people in the village. The school and the church had been at Noatak for over fifty years.

Although the men agreed that they needed a sawmill there was no plan suggested so that they could cut the trees for building materials. A wooden sidewalk would have been helpful too, even though the ground was frozen most of the year and the mud would soon be gone.

In one of the plywood houses lived Charlie and Quavuk. Instead of hauling logs from the surrounding forest, Charlie paid high prices to have plywood brought in by barge from Kotzebue. Some of the men who worked for wages all summer found it easier to build with plywood; however, the houses required a good deal of insulation to keep them warm. Charlie and Quavuk's house was built high off the ground and had wooden cupboards and a hardwood floor, all built by Charlie who was a good carpenter. The kitchen had three stoves, a modern gas range, a wood-burning range, and a two-burner primus stove. Their bedroom accommodated three beds. Quavuk showed me where I would sleep, for I had promised to share my time with her as well as Okukchuk. It was an alcove off the kitchen, large enough for a big clean bed, and it looked so inviting and I was so tired that I drank my tea, took off my boots, and upon the good suggestion of Quavuk's took a short nap.

When I woke up, I chatted with Quavuk a while before going back to Okukchuk's house to spend the night. Quavuk was one of three village midwives, but with Puyuk and Ethel, the others, gone, she would deliver the village babies herself.

Most Eskimo women who had many children gave birth easily with only a few hours labor and occasionally the children was born before the midwife arrived. A few of the women had their babies while traveling; they were put ashore to give birth. The woman then cut the cord herself, scraped earth over the afterbirth, placed the baby in her parka, then ran up the beach to catch up with the boat.

A doctor at the Kotzebue Hospital told me that Eskimo women have no fear of childbirth. He said their record of midwifery was remarkable; there was no higher incidence of infant mortality at birth in the hospital than there was in the most distant village.

But the infant deaths during the first year were high, for they die of pneumonia and other diseases and hardships. If the baby survived his first year, he was considered pretty tough.

When Ethel, the former Noatak postmistress, was in the Kotzebue Hospital resting after an operation, the girl in the next bed started labor pains. Ethel got out of bed and delivered the baby. By the time the doctor arrived she had neatly tied the umbilical cord and mother and baby were doing fine.

But some women had breech births or difficult delivery. I asked Quavuk about this.

"A long time ago the women had to go by themselves and deliver away from the village in their own tents without any help; later they let other women help them," Quavuk told me. "In those days they forced the baby out, making the women get on their knees. Many women ruined their insides this way, forcing the womb. The doctor taught us how to let the woman lie down and we wait now for the baby to come. We are patient. Sometimes I have to wait all night."

"What do you do if the pain is bad?" I asked.

"I give the woman some hard candy."

"No medicine, shots or pills?"

"Nothing; no, nothing. We hardly have trouble, we lost no babies," she answered. "Now some of the young mothers go to Kotzebue Hospital to have baby; not many, but some do."

"Do they rest after the baby is born?"

"We hope they rest a few days, but some don't," she replied. "They get up right away."

After a good night's sleep I awakened to the fragrance of coffee and a cozy crackling fire. Jack was tiptoeing around. "Hello, good morning," he said cheerfully, sorry that he had wakened me.

Okukchuk whispered loudly from the bedroom, "See, I told you to sleep late so you wouldn't wake her, but no, you had to get up."

"It's okay," I groaned cheerfully.

Tiny in her flannel nightgown and beaded slippers, Okukchuk quickly dressed and made us delicious hotcakes. Her sole function and purpose in life was as helpmeet to Jack; if she looked out the window and saw Jack pushing the boat, she quickly put on her coat and ran down to help him push it; if he carried a load of wood in, she helped him; on the boat trip she had grabbed a pole to push him out of shallow water. They did everything together, for their children were grown and married.

Over more coffee Okukchuk related, "We go camping together in the mountains. Take the dog team and stay a week or two. We hunt fox or muskrat. That's how I got my foxes." Hung on the wall of her bedroom were two huge foxes, one silver and one red. "We go caribou hunting, before ice comes on river, we go home with boat."

According to the other women, Okukchuk had some of the finest furs in the village. She wore only the choice ones, fashioning the skins in beautiful designs and knowing the worth of each skin. Her shed was full of caribou and other skins, including the scraped caribou skin she had dyed with willow root to make a red trim for her mukluks.

Her new muskrat parka was made of matched muskrat belly skins, "The belly for the woman's and the backs for the man's," she said, caressing the fur. "The bellies softer, tear easier." She had trapped each muskrat and tanned, cut, and sewn the skins together with fine caribou sinew. A three-inch border design of white and black calfskin completed the bottom of the parka and the tails of other animals hung from the sleeves and the back of the hood. Her coat hung longer in the back because, she explained, "My daughters like to use my parka to pack their babies and it stretch the fur."

She showed me the caribou pants she had made for Jack for winter hunting, also three kinds of mukluks she had sewn for him. The long caribou leg mukluk, the sealskin one for rain and wet wear, and the shorter one trimmed with beads; all had pleated ugruk soles. She used pliers instead of her teeth for pleating because she had lost all her front teeth.

"My muskrat parka, warm mukluks, and gloves are all I need to sit and hook fish on the ice in the coldest weather," she said.

Okukchuk was the only one in the village who had planted a small patch of lettuce and turnips. The plants were equal to any in Fairbanks. Her daughter had weeded the little garden while she was gone and the rain had done the rest. The soil was rich and black. "I dry the turnip leaves and use them in soup. I give them to the schoolteacher who has no garden," Okukchuk said.

Four kinds of berries were stored in their cache: barrels of pale orange, clustered salmonberry or *ahpik*; the small, black, globelike black crowberry with large seeds; the red lowbush cranberry; and the blueberry. All were packed with a little seal oil as a preservative over the long winter.

Okukchuk went out daily to find the blueberries remaining on the reddened leaves. They were hard to find but fully mellowed and wine colored; they were a feast with a bit of sugar.

In front of Okukchuk's house flowed the broad Noatak River carrying dead wood and multitudes of salmon and other fish. From the banks one could see the wilderness spread for miles across streams and hills. Bands of orange haze indicated the autumn birches in the distance and the sky was streaked with clouds.

Jack's relatives had fished all summer and on their racks were fish, a plentiful supply of fish, huge *kalugrok*, or the brutish dog salmon, with sharp ugly teeth and reddish strips, mouths open in a wicked leer; silver salmon, the river's prize eating; trout with lemon-colored flesh; and grayling—enough fish to crowd the nets at a hundred a haul. The dogs were sleek and fat, so stuffed that they ate just the heads of the salmon, leaving the large bodies to rot by the banks. Some of the fish were wrapped in sacks and put to freeze in the frozen earth, and some were dried for dog food. As far as I knew, no one used the fish commercially and few canned them; drying was the popular method of preserving.

Several moose had been killed, already heralding the fall season, and the meat had been divided among several families. This was a year of plenty; no one was hungry. But they had known years when the run was poor.

Reverend Thomas had told me how kind Jack and Okukchuk had been to him. "These people are the salt of the earth," he had said.

"We try to live a good life," Jack said modestly when I told him. He was from Kobuk, had been straight and strong as a young man, with swarthy skin and a hawklike nose. He had met Okukchuk in Kotzebue where they were married; it was a love match.

A long time ago there had been jealousies and wars between the Noatagmiut and Kobuk peoples. A legend related how the Noatagmiut had invited the Kobuk people to visit them but secretly planned to kill them. A Kobuk woman married to a Noatagmiut man had warned her people and when they began to shoot bows and arrows, some of the Kobuk people escaped.

Then the Noatagmiut grabbed the Kobuk woman and set her on top of a high cliff. It was winter and cold. They took off her clothes and let her fall over the cliff. "Why did you tell the Kobuk people?" they asked. When she got to the bottom of the cliff, they pulled her up and then let her slide down again. Her husband was around, but he could not help her. Her breasts were frozen and cut up but they kept doing that until she died.

"They call that place Siesiegukrok. When it gets real cold there in the wintertime, the willow bark always comes off," said Okukchuk.

When the sun appeared, the hills were a golden offering. The river, now calm, had dropped and I could see gravel bars that had not been there a few days before. Fish nets were drying in the wind and smoke rose from the cabins.

I left the house each morning with paints and pads, followed by children. One of the young women who lived near the river banks spoke to me and I asked her if she would pose. The huskies tied near her house made a good background. I asked her how many children she had, as a little boy was climbing into a wheelbarrow.

"Three."

"And what is your husband doing now?"

"I have no husband." Sounds of activity came from her house. The baby had gone in the house and must have fallen. One of the dogs chained outdoors made grotesque sickening upheaval motions and finally retched.

Too much fish.

We parted, the watercolor finished. A crowd had gathered to watch. I walked farther into the village and began a watercolor of an older woman with the hillside bathed in sunlight behind her. It was a painting that revealed nothing of the mud, of the old houses, but the best of Noatak—the people. A black raven flew by and I painted him in with my brush just as a youngster fell over the high river bank, picked himself up, and crawled back up to watch again.

Running toward us was a woman I recognized as having met at Sheshalik. Narvuk and her husband had been kind to me then; now she was in her seventies and ill. We met halfway up the hill, greeting each other.

I left the painting and went with her to her cabin. "I took the boat trip to Kotzebue but was so weak and frightened at the rough water that I spit blood. They put me right in the hospital," said Narvuk, puffing.

She showed me photos of her mother taken when they had lived along the river shore. Her father had been an angatkok at Kobuk and Narvuk was thirty when they stayed in one place during the winter, calling the village Noatak.

They picked Noatak because it had high banks safe from river overflow and was near good fishing. In 1908 the Friends opened a federally supported mission school and church there. "About one hundred people moved to the village to educate their children and to learn about Christianity. The first houses were sod covered but the missionaries, Reverends Robert and Cary Sams, taught us how to make log cabins," said Narvuk. "Before that we had willow frame houses with caribou skin covers."

Narvuk took me to see Erahooruk, the oldest woman in the village. Her entranceway was obscured by a fish rack. Five dogs guarded the modest dwelling and bits of intestine and fresh meat hung from a pole over the wood pile.

"Erahooruk, Erahooruk," called Narvuk.

Out of the entrance came an old woman with alert eyes and an intelligent manner whom I recognized as someone I had sketched once five years before. She gave the appearance of good health and walked with an easy free stride. Half a century before, she had worn her teeth down to stubs chewing seal hide and now even the stubs were gone. The black tattoo marks on her chin were also worn. Walking

Tiglut, Pt. Hope

without aid, she moved to a stump and sat with her head bent forward. Her cheeks were covered by a network of wrinkles, an inscription that years of struggle had written on her flesh, each indentation attesting to her stamina and will to survive.

Narvuk explained who I was and asked if I could paint her. Without any ado, she agreed, sat down on a log. As I carefully began the drawing in pencil, she remarked in Eskimo, "Now I will not be forgotten."

I was struck by that because none of the other Eskimos had ever thought of it that way. It made me ever so careful to do her well. I told Narvuk to say, "I will do my best for you."

She nodded her head, peering steadily at me with earnestness; with all her being she was helping me to paint. I had never encountered that either; she willed me to do well of her. When the children crowded too close, she shooed them away sternly. She refused to talk to Narvuk for fear it would spoil the pose.

I asked Narvuk to tell her that it was an honor for me to paint her. Erahooruk nodded and then Narvuk translated what she said, "She wants you to come in the house when you are finished; she wants to give you something."

What an ancient face! She behaved with dignity although dressed in a faded dirty calico full of holes. Her parka covering was no better; the fur ruff was moldy and worn at the edges like herself.

She peered at me with shrunken, narrowed eyes and widened nostrils as if she were smelling me as well as seeing me. I painted her hands and was surprised to notice how young they were!

Her stubborn will had set her mouth in rivulets of wrinkles radiating to her nose and down to her chin, wrinkles which met and crossed when she laughed. She squinted at the river with her wise old eyes, alerted to the raven that had lit on her fish rack. When the painting was done, I followed her into the storm porch where she kept her seal oil, tools, and assorted paraphernalia.

Erahooruk drew out a wooden bowl filled with tools and spread them out on the floor, offering me a choice of one. There were bits of carved ivory and harpoon heads. One tool caught my eye; it had a carved wooden handle, with a series of circle-dot designs all over it, and a sharp iron blade.

"It was her husband's," said Narvuk. "He used it to scrape skins like this." She proceeded to show me how the tool was held. "She said you can have it if you want it."

I followed Erahooruk deep into the small room while Narvuk shut the door. Immediately I felt claustrophobic; the air was fetid, close, and overpowering. The bed and floor were covered with caribou skins, and the room contained a stove, a bed, and assorted clothing, the bare essentials.

Erahooruk drew out an object from under her bed which resembled a chamber pot. It was a chamber pot! For a moment Narvuk and I looked at each other, wondering what next. Erahooruk opened the lid and lifted out one of the contents for our inspection. It was a miniature bird feather parka, complete in every detail; the hood and the fur tails hanging down the back were made of loon feathers, in intricate matching designs of black and white. She motioned for me to keep it.

"*Quayana,* Erahooruk," I said. With that she put the lid on her secret storage pot with a satisfied air.

I asked Narvuk what Erahooruk would like me to send her and she translated. "She's always wanted a real kerosene lamp like Noyuk's." My heart sank for I knew hers was an antique but I said I would try. I knew that at least I would send her coffee and other foodstuffs, for I felt greatly indebted to her, not only for her gifts and her courtesy in modeling, but because she was the oldest woman I had ever met. Her presence was a triumph of spirit as well as body.

Erahooruk said after seeing my painting of her, "I should have smiled!" The vanity of women! I told her I'd try to do a smiling one later one.

Word about the portrait must have spread through the village because several men and women came over to see it.

Usually at other villages not much interest was shown in my work, but here they marveled at the likeness.

"It's Erahooruk," they exclaimed to one another, "really Erahooruk."

"She had the hardest life I've ever heard," said Narvuk.

Trained in hardship, she had responded with stoicism. Even her name, Erahooruk meant berry seed, the seed of the ahpiks which grew close to the earth and were hardy.

No one knew exactly how old she was; they didn't record births when she was born. "Maybe one hundred years," ventured Narvuk.

Erahooruk fascinated me and I visited her often, taking Narvuk along to translate. Her earliest memory was of her uncle putting on her chin tattoo. She remembered the needle going in her chin and how she had started to cry. Soot was rubbed in the cuts to make three vertical chin marks that have remained.

Erahooruk had one sister and two brothers. "I had one more brother but they threw him."

"Does that mean he died?" I asked.

"Yes, they left him and went away."

"Was he alive, nothing wrong?"

"No, he was good," she answered. "It was the time when the people starved. My father was still alive and I was about sixteen when it happened.

"We came upriver and the Noatagmiut were starving. My uncle walked upriver to look for his people. He walked along the west side of the river until he saw somebody sitting under a tree leaning against it. It was his wife. He got close and saw the top half of a body hanging from a branch in a tree. He sat down and told his wife, 'You still live. Let's go home from here.'

"She said, 'No, I'm not fit for that any more now.'

"He wanted to take her but she didn't want to go. He asked, 'Where are your parents, your sisters and brothers?'

"She answered, 'They all starved except for my brother. He is still alive. He took a knife and tried to kill me for food.

That half body up there is one of my parents. I took it along for food when I ran from my brother.'

"Her husband asked, 'Where's your younger brother?'

"She answered, 'He was alive but my older brother killed him.'

" 'Come home with me,' said her husband.

" 'No, I can't come with you. I am going toward Point Hope. You go home. If I get real hungry I have that half body yet. I will eat it.' She went to Point Hope and he went downriver. She got married to a man at Point Hope and got a big family and he got another wife.

"All the old people I used to know are dead. Except me," said Erahooruk. "During these starving times it was hard. On the way some people always throw those who starve or those who are too weak to go. They leave them on the trail."

The old, the sick, the starving, and the newborn were left behind. Erahooruk's was an old heartbreaking story of the struggle of a people to survive.

Narvuk and I visited Erahooruk again and found out more about her life. When Erahooruk was young, her family moved to Kotzebue. Her father never knew about the moose, she said. "No one had seen a moose, or moose tracks," until recently.

When she was a young girl, she used to hunt and walk upriver with the men. They had no dog teams then. They fished with spears and gaff hooks and after the river froze, with hook, line, and traps. They were poor and had no white man's food and little clothing. "When food was scarce, they would dig for dead salmon; that's how they lived in those days," she said. They did not have a tent, just a sod house; no stove, just a campfire in the middle of the *ebrulik*. Their tent in the summer had a caribou skin covering; for the opening they sometimes used bear hide.

In those days they made clothes in the winter because a taboo forbade sewing caribou skin while they were on the coast; only the sewing of sea mammal skins was permitted on the coast. They believed if the taboo were broken, they would die. They even had to cut caribou before they left, as they could not cut it on the coast at Sheshalik.

"A woman had a pot for taking food to the galegi and her own pot for the family. After eating seal or ugruk, we had to clean teeth with piece of wood before we went back upriver. We had to burn all the seal bones; if we did not burn good, someone would die from our family.

"I was pregnant with my first child when I got married," said Erahooruk, "I had my first baby away from everyone. People believed if they help deliver a baby, they die; so no one help me. I had no water when have baby. It was a boy and he had a cracked head because no one help me.

"I lived below Noatak village in a little tent and cook on campfire outdoors around December. Have baby outdoors, make a little thing to lay down and stay about four days. It was cold.

"Right after that I went with husband and three dogs to Kivalina because we were hungry. My husband died young from kidney trouble, then I marry two years later, a Kotzebue man name of Taluk. We had to hunt upriver and at the coast or starve. Around this time people had fish and *masu* [sweet potatoe-like root]. They stored it and when they ate it, they died—it was just like poison!

"Around this time I have my girl. The women help me this time. They think I die. They pulled my hair because I don't move, like dead. They don't know what to do. They break my two little fingers," and here she showed me her two small fingers of each hand. I had not noticed how broken they were.

"Ayeeee," I said.

"Okukchuk's mother have same thing from time she was just like dead. No doctor," said Erahooruk. "I came alive.

"Sometime the angatkoks help woman have baby," Erahooruk continued. "A woman is lying down on the floor trying to have baby but she is having a hard time." Era-hooruk took a stick and made a digging motion with it at the floor. "If they don't know if a woman is going to have her baby, they tie a string around her head as she is lay there. They put the stick through the string and if her head is heavy to lift, she is going to have the baby; if it is light, she won't. If it is light even though the angatkok is working, the woman is die because she can't have her baby." Erahooruk demonstrated this for us, kneeling with her legs wide apart and making contracting motions.

"That is how Outoyuk was born. His mother was going to have her baby and an angatkok had to work on her. Her husband crawled over the floor because he was suffering. She was about ready to die. All kinds of angatkoks worked on her but she couldn't have the baby; even her mother-in-law, tried to help her. She took off her clothes and held her daughter-in-law, trying to let her live. She worked on her till she have a baby, a big boy.

"But in those days if you went in a tent where they were having a baby, you would die. Her mother-in-law didn't even live through the night. She died because she let her daughter-in-law have baby and the angatkok's devil got her."

Narvuk interrupted to say, "Sometimes woman have twins or four babies but they didn't live."

Erahooruk continued, "I tell you about a woman angatkok. I saw her with my own eyes stuck a knife in her belly button. It went in and came out through her mouth and started moving just like a tongue. When the point come out, she swallowed it again. The handle came out her belly button and she pulled out the knife."

Narvuk interrupted. "They all quit angatkoking when they heard about the Bible. Never continue after Christ came. A person became an angatkok when the devil got into him, that's how strong the devil was long ago. People went to see angatkok because they wanted to listen to the devil talk. Some agatkoks get rich when they helped people."

Narvuk said, "In those days people lived in fear, even

afraid to help one another, but after Christianity they were kinder. They used to worship idols, charms; some had weasels or other animals."

"A woman was dying," Erahooruk went on. "Her relatives gave the angatkok gifts to work on her. They promised if the woman got good, he could use her. He stood her soul on his drum and it kept falling off. He tried to inhale something through his drumstick. He had it in his mouth and then took it out and set it on his drum. It was her *inyua* [her soul]. A lot of people were around watching; it was winter and the seal oil lamp was burning but it was covered, not too bright. The inyua fell and he put it back up on the drum. It fell because the woman was dying. Finally the soul stood up by itself and started going around, jumping by itself all over the drum.

"The angatkok got a hold of it and put it on the dying woman's head, then it went back in her and they didn't see it any more. The woman came alive."

"What did you really see?" I asked.

"The inyua was a small thing," Erahooruk showed me her hand, "dark color, maybe like a little doll. People sang when the angatkok beat the drum. The woman had bad pains; she would have died if he not work on her. When she got well, he used her."

"What do you mean?" I asked.

"He slept with her."

Okukchuk had a good supper of salmon, turnip greens, and lettuce. "I was worried what to feed you."

"I like everything," I answered.

For entertainment Saturday night Jack played tape recordings of music and messages from other villages. The neighbors came to listen and heard their relatives from Point Hope, Point Barrow and Kotzebue.

"I even got a tape from Aklavik in Canada; their language is the same as ours," Okukchuk told me.

Most of the songs and messages were religious in nature. The Noatakers and Point Hopers had a friendly competitive relationship and people had a friendly competitive relationship and people of both villages liked to visit back and forth by dog team. They invariably looked around, visited, went back convinced that their village was better.

The Eskimos had mingled with the Portuguese, Irish, Negro and other whalers. One of the Noatak men told me, "Most of us have some white blood in us."

I sat on the steps of Narvuk's cabin overlooking the river, the hills, and the whole village while the sun went down. One of the children reported that Erahooruk was visiting a neighbor and would soon come to Narvuk's, so we all waited. The wind had shifted and was bringing the stench of fish to our noses and someone said, "It smells terrible."

I began to have violent cramps in my upper abdomen; I didn't know what was wrong but soon found out. I had been drinking unboiled water from the river and it had been causing dysentery. I had brought Kool-Aid for the children and they had mixed it with river water, which, of course, they were used to drinking.

Erahooruk appeared with another woman named Summerun, a widow who had formerly lived at Point Hope. She couldn't speak any English either so Narvuk translated. Summerun asked Narvuk why I hadn't painted her, and I gladly obliged. One of her cheeks was badly scarred so I painted the good side in watercolors, and because she asked me, painted the gold ring on her finger. When the portrait was done, she asked me to follow her.

One of the children came with me to her cabin which was in dilapidated condition. Summerun pointed out the leaky roof and the moldy walls; the place resembled an abandoned cabin except for the clothes hanging on lines strung from the ceiling and the fresh meat above the stove. It didn't look inhabited; it looked camped in. In the dark outer room was a cot, and from this room Summerun brought out a small package wrapped with scraps of material. Small pieces of old ivory came to light and she selected a needle case and an ivory ring for me. I motioned that I did not want to accept the gifts, but she insisted I take them so I thanked her. I promised to send her rubber boots and other things which she needed badly.

The sun shone until late, illuminating the shabby houses with its fiery glow and coloring their brighter sides lemony orange which contrasted with the somber shadowed sides. The salmon racks stood out in relief against the silvery river waters. The wind blew in another direction, wafting the fish odors the other way, at long last, and giving the villagers a respite.

Erahooruk was stirring fish heads in a tub to make dog feed when I passed by. She grinned delightedly at me. Smoke from her fire enveloped her as the evening rays sank into the river.

Charlie and his grandson, Billy, had been fishing.

"How many?" hollered Quavuk down to her husband.

"One hundred twenty-seven," yelled Billy excitedly.

"Good," she answered and set out a pot of soup, dried ugruk, seal oil, bread, and coffee for our meal.

Billy had white skin and freckles but spoke English with an Eskimo accent. "He likes white man's food. Won't eat Eskimo food," said his grandmother.

"What does he eat for breakfast?"

"Potatoes, fried eggs, if we have them."

"Billy, you should eat Eskimo food," I scolded taking a bite of ugruk. "It's good."

Billy grinned at me. We all went down after the meal to see the load of fish they had netted.

Trout glistened in the sun and large king salmon, some weighing over twenty pounds, were thrown across dog salmon. Smaller flounder and other fish lay in the bottom of the boat; some of the salmon had had a twig forced through their mouths for easier handling. Quavuk moved quickly and with her ulu proceeded to cut the fish, gutting them and adding them to her groaning racks.

Charlie talked about going to Kotzebue to buy gas, which was "twenty-eight dollars a drum there but forty dollars at Noatak." It paid him to go to Kotzebue for three or four drums of gas. Also he and Quavuk wanted to camp and pick berries and hunt along the river. When they asked if I wanted to go along, I did not hesitate to say yes, since the trip upriver had been mainly at night and I had waited to see the country in daylight.

Quavuk repeated, "Stay in us," meaning, "Stay with us."

"We're leaving early the first nice day," Charlie warned.

I walked over to the end of the village to get my gear and to thank Okukchuk and Jack and their relatives for their warm hospitality. They were listening to the doctor at Kotzebue give medical advice over the radio to all the villages. The village of Kiana reported that a child lay ill with flu, runny ears, and a temperature of 104. The doctor advised, "Put her on the next plane to Kotzebue Hospital."

"Roger, over."

It seemed to me that listening to this "agony hour" as it was called, produced a lot of hypochondriacs.

A call of serious nature came one day from Bethel; the symptoms described were those of a coronary attack. The doctor told the Eskimo to get to the hospital as fast as he could. They waited for three days but as the weather was bad, there was no sign of a plane or an Eskimo from Bethel. Finally he appeared—he had walked the forty miles!

"In the days before we had a doctor," said one woman, "if someone cut himself we used to sew it up with human hair; if we used sinew, the wound would have pus. For headaches the angatkok would poke in the back of the head to let the blood out and if someone broke an arm, they set it and bound it up with wood until it healed. When a person got very sick with pain, the angatkok used a drum to make him well."

CHAPTER 30 *Saga of Kahhoaruk*

There are ill rumors abroad,
Of some who starve in the far places,
And can find no meat. . . .

NOYUK'S FAMILY lived in a house surrounded by many sheds and heavily laden fish racks. To one side was a fancy sled with curved sides and a bearskin draped over it. In their large log house everything was in one room, like a homesteader's cabin, with an old kerosene lamp giving off light.

Noyuk looked down at her swollen stomach and patted it. "I may as well have Quavuk deliver my baby. It's too much trouble going to Kotzebue Hospital."

Nearby in one of the small shed-like shelters sat Noyuk's old mother Kahhoaruk. She wore a brown print calico with an old fur ruff and sealskin mukluks. Her right eye drooped shut in her withered, wrinkled face and she sat on a caribou skin, leaning her body forward in an awkward jackknife position. As we drank coffee with Noyuk's biscuits, I noticed Kahhoaruk quietly observing me with her one good eye.

From Noyuk and other Noatak people I gathered the story of her life. Kahhoaruk had become a legend in her lifetime.

Before Kahhoaruk was born, her mother had angered her parents by marrying a man whom they disliked. The young couple ran away to the coast.

Thirteen years later the mother returned without her husband and with her children, Kahhoaruk, who was about nine, and her four-year-old brother. She had driven the team by herself from the coast, exhausting herself and her own small food supply. There was little food in the village, for it was a year of few caribou and it had been a barren cold winter. The tribe had moved from camp to camp along the Noatak River, hunting and trapping. The stronger hunters had gone into the higher tributaries of the Noatak far into the Brooks Range, searching for caribou. One group of families had followed the Colville River to the northern Canadian coast. They had not found caribou but had lived on sheep that winter.

It was nearing the end of winter and the Noatagmiut were starving. They usually shared food, but now families were hoarding last containers of oil and meat, giving some to the strong ones and keeping it from the old and the very young. Many children had not made it through the winter

and the ones who were left had little bones projecting, and
their cheeks and eyes were sunken, an accusation to their
parents.

The people were afraid of death. Their mangy dogs
snarled constantly and when one died, it was fed to the
other dogs to keep them alive. Soon they would have to eat
the dogs themselves.

Where had the caribou gone? They could only believe
the explanation of the angatok who said that someone had
frightened the animals away; someone in the village was
harming them by breaking a taboo. He looked around
threateningly. It could only be the newcomer who had dis-
obeyed her parents. The villagers began to ostracize the
little family; even the relatives shunned them. One day a
child taunted Kahhoaruk, saying, "If the people leave this
camp, you and your family are going to be left behind to
starve!"

The prophecy came true and the people left the camp
to move toward the coast in search of food, leaving behind
the sick mother and her young, helpless children. Two older
women stole back at night when no one would see them and
left some seal oil and a little meat with the sick woman. One
of the women took pity on the little boy and wanted to save
him, but he cried and would not leave his mother's shrunken
breast. The older woman picked him up by force, stowed
him in her parka back, and fled.

The mother was getting weaker. After they ate the
meat, they ate the last of their dogs and some hardened
intestine used for windows. They set snares but did not
catch anything except for one porcupine which they boiled,
drinking the juice and chewing the bones for nourishment.
Finally they decided to walk back to the coast. The mother
was very weak but she told Kahhoaruk over and over again
the directions, the landmarks and the rivers she must cross
to reach the coast. She knew she was dying, yet she would
not give up her life.

That night they slept near the fire and in the morning

Kahhoaruk

began the long journey. Kahhoaruk walked ahead, turning back to see if her mother was following. They had to rest often, making camp in dry places along the river. Her mother crawled, dragging herself on her knees through the thick brush. At night they slept close to the river's edge among the thick willows.

They ate a little oil, a lick at a time, hoarding it. New snow fell overnight, covering the trail. If only the willow leaves or berries had been out. They saw no animals; but even if they had there was no gun, only an ulu, and so days passed without food.

From weakness and hunger the mother became delirious and lost consciousness. Her face bloated and began to turn black. The child began to cry from fear and loneliness.

The mother in her delirium cried out, "My little son, my son," rocking her empty arms. Then in the middle of the night she awoke, crying, "Kahhoaruk, my child, what will become of you?"

It stormed icy flakes of snow that night. When Kahhoaruk woke in the early morning, she touched her mother and found her cold and oily. During the night she had spread their remaining oil all over her face and now she was dead.

Kahhoaruk built a fire and wept as she gathered the frozen willows and boiled snow water to drink, then lay down on her caribou skin on the ground and tried to warm her mother. "*Ahkah*," she mourned, "*Ahkah*, I am alone; help me."

The next day the trail which led to the coast was covered with snow but she kept walking until she reached the place where her mother had said she would see two hills and find the old camping place. She found a discarded ugruk boat skin and sucked that. She discovered some ptarmigan droppings and ate them, stopping to boil some snow water again. Then she began slowly to climb the hills, wrapping her feet in rags as her mukluks had begun to tear.

When she came to the river, she crawled across it, afraid of breaking through the ice. The wind had swept away some of the snow and she stumbled over the frozen ground, over bare willows, hummocks, lichens, and rocks. The snow held fast in the mountains and her small figure steadily climbed the trail between the two hills, plunging ever deeper into an unknown wilderness.

At the top of the hill she looked out over a wide area and did not see a single living creature, only icy tundra and barrenness. It was a hungry land. A caribou trail, once filled with thousands of tracks, was now empty—not a sign of game.

As she walked through the willows, one of the branches hit her eye so that she could hardly see. She couldn't stop although the pain was intense, blinding her. When she came out of the forest into the flat country, the trees were sparse and far between. The farther she walked, the fewer the trees, until there were no trees at all, just very low willows bent by the wind. The land was crisscrossed by frozen bogs and lakes and she was careful to test the ice before she ventured to cross them.

Struggling to keep herself warm she slept fitfully, her eye throbbing. Fear, hunger, and cold traveled with her. She was at the end of her strength; only thoughts of seeing her brother kept her alive. She found rabbit droppings and ate them, for death lay hard and cold within her belly. Ptarmigan flew overhead and she watched their white fluttering bodies helplessly, her arms outstretched toward them. Then she sat down and cried, her back humped against the bitter wind.

She was exhausted; it would be so easy just to lie in the snow and sleep forever. When she awoke, she saw something moving on the ice and a dog team came toward her.

The woman on the sled called, "Who are you? Who are you?"

Kahhoaruk answered, "It is I, myself."

The couple moved closer.

The man was an angatkok and full of superstition.

They would not come close to her for fear of touching her, as that might contaminate them and they would die. They told her she must change her clothing, for it was taboo to mix caribou with seal. They had no extra clothes with them but when they saw the pitiful condition Kahhoaruk was in they gave her some seal meat, leaving quickly because they were afraid of the consequences.

Later two men found her and put her on their sled and took her to the coast. She stayed with Muniksakk and his wife, who were Quavuk's grandparents. Warm and fed and given new skin clothing, she grew stronger. When the sun came out and warmed her, Kahhoaruk knew she was among the living once again. She learned her brother had died but they told her not to grieve. Muniksakk's brother-in-law was especially kind to Kahhoaruk and when she was old enough, she married him.

At Noatak, surrounded by grandchildren in her old age, she had not suffered want or hunger again but she had lost the sight of one eye. Noyuk, her daughter, took care of her and loved her greatly.

Kahhoaruk posed for me, sitting outdoors, and her wise, all-knowing eye, that had seen and experienced so much of life, looked contentedly at me. Erahooruk and Summerun, her old cronies, came to join her for a game of Chinese checkers on the caribou skin.

Kahhoaruk gave me a treasured gift, a raincoat made of ugruk intestines such as is not made any longer. The skin was hardened and transparent like old parchment and upon it were sewn hundreds of tiny sinew stitches to make it waterproof.

One day I noticed Kahhoaruk writing something and I asked Noyuk what the strange markings were. Noyuk explained that in her eagerness to understand and remember the printed words of the Bible, her mother had created a language of her own.

I copied down her symbols and meanings:

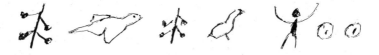

This meant: "But the fruit of the spirit is love, joy, peace . . ." (Galatians 5,22).

Neither Noyuk nor I could know that her mother would not live to see her eighth grandchild, which Noyuk endearingly called "Mother" or "Ahkah" after Kahhoaruk.

CHAPTER 31

Downriver

Rarely I see the water calm,
The waves cast me about;
And I tremble, I tremble at thought of the hour
When gulls shall hack at my dead body.

WHEN IT WAS TIME to leave we made quick work of loading the boat, for there wasn't much to take down the hill, only the primus stove and some dried meat and fish, the coffeepot, the tent, and other camping supplies. The boat looked empty compared to the one coming upriver.

The morning was dewy and the water effervescent. I felt light as a feather, washed, free from all doubt, dreadfully tired but floating like the river boat. Quavuk, her friend Cora, and I sat in the middle of the boat leaning against whatever we could. The tent was spread as a tarp over the articles in the boat in case of rain.

The women and I put on heavy fur-lined parkas for protection against the wind and settled down, fur ruffs raised over our heads. Charlie stood calmly as if fastened to the motor, a slicker thrown over his shoulders. Cora jumped up, her agile mukluk'd feet swift over the empty drums, and grabbed a long pole to help push the boat. A load of partially dried salmon was placed on top of the drums and now the wind shifted the scent to us.

Oh, no, I cried inwardly.

About seven minutes out of Noatak, Quavuk called out, "Charlie, your glasses."

He smiled and patted his pocket.

The banks glowed with yellow shrubbery and spruce trees, all rather thin and stunted, and in the distance fog covered the bald mountains. When it began to drizzle, we ignored it until it was impossible to any longer, then ducking underneath the tarp we peered out and the rain washed our faces.

The impending storm broke upon us and the rain fell, needling the river. The Noatak pursued a tortuous course, winding in and around the banks, which in spite of the wretched weather were wild and beautiful.

The rocky cliffs were worn to fantastic shapes. We passed the place where the sea monster, or *direechee*, supposedly lived deep in the murky waters and hurried past it; not that I believed in a direechee, but I shivered just the same. It was shady there with rocks on shore giving a feeling of impending disaster. A woman had committed suicide there a long time before. She threw herself off the cliff with her baby on her back, singing, "My poor son, my poor son." It seemed that she was punishing her husband, who continually beat the son with the stick he used for poling the boat.

We passed a crude shelter that resembled a wigwam; it consisted of a number of poles tied together at the top. "In there is the bodies of the men who died a long time ago," said Quavuk.

I remembered seeing a grave like that at Sheshalik. One old man had told me that "when a man died long ago, they just wrapped him in piece of old skin. Sometimes just leave him, high off ground, in trees, or else build tent of poles over him. Sometimes we used to find an arm near river. Missionaries taught us how to bury in ground."

I remembered Erahooruk's telling me about her father's death. When he had died at Kotzebue many years before, she had to drag him through mud and water to the graveyard. No one would help her in those days. They were afraid to stay in the place of death and left their tents. They feared even to drink water from the tent of a dead person.

"My father's back was torn from dragging him," Erahooruk said. "The dogs ate him.

"Mr. Sams, the missionary, came to my tent afterwards and told me not to cry because my father was in heaven. He asked me why I didn't call him to help. That's why I tried to be Christian. I dragged my father to the other side of the lagoon and covered him with cloth. Mr. Sams came to my tent and drank water from the bucket. Before this no one would do it. He told people to move back into their tents; before that they moved away when someone died.

"Mr. Sams told them to make a box to put my father in, but it was too late. He taught me how to pray, 'Our Father who Art' so that we would be forgiven. He said that even though we shed our tears in this world, God will wash them away. That was the first time people heard about the Gospel. After that they had big meetings in Kotzebue and then buried a dead man in a box."

The rain stopped as the boats swiftly moved downstream. So far the trip had been calm, but now we hit rough currents.

"It's the Agashashok River. It comes into the Noatak real rough," said Quavuk.

The women called excitedly and I could see two boats coming upstream. It was the rest of the Noatak people returning home. Little Frances, my inseparable friend of five years before, came into sight perched on an oil drum in the first boat. It was laden to bursting point with three dogs in the prow. Leela and Gordon were in the next boat; Leela was sitting contentedly among the fishes, the sacks, and the dogs.

"Good-bye, good-bye," we cried, our voices drifting away from one another.

The boat came into a flat marshy area, desolate looking, with numerous lakes deep in the country. "This is rat country," explained the women. "Where we get many muskrats."

It was raining hard and we were cramped, so we stopped at the Sauers' camp, the only dwelling on the river. The old man came down to our boat; his wife had gone berry picking and we were sorry to have missed her. I was eager to get to Kotzebue, but the others wanted to stay, pick berries and camp overnight. Just as we were entering Sauer's cabin, a small speedboat with a large motor pulled up. A young Eskimo with gleaming white teeth landed, handling his boat as a child does a toy. He had stopped just to say hello.

Quavuk asked the man if I could go with him to Kotzebue and before I could say anything, he had dumped out a sackful of rocks that he had used as ballast and motioned for me to jump in. My duffel bag was transferred quickly and I embraced Quavuk and thanked them all.

I sat on the bottom of the boat near a little girl and we were off before I could really think whether I wanted to risk the crossing in this speedboat with the grinning youth. Peering at him through my ruff, I wondered whether he was old enough or experienced enough to handle the boat but there was no turning back. The little girl's hands were warm but mine were freezing even though I wore long underwear and full winter regalia and she had only one thin coat and bare legs.

Except for being drenched and uncomfortable sitting

on the bottom, I was fine as long as we were on the river, but coming toward the Sound was the rough part. I had heard that the waves could turn a little boat over and I was apprehensive.

Great was my relief when the pilot pulled over to shore just at the mouth of the Noatak. "I'm waiting for another boat," he explained.

The men never crossed this place alone if they could help it and he had left Noatak with another boat but had passed it. It was reassuring for a moment to know that we would be accompanied, but really of what use would it be? We had no life jackets—Eskimos scorned them.

Even with life jackets, three minutes in Arctic waters was about the limit for survival. The other boat might reach the person in the water in time, but then it might not. I looked at the little girl—I was not much of a swimmer and with heavy clothes . . .? We drew closer and I put my arms around her and she looked up at me to see if I was afraid. I in turn looked at the handsome pilot for confidence. He kept grinning, his face wet with drops of spray. The other boat passed us and we shot out to follow.

Both boats made straight for the middle of the sea; no aiming for the safe point of land which offered some protection but directly toward Kotzebue, out of sight of land. The small boat seemed helpless against the huge waves and rough sea water. I was terrified. I had no Okukchuk this time to sing "The Lord is my Shepherd."

The little girl clung to me and to make conversation I asked, "Where are you going, honey?"

"I'm going to stay with my grandmother at Kotzebue."

I looked at the pilot again and he looked pale, not as sure. The frail boat came down with a whack, almost jarring my teeth each time, pounding the water hard with each advance over the waves.

In the other boat a drenched woman sat hunched with an infant on her back while her husband ran the motor. Later I saw her in Kotzebue Hospital, for her newborn baby was ill.

I couldn't see a thing, the water splashed us with each impact. I balanced the boat, thinking that maybe my pilot should have left the rocks in but telling myself surely he knew what he was doing. I had heard that Eskimos were magnificent navigators but reckless and I wondered who had told me that. "They will take no chances no white man will take." Ridiculous, I said to myself.

"Oh, God," I prayed, "take me to shore alive and I'll never leave home again—my nice safe home with loving husband and kids who need and love me." All thought of painting was gone, only the motion of the boat and the struggle against the sea were real.

At last we saw dark specks rising on the shore ahead. I pointed them out to the little girl, watching the shore came closer. I looked helplessly at the pilot whose white teeth shone as he grinned confidently at me. The boat was filling with water, but we could see land.

I'm not a sea woman, but an earth woman, a land lover, uneasy in sea and air. We were close to shore now and I felt like kneeling down to kiss the salty gravel beach of Kotzebue. I jumped out with my things and the boat pulled off quickly as I waved good-bye, shouting, "Thanks."

I arrived wearing heavy clothes, with a severely reddened, wind-burned face, wild looking, and terribly dirty, smelling of fish.

The Jensens, blessed people, were peacefully eating hamburgers and cocoa at the kitchen table. Their routine was so sane! They fed me while I mumbled, more exhausted than I realized, then sent me off for a bath. I took off my clothes and soaked. Oh, heavenly luxury! How docile was that tame water, pouring out of white, white plumbing, how marvelous!

The weather was so bad that evening that I doubt we could have made it across the open water had we waited. The flight to Fairbanks was canceled after I had sat two hours at the airport. The radio message to Kotzebue was: "Have to turn back to Nome, can't land here."

The next day I left for home. As I looked down at the snow-covered mountains, the frozen land, and the sea where the people lived, I felt their great spirit and I knew I would return.

At our Fairbanks home along every window ledge are starfish, bulga bones, the neck of a seal that an Eskimo child played with, and a branch of a stunted willow from the mouth of the Utortqaq River. The jade adze, masks, and a huge whaling harpoon that Asatsiak made, hang on our walls among my paintings. Erahooruk's loon parka and Kahhoaruk's raincoat, David's mukluks, and Eskimo carvings lie on the shelf in my studio. Things that tie my mind and heart to the Arctic . . .

About the Author/Artist

Claire Fejes was born and raised in New York City. She studied painting and sculpture at the Art Students League and the Newark Museum, but left a promising metropolitan career after World War II to follow her husband to a mining camp in the Alaskan wilderness, then to Fairbanks 44 years ago.

In 1959 Claire spent time painting in the nomadic whaling camp of Sheshalik and this proved to the beginning of her career as a painter of Native Alaskans and the Far North. Since then she has had thirty one-woman museum shows throughout the United States, including the Frye Art Museum in Seattle, the Charles Bower Museum in Santa Barbara, California, the Norfolk Museum in Virginia, Washington State Museum at Olympia, as well as at all the museums in Alaska.

Her works are in the permanent collections of the West Point Museum in New York and the Williamstown Museum in Massachusetts, as well as in the Michener Collection at the Archer Huntington Museum of Texas, and in several important private collections. Claire has exhibited in New York's Roko and Larcada galleries, and in Israel, San Francisco, and London. She has exhibited for ten years with Japanese national artists in five museums in Japan, opening at the Tokyo Metropolitan Museum.

Claire Fejes has written and illustrated three books: *People of the Noatak, Villagers,* and *Enuk, My Son.* Her fourth book, *Cold Starry Night,* will be published shortly. Fejes was recently commissioned by the Marshall Islands to design three postage stamps commemorating Alaska Statehood.